MW01282266

Praise for *The First Season*

"Coach Carter helped me bridge the gap from the playground to the NBA."

–Vinnie "The Microwave" Johnson
Detroit Pistons, NBA Champions 1989, 1990

"I grew up in the small east Texas town of Alba, which had a population of about two hundred. Our high school was a Class B school and basketball was the only sport we had because we didn't have enough students to field a football or baseball team. *The First Season* brings back many memories of my playing days in the 1950s and of the people and teachers who helped shape and form who I am today. The small schools seemed to have a lot of "can-do" people and although there was never enough money in the budget, they always seemed to get things done.

Kennard High School, another Class B school in east Texas, was looking for a basketball coach in 1966. The school did not have enough money to lure an experienced or proven coach, but they did look for a man of integrity and ability and a man who had a dream. Enter Coach Johnny Carter, who was the right man at the right place at the right time. Johnny's story is not just about winning championships; it's about the process he went through to become a coach and a leader and about winning the respect of his players, their parents, and the community.

This story would be a good read even if it were fiction, but the fact that it really happened makes it extraordinary. I think everyone who has a dream—and we all do—will enjoy this book and have a very good feeling after reading it."

—Carroll Dawson
Senior Consultant, Houston Rockets
Former Assistant Coach, Houston Rockets
Retired General Manager, Houston Rockets

i

"I was excited and honored to be playing for the first all-black school in the Texas State Basketball Tournament. With integration coming, we knew that 1967 would probably be the last year for our small school, Booker T. Washington High School in Plainview, Texas, to be in existence. Our team was definitely motivated to play our best."

-Lawrence McCutcheon
Los Angeles Rams

The First Season is an exciting book to read. His knowledge of the game, for a twenty-three-year-old, is astounding; truly a winning combination of the coach, his parents, and his team, all working together. Coach Carter handled the integration of his team with no incidents. It actually reminds me of Elvin Hayes' and Don Chaney's first year playing at the University of Houston. On the road, there were slurs some of the time, but on campus and amongst our fans, they were accepted right off the bat. This book is a good learning tool for coaches, players, and fans. Coach Carter is like a psychologist in the way he talks to his team. He is a devout believer and his prayers were answered."

-Coach Guy V. Lewis
Retired Head Basketball Coach University of Houston

"Johnny Carter captures the essence of high school sports in his book. It is a must-read for every coach, especially those just entering the profession. Coach Carter captures the life values that can be learned from sport. He teaches us how young people learn from coaches and how adults can learn from kids. A championship read, written by a championship coach about a team of champions!"

-Dr. Charles Breithaupt
Executive Director, University Interscholastic League Austin, Texas

"This unique story combines the rich human relationships of *To Kill a Mockingbird* with the sports drama of *Hoosiers*. It's a great read for anyone, but if you're a basketball fan, you won't be able to put it down. Written by Hall of Fame Coach Johnny Carter, it details his first year in coaching in the small east Texas town of Kennard in 1967, when the school had just become racially integrated. Carter's story starts with his interview for his first coaching job and goes all the way to the state championship. In a totally amazing season, Coach Carter's Tigers brought a community together while many others struggled during this very difficult time in our nation's history. After this incredible first season, Carter's teams went on to win over 900 games and capture two more state championships. In 2013, Coach Johnny Carter was selected to be inducted into the Texas High School Basketball Hall of Fame. After you've read *The First Season*, I'm sure you'll join me in asking when the sequel about his legendary career will be written!"

Rick Sherley
Executive Director, Texas Association of Basketball Coaches
Sugar Land, Texas

"Johnny's book parallels State Tournament history with an amazing story of team togetherness. I highly recommend it."

-Billy Tubbs
Retired Head Basketball Coach
Lamar University, Oklahoma University, Texas Christian University

"Coach Carter helped me prepare for life with lessons from the basketball court."

Sam Worthen
Chicago Bulls

"Johnny's story is a great example of the power of athletics—not just in winning State championships but something more important: the power of accomplishing great things when people have a common value system and a shared vision. Athletics provides a solid foundation for young people to learn the basic disciplines that they can carry forward in their lives. This 'education' gives them a true competitive advantage if they are willing to work hard, stay focused, and maintain their passion for excellence. I am pleased to have coached Johnny and I am proud of the success he has had on and off the court. He should be very proud of his accomplishments and the positive role model he set on these young athletes' lives. Job well done!"

–Leon Black
Retired Head Basketball Coach University of Texas

"In *The First Season*, we get a glimpse into the personal thoughts of a young man entering the coaching profession and his need for love and understanding from family, friends, and fans. Coach Carter's book is a work of love and inspiration that captures the vitality of a coach with the desire to excel by inspiring his team to be able to say, 'We did it! We did it! We're state champions!' While this book bears Coach Carter's name, it is also his parents' story as he tells of their love, counsel, and support for him as he embarked on a new era of his life. Thanks for sharing those games with us; I have replayed them many times in my head——and I still come up four points short!"

–Bob Derryberry
Retired Head Basketball Coach, Howard Payne University
Sam Houston State University, Southwest Texas State University

"Johnny Carter has written a superb sports story—first-year coach taking a small east Texas town to the State Basketball Championship. The book is a triumph of excitement and exhilaration and so much more than a sports story. It is the story of young boys becoming men. It is the story of a basketball team uniting blacks and whites in the 1960s. It is the story of a young coach and his basketball team coming to love each other. You didn't miss *Hoosiers*. Don't miss *The First Season!*"

-Jeff Wells
Senior Pastor, Woods Edge Community Church
The Woodlands, TX

"For anyone who loves the game, *The First Season* is a great read. It will inspire the aspiring coach, make old memories fresh again for the experienced coach, and motivate players of any age to press on toward their dreams. What rabid fan wouldn't enjoy re-living their time in the bleachers as they battle with Coach Carter and the team toward the State Championship? They say that when preparation meets opportunity, you experience success. The dream drove the preparation, the game provided the opportunity, and success was the blessing. Congratulations, not only on a great read, but also for sharing the day-to-day dedication it takes to make dreams come true."

–Ken Henson
Retired Head Basketball Coach Howard Payne University

"Coach Carter was my junior college coach at McLennan Community College in Waco, Texas. He displayed the same passion, enthusiasm, and love for the game and its players with my teammates and me as he did in the book with his first team at Kennard High School. *The First Season* is an amazing story about a young man's first opportunity to do what he was born to do — coach basketball. His trials and tribulations in his first season of coaching are something to which all of us fellow coaches can relate. The book is about high school basketball, the human relationships involved, and the work, time, effort, and luck required to win the State Championship. An outstanding read!"

–Danny Kaspar
Head Basketball Coach
Texas State University

"Johnny Carter, as a player, was the ultimate teammate: unselfish, dedicated, hardworking, and committed to excellence. As a coach he was unparalleled, winning three State Championships. However, what I have admired the most about Johnny Carter is that his life is a testimony to his Christian beliefs and values, and in the final analysis, that is the goal we should all be trying to achieve. *The First Season* is a reflection of his Christian beliefs and values, and provides the reader with a keen insight into the player- coach relationship, the influence that a coach has on the lives of the players, and in return, the influence the players have on the life of the coach. I hope you enjoy reading this book as much as Johnny has enjoyed writing it. Go Mustangs!"

–Thomas Poe, Executive Director
Education Service Center, Region VI, Huntsville, Texas

"Every high school coach's and player's dream can be lived through reading this book."

-Ronnie Arrow, Head Basketball Coach
University of South Alabama

"Coach Carter was one of the most influential people in my career. I have taken eight different teams to the Final Four in the Texas State Championship and have won three State titles. I owe that to Coach Carter, who taught me the press that they had used at Kennard. I also used some of his drills and mainly just his philosophy of an aggressive full-court press. Our last two years playing at the 5A State level and making it to the final game two years in a row (2010-2011) show that this type of system still works. Thanks, Coach. This is a great book to read and to develop what he taught me."

-Tony Mauldin
Head Basketball Coach, Garland Lakeview Centennial High School,
Garland, Texas

"The First Season should be required reading for anyone contemplating going into the coaching profession. Johnny Carter has put into print the many trials and tribulations of a first-year coach. He has put a positive spin on the pure innocence, the lack of fear of the unknown, and the true ignorance of reality, at times, of all first year and many veteran coaches in their desire and attempt to make their team winners on and off the floor."

-Sam Tipton
Executive Director, Texas Girls Coaches Association Austin, Texas

THE FIRST SEASON

The True Story of How a Rookie Coach Took a Newly
Integrated Team to a Texas State Championship

Coach Johnny Carter

Coach Johnny Carter

© 2011 Johnny Carter

The First Season
The True Story of How a Rookie Coach Took a Newly
Integrated Team to a Texas State Championship

Printed in the United States of America
10 9 8 7 6 54 3 2

For more information, please visit www.CoachJohnnyCarter.com.

ISBN-13:978-1492252627
ISBN-10: 149225262X

Dedication

I dedicate this book to my mom and dad, John Dean and Mary Frank
Carter, and my two brothers, Billy and James Otis. We were raised in a
Christian home and were blessed to have two very special parents.
This story would not have taken place had it not been for my
family's influence and support.

Thanks to our Heavenly Father for guiding me along the way.

"Don't let anyone look down on you because you are young, but set an
example for the believers in speech, in life, in love, in faith and in purity."
—*1 Timothy 4:12 NIV*

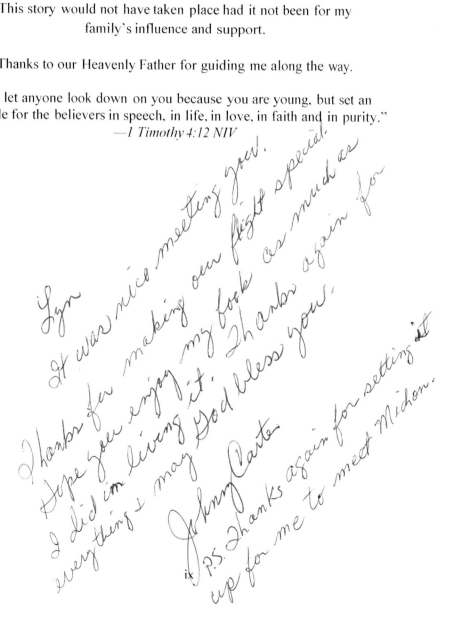

Lyn
It was nice meeting you.
Thanks for making our flight special.
Hope you enjoy my book as much as
I did in living it. Thanks again for
everything + may God bless you.
Johnny Carter
P.S. Thanks again for setting it
up for me to meet Michon.

Coach Johnny Carter

THE FIRST SEASON

Coach Johnny Carter

Contents

Coach Johnny Carter

Acknowledgments

To all the coaches that worked countless hours with me: Bob Ford, James Walker, George Autrey, Floyd Dickens, and Leon Black—plus all the others too numerous to mention whom I visited or listened to at coaching clinics.

To all the players I played with and against—in particular, the other four starters my senior year at Madisonville High School: Tommy Poe, Tommy Ferguson, Charles Grizzle, and Kenneth Standley.

To all the teachers, administrators, and those wonderful fans at Kennard who helped carry us through each season—especially the Harley Myers family. Mrs. Myers was like a second mom, having me over for dinner countless numbers of times.

To Bob Currie, a devout fan and friend.

To all the student athletes who played for me in my forty-plus years of coaching. In particular, the Kennard players who worked together, unselfishly establishing a great tradition that made my four years there a sheer pleasure.

To all the coaches, teachers, and administrators with whom I worked at Howard Payne University, McLennan Community College, University of Oklahoma, and Madisonville High School.

To Craig Smoak, a friend, a player, and a tremendous recruiter.

To the late Landon Holomon, thanks for your help with several Bible verses.

More Acknowledgments

To the late Johnny Wooden, who spent an entire day out of his very busy schedule to counsel and enlighten a young, very inexperienced coach on the finer points of coaching.

To Missy Allen, who helped type up the original manuscript from my handwritten copy to CD form, allowing for a workable format.

To Cynthia Stillar and her team for their patience while working with a first-time author.

To my wife, Sallie, for acting as my secretary.

To Sallie and my son, John Reid, for showing incredible patience with me in the amount of time it took to write this book. I would also like to thank my adult children, Candice and Ben, for their support.

To all those that endorsed this book or took the time to read the original manuscript, thus providing some very appreciated comments.

To Carol Zimmerman (The von Raesfeld Agency, Henderson, NV) for her tremendous help with updating and republishing this book.

To Dorothy Hardy for her wonderful job with updating and revising the cover of this book.

To Jan Blair Felcoff for orchestrating the revisions to and republishing of this book. I certainly could not have done it without you.

Thank you all!

Texas Basketball Hall of Fame

Coach Johnny Carter Inducted Into Hall of Fame

Getting Into the Hall
By Jason Chlapek Sports/Education Editor
The Madisonville Meteor

Effort is something former Madisonville boys basketball coach Johnny Carter thrived on throughout his coaching career.

Carter's efforts did not go unrecognized either. He recently found out he will be a member of the Texas High School Basketball Hall of Fame's Class of 2014.

"I was at the a long table at the entrance to the St. Mary's University gym selling books when Sam Tipton, Executive Director of the Texas Girls Coaches Association, tells me, 'Coach, you're working too hard. Have a seat,'" Carter said. "Sam then congratulated me, but I didn't know why he was congratulating me. Then he told me I was voted into the Hall of Fame."

The congratulations turned out to be news to Carter. In fact, he was shocked.

"The shock still hasn't worn off," Carter said. "It's quite an honor and I feel blessed."

Carter's coaching career spanned nearly 40 years, with most of them taking place in the high school ranks. He coached at Kennard High School (1967-70), Howard Payne University (1971-73), McLennan Community College (1974-80), University of Oklahoma (1981-82) and Madisonville High School (1984-2005).

If there is one thing Carter says he owes his coaching career to, it's the full-court press defense. Carter's teams employed the full-court press, and it took a desperation situation of Kennard's 1967

Class B region championship game to evolve into his way of coaching.

"We were down in the fourth quarter, and needed to get back in the game," he said. "We were not a pressing team until that night, but we were not only able to force turnovers and get a few transition baskets, we were able to come back and win. Driving back from that game, I was thinking about how I could incorporate pressure defense in the future instead of being elated that we made it to state."

Following the 1967 season, Carter spent a lot of time at Sam Houston State University talking to then-coach Archie Porter.

"Archie Porter won a state title at Dallas Jefferson running the full-court press so I picked his brain every chance I had that summer," he said. "Full-court press defense is based on five guys with one focus, and the guys on the bench having that same focus. If one guy messes up, it's costly."

Carter's 1970 team, his last season at Kennard, was a prime example of what all-out effort can do as it went 43-0 en route to its third state championship in four years.

"That team was a very good pressing team," he said. "They overcame a lot of obstacles, and they were very much what I call, 'overachievers.' Good pressing teams give maximum effort. When you give maximum effort, good things happen. That team did that consistently, surprising everyone with an undefeated season."

While Carter is retired, he helped the 2012-13 Madisonville basketball team as a volunteer assistant. The Mustangs were 25-8 this past season — Brian Thurmond's sixth as their head coach.

"I talk to Brian on a regular basis," Carter said. "One time he asked me if I could come up to practice and teach his players full-court defense. It certainly rekindled some old coaching vibes in me, but the thing that made the press successful this past season was the fact that the players bought into it."

The mantra of "run and press, forget the rest," was a way of life for Carter-coached teams. But he credits his teams' efforts for his successes.

"I always told my players that other teams may have more talent, but they won't outwork us," he said. "Effort applies to everything in life. The best thing about coaching is convincing kids to go beyond expectations through effort."

It's all about effort.

Coach Johnny Carter

Foreword

My childhood home was sandwiched between our church and the high school in Buna, Texas. The front door to the gymnasium was less than one hundred yards from our house. The back door to the church was less than fifty. In fact, I left a furrowed path through the preacher's backyard on my way to the gym. I got a heavy dose of the two *Bs:* the Bible and basketball. In many ways, I probably had an unhealthy dose of the latter.

No doubt that interest was piqued because of the enormous success of the Buna Cougars, our high school basketball team. Led by legendary coach M.N. "Cotton" Robinson, the Cougars won seven State championships between 1955 and 1963. I was a witness to a large number of those victories and I was hooked.

One of those wins came at the expense of Madisonville High School in the finals of the Conference AA Regional Tournament in 1961. The Mustangs were led by the talents of Johnny Carter, a superb six-foot guard. Buna eked out a narrow 48-43 victory at G. Rollie White Coliseum on the campus of Texas A&M University, then went on to win the Texas UIL State Basketball Championship with a 43-0 season record.

After that game, Johnny Carter would remain on my radar screen. As a frequent attendee of the State Basketball Tournament, I witnessed his coaching prowess as he guided his Kennard Tigers to the State Title in 1967, in his very first year to coach.

By 1967, Buna was no longer making trips to the State Tournament, but what occurred was the basketball version of the six degrees of separation. How many former players or coaches had a connection to the Buna basketball dynasty in some form or another? Coach Carter was one of those connections.

I continued to follow Coach Carter's career. He went on to great success in the junior college ranks and at the highest level of Division

I collegiate coaching. His early foundations and principles of excellence served him well at every level. The success he attained at Kennard High School was simply a precursor to an outstanding career in coaching.

What he accomplished with those young men in those turbulent times is a story for the ages. This book should be required reading for every coach involved with interscholastic sports. Developing young people to their fullest potential is the essence of educational competition. Coach Carter shows us how he positively impacted the lives of his students and, in turn, his community.

This book chronicles a season in the life of a coach. Not an ordinary coach, but a fresh, young coach who took a directionless team and made them into champions. This team overcame racial prejudice and stereotypes that were prevalent in the South during the '60s. They bonded together to represent the epitome of interscholastic competition.

Having served the students of Texas as a teacher, coach, and administrator since 1975, I have witnessed many championship events. I have had the unique opportunity to watch students and coaches work together to achieve their dream of a State title. None of those stories is better than the story of Coach Carter's Kennard Tigers.

As co-author of *King Cotton* with Fred B. McKinley, a biography of Coach Cotton Robinson, I hope we captured the essence of high school sports and the impact those sports have on our society as well as Johnny did. Johnny's story about his first team resonated with me. I hope you enjoy it as much as I have.

–Dr. Charles Breithaupt, Executive Director,
University Interscholastic League, Austin, Texas

Texas State Basketball Tournament

The Texas State Basketball Tournament has an amazing history going back over 90 years. Indeed, during that time Coach M.N. "Cotton" Robinson's legacy of seven State Championships stands out among all the others. From the small community of Leona, Texas, Coach Robinson credits his high school coach, Bill Bitner, as the most influential person in his life.

Growing up in Madisonville just ten miles south of Leona, Johnny Carter graduated in 1961. His Mustang team faced Buna that year in the Regional Finals, losing a close game to Coach Robinson's undefeated squad. Ironically, five years later Carter was sent to Kennard High School for his first coaching job by none other than that same Bill Bitner. He would win three State Championships in his four years there. Coach Carter's heartwarming miracle story, *The First Season* follows.

Coach Johnny Carter

BOOK ONE

In the Tigers Den

Coach Johnny Carter

1

Almost Drafted

The first day of August was a typical, torrid summer day as I drove through the east Texas Piney Woods of the Davy Crockett National Forest. I was headed toward the tiny community of Kennard to interview for their vacant coaching position. For a twenty-three year-old just out of college with little experience to speak of, trying to convince someone that you were fit to teach their children was a hair-raising notion, to say the least. It really wasn't that long before that I was *playing* high school basketball, the red and blue colors of my hometown Madisonville Mustangs draped across my shoulders.

My senior season of 1961 was extraordinary for our team, despite our school being reclassified with the UIL. We were moved up into the 2A bracket with the larger schools though we were only a hair over the classification number. Even as a little fish in a big pond, we managed to knock on the door of the State Championship, only to have it slammed in our face. It was a tough loss to take, particularly because of the regimen I devoted to personal excellence. I would be lying if I said that loss didn't still sting.

Later that spring, my friend and teammate Tommy Ferguson and I got basketball scholarships to Lon Morris Junior College. I wish I'd known I was planning on becoming a coach while playing for two years under Coach Leon Black. He was a student of the game and I could have learned a whole lot more about basketball if I had approached playing for him from a coaching perspective. My focus, however, was on my radio and television career. I'd dreamed of being a sports announcer since childhood, announcing remembered or imagined games featuring the White Sox, my favorite team, as I mowed the lawn. I gave up my basketball career after junior college and transferred to the University of Houston because they had the best Radio & TV Department in the South. Later that semester, I was actually in the process of changing my major when I heard the tragic news: President John F. Kennedy had been assassinated in Dallas. Anyone who was alive during that time will never forget where they were, who they were with, and what they were doing.

A couple of years later, I had graduated from U of H and was in the process of getting my master's degree at Sam Houston while working at my dad's store. One day, Bill Bitner, the superintendent of Centerville High School and a good friend of my dad's dropped by the store to say hello. Within the course of the visit, the conversation turned to an opening for a basketball coach at Kennard High School. Bill's brother was the superintendent at Kennard and that was when he said the words I wanted to hear——his brother was desperate. Their old coach had transferred schools, the semester was about to begin, and he still didn't have a replacement. I was classified 1A by the selective service, had already passed my physical, and was expecting the call from Uncle Sam any day. I figured that Bill's brother couldn't be any more desperate than I was. A telephone call later, I was on my way.

~~~

There was a lump in my throat as I walked through the doors. Schools have a particular smell, especially during the summer. The smell of varnish and wax lingers, following your every step, and fresh paint wafts up as you turn each corner. The familiar smell helped and by the time I found the superintendent's office, I was at least able to breathe normally.

Mr. Bitner was sitting behind his desk. When he saw me, he smoothed back his graying hair, his mouth gnawing away at a piece of gum, and looked up over the rim of his glasses. A frown spread across his face.

"How old are you, boy?"

I told him I was twenty-three. "You could pass for eighteen."

What little confidence I'd been able to muster deflated as I took a seat.

THE FIRST SEASON

We covered coaching experience and I told him that I'd coached a bit of Little League; I do believe his frown deepened. We covered my experience as a player and I managed to score some points when we talked about Leon Black and my scholarship at Lon Morris. It turned out the superintendent was a fan of the game and Coach Black was a name that meant something to those who were in the know. However, that was quickly followed by a sore spot.

"The Mustangs—I know you played on some real good teams at Madisonville. I saw the Madisonville versus Huntington game a few years back; they beat y'all by one point. It was a heartbreaker; I remember that poor kid missing that last second, game-deciding shot." He shook his head. "What a game. A sports writer told me the winner of that game would be the State Champion and boy was he right. That would have been about the time you were on the team, right?

I tried to mask the sadness in my eyes with a smile. "Yes, that was my junior year. I was the guy that missed that last-second shot."

Mr. Bitner stopped chewing, "Sorry I asked."

I shrugged, "That's okay. It's one of the reasons I was driven into coaching. Besides, in the end, you win and lose as a team." I thought I saw a smile at the corner of his mouth, but it was hard to be sure.

My hunger for the position only increased when we talked about my selective service status. He informed me that if I got the position, a deferment would be in the works. There was a shortage of math and science teachers, subjects I would be required to teach three to four times a day.

"If you sign with us," he said, "I'll make an application with the draft board and you'll probably have a work deferment by next month. Are you ready to handle that?"

I smiled. "Where do I sign, sir?"

"I haven't offered you the job yet, son."

I swallowed deeply, slouching in my chair.

He pretended not to notice. "Why do you want to coach?"

I looked him in the eye. Sir, it's my passion. It's become my dream and I know I can teach guys what it takes to win."

There was a slight smile on his lips as he stood and moved to the window. He asked me about my goals and I told him that I only had one to take the team to the State Championship.

His smile encouraged me a little. "I like that answer, but let me warn you, son, your chances of taking anybody to the State Tournament this year are pretty far-fetched."

"Well, if you shoot for the stars, you just might hit the moon."

"You also have to be realistic and have a reachable goal."

I nodded my head in agreement. "You're right, but State will *always* be my goal."

We talked about other things—my coaching philosophy, my feelings on what makes players great, and the best qualities of great teams. I told him that our team would never lose because we were tired and that I wanted to play a running game, utilizing layups and high percentage shooting.

Mr. Bitner had yet to sit back down and his jaw worked nonstop in its attempt to grind his gum into oblivion. "This is a very poor school district. We have insufficient funds to handle what we do here, so expansion on our programs is not really an option. We're not an ISD; we're one of the few common school districts in the state. We don't have the same tax structure, so we get less help. Does that bother you?"

I shook my head, getting another half-smile out of the man.

"Come on, son," he said as he popped another piece of gum into his mouth. "Let's take a walk. I want to show you our so-called *friendly confines*." When he said that, I figured he was a Cubs fan so there was no way I was going to admit to being a die-hard Sox fan.

We made our way back out into the smell of restoration that permeated the school and walked down the hall, turning into the gym.

"We just finished our floor last week, but for an old gym, it's in great shape. Now it's not Madison Square Garden, but it is home and where you would play about half your games." There were dark wooden bleachers on one side and a stage on the other end.

"Some of your biggest critics will be on the front row of that stage." He had his fists on his hips as he locked eyes with me and motioned around the place. "Well, what do you think?"

I glanced the building over from top to bottom. "It's got goals ten feet tall and a nice floor. What more could a coach ask for?"

We were about to head back to the office when Mr. Bitner stopped me. "Oh, one more thing—and maybe the most important thing that we have yet to discuss. This year our school will be fully integrated for the first time. We've already had several kids from our black school enroll. Problems are... anticipated. How do you intend to approach it?"

It took me a moment to get my words together. Integration was something I had never worried about. I'd grown up in my dad's grocery store working with blacks as well as whites.

"My father taught me that one man can work as hard as the next; you just have to find the ones that are *willing* to work that hard—and they come in all colors. They're human beings just like we are. If you treat them with dignity and respect, there shouldn't be any more problems than with any white student. Problems will probably come more from the adults than from the students."

Mr. Bitner was nodding, but his frown was back in place as we walked down the hall and back to his office. "Things probably won't be quite as smooth as you think. This is the South. We're about to explore new territory and quite frankly, I don't know what to expect. You could play a key role in bridging the gap with your coaching. How are you going to handle it when some irate parent comes up to you and says, 'You're prejudiced; why aren't you playing my son?'"

I set my shoulders. "I would let them know the truth. My players will determine every day in practice just how much—and if—they get to play. I would let them know that I am out there in that gym each day for one reason: to put the best team on the floor that I can. If any player proves to me that our team will improve if he plays more, I can promise you that he will. If they want it and work for it, they'll get it."

Mr. Bitner appeared pleased with my answer. We were just in his doorway when the phone rang and he moved to pick it up. I was trying to assess how the interview was going when his face turned as white as a ghost. He seemed to have forgotten about me as he placed the phone back on the receiver, staring at the wood grains on his desk. After a moment, I asked if he was all right. Recognition flickered in his eyes as he shook his head.

"Son, you're hired. That call was from Austin. Some nut is on top of the University of Texas Tower with a rifle, shooting people. My daughter is in school up there. They're warning the parents to be prepared."

I was barely able to think about my being hired as I walked out the door and back into the Texas heat.

5

Coach Johnny Carter

Driving west on Highway 7, I listened to the radio about the UT disaster. I had to stop in Crockett and call back to see if Mr. Bitner had heard anything about his daughter. She was okay and had called only a few minutes before. My thoughts and prayers were with all the other parents who were worried about their kids.

My family was at the supper table when I walked in. I shared the good news first and then we spent a good amount of time in prayer for the families of the tragedy.

The next day, I called my friend Tommy Ferguson and shared the good news with him. Tommy had secured his own first-year coaching position a little over a month prior at Richards High School. I think we were both more than a little relieved to have someone else going through the process at the same time. We talked about coaching philosophies (something neither of us had at the moment), our schools, and drills. Tommy and I had been good friends on and off the court throughout high school and on into Lon Morris, but we were also fierce competitors in everything we did.

Tommy was an only child. Not having brothers was probably the main reason he was constantly challenging me to play him. There's no telling how many times we battled each other in our backyards after school. We had some intense one-on-one battles and I'm convinced that we made each other stronger competitors.

Kennard was a small school, Class B. At the time, Texas had five classifications of schools, with Class B as the smallest and 4A the largest. Each classification had its own State Championship. You have to under-stand, Class B basketball in east Texas was extremely competitive and many schools had rich traditions in basketball going back for years. Success breeds success and the schools with established traditions had already won half the battle. Kids grew up in the shadows of teams that had won for years and they started each season fully expecting to win. A positive attitude was ingrained in those schools before they ever started practice. Kennard had won District the past year, but had lost to Magnolia in the first round of the playoffs. Their advancement in the playoffs prior to the District win was erratic. A high point was that they had two starters returning from a team that went 25-11. The fact that twenty-five victories was on their record from the previous year was a great starting point.

2

Meet the Tigers

Another hot summer day heralded the first day of school and I was apprehensive about meeting the seventy-plus students that I had to help register. As I walked down the semi-deserted hallway, an older female teacher spotted me and began walking my way.

"I know every student in this school; you must be a transfer." She pointed down the hall behind her. "You need to go down to the gym and register."

My stomach dropped. I stood there almost dumbfounded. It took longer than I would have thought to assure her that I was older than I looked and that I was the new basketball coach. She apologized for what seemed like ten minutes, none of which helped repair my dented ego.

As the students began to file by the registration tables in the gym, I slowly became acquainted with a few of the players. One of the new black players was the first to introduce himself—or at least to mumble something about the team. It took me a few tries to get his name— Haywood Henderson, Jr.—and that guy was a physical specimen. Two brothers, Fred and James Pilkington, were introduced to me later by Mr. Bitner. Fred, a senior, was about my height—six-foot-one or two—and was a distance runner who'd gone to State the previous year in the mile. His brother James was much shorter, which had earned him the nickname "Nubbin."

About ten minutes later, another young black kid put out his hand to shake mine. "I'm Roy Harrison. I'm looking forward to playing for you. I'm not that tall, but I can play post." The guy wasn't five-foot-ten; he was probably barely five-foot-eight. All I remember thinking was, *This guy better be able to jump out of the gym.*

The next student to come by was only a little taller than James and looked like he might need to shed a couple of pounds. "This will be your best shooter." The voice came from behind me. As I turned, the man reached out and shook my hand. "I'm Benford Frizzell. I'm the Ag teacher."

He wore a smile that oozed confidence as he rested his hands on the kid's shoulders. Standing there, he reminded me of a young Mark Twain, minus the facial hair. "Coach, let me introduce you to Herman Myers. This guy doesn't look like a basketball player, but I assure you he shoots like one. He can fill it full from downtown."

I knew I was wet behind the ears in coaching, but the faculty's two cents was beginning to wear on me. I gave the pair a friendly nod. "The starting five will be determined by what they do when we start practice." Frizzell just winked at me, disappearing to help other students. Herman stayed to shake my hand before moving on to register.

Later that day, I looked into the young faces of Kennard basketball hopefuls. My wannabe players were lining the bleachers, looking over their competition. It was a decent turnout.

"My name is Coach Carter, but you can call me Coach. I want to lay out for you my expectations for this team. We will always be competitive and you will take pride in that fact."

I stared into my players' faces. "You're going to beat teams down the floor. I firmly believe in this style of play and I am committed to it and so are you if you plan to play on this team. I expect you to play hard-nosed defense. When a team scores on you, I expect them to have earned it.

"I will grade you every day, every game, on your defense. If you give up easy baskets, I promise you, I'll make you pay for each one. You might as well start conditioning your mind today because as far as I'm concerned, defense is the name of this game. Being consistent offensively is almost impossible. If a team hits 50 percent of their shots in a game, that's considered a great game. You show me a team that plays defense *50* percent of the time and I'll show you a team that we will kick up and down the floor every time we play them.

"You will play as a unit. I cannot stress enough the importance of team chemistry and before this year is over, you not only will see it this way, you'll eat, sleep, and breathe it! We will, in turn, either win or lose as a team. One person never wins or loses a game. The team does. Individual statistics mean nothing to me. It's all about *team* statistics. Some of you may average twenty to twenty-five points a game; if you do, it will be within the team concept that we establish as the season progresses. Every guy on this team will have a specific team role and I expect you to play that role to the absolute best of your ability. One more thing: I believe that there is no substitute for hard work, so get ready. I *will* work your butt off! Don't get me wrong, we'll have a lot of fun. But when it comes time to work, believe you me, we will. Any questions?"

Their hands stayed at their sides and one or two looked like they were second-guessing their decision to try out. "It's nice to meet you guys and I'm looking forward to working with you. Get a good night's sleep because practice starts tomorrow."

~~~

The long, sizzling summer of 1966 came to a close as I began to prepare for my classroom duties. The classroom was the major part of my job, something that came as a bit of shock since I couldn't get my head out of basketball. The fact was that I had four different classroom preparations each day, duties that would keep me busy well into the evening as I tried to stay one step ahead of my students. I once was told that what a teacher *is* is much more important than what he teaches. Daily, it became more and more obvious to me that a teacher exemplifying that statement would become a much more successful one.

In my third period class, I noticed two faces that I already knew, Lester Hutcherson and James Smith. They were the two best freshman basketball players in our school. Lester was a wiry kid who looked like he'd fall back on the seat of his pants if you sneezed too hard. If I had judged him solely on physical appearance, I would have said there was no way that frail-looking kid could ever be a basketball player. You could hide him behind a radio aerial. James Smith, on the other hand, was a little more filled-out and shorter than his teammate. I hadn't thought about getting to know my players off the court. It would be nice to get to know them outside of the game and, better yet, to make sure they were keeping their grades up. I didn't want any of my guys failing out.

Outside the window, clouds were rolling in, which was perfect because we were going over weather and atmospheric conditions in the lesson plan. Things were going pretty smoothly and I thought we were making good time, but we weren't halfway through the lesson when my eye again wandered to the window and out past the parking lot to the Ag shop. My train of thought broke down completely when I saw the shop's doors swing open and the entire class file out. I glanced back down at my watch to make sure it was running. There were almost thirty minutes left in the period, but there they were, standing around, laughing, and shooting the breeze. Mr. Frizzell was nowhere in sight. Eyes were beginning to wander to the window, so I cleared my throat and hurried on with the lecture with growing anticipation. Thirty minutes later, I was finally reassured when I heard the bell ring and watched the students across the lot head to their next classes.

It was finally time for lunch so I made my way to the cafeteria. In the lunch line, a pleasant lady behind the counter introduced herself.

"I'm Nona Baker, Coach. May I help you?"

I looked down the line. "I think I'll have chicken and two rolls, please."

She looked me over, placing the backs of her hands on her wide hips, one still holding a ladle. "You look like a growing boy; I think I'll give you three."

"Three!" I turned as I recognized the voice of Benford Frizzell, who had a sneaky smile on his face. "This guy must be something special to get three rolls on the first day of school. It took me five years to get that far into Nona's good graces."

I looked the man over. "Mr. Frizzell, you *are* the Ag teacher, aren't you?"

He raised an eyebrow and nodded.

"Then can you tell me how it is that I'm right in the middle of third period when I look across the parking lot and see your guys coming out of class? Apparently you were done teaching when I still had thirty minutes of lesson left! Do you know something I don't?"

With a deep sigh, he threw an arm across my shoulders and pulled me in close, glancing around conspiratorially. "Well, you're a rookie at teaching yet, so I'll let you in on a little secret. When you've taught as long as I have," he let his voice drop even lower, "you learn to teach *fast.*" He released me with a smile and picked up his tray.

I stood there dumbfounded with my mouth hanging open. Finally, I shook myself. "Teach *fast?* That's ridiculous!"

Mr. Frizzell looked hurt as he shook his head. "No, Coach. Seriously, it's a new technique I'm working on. Have you ever heard of the 'speed-reading' system? It allows you to read a book in a fraction of the time it normally takes while still retaining the knowledge. Well, I've taken it and incorporated that technique into my classroom procedure. Man, it works *great.*"

My eyes were getting bigger as I thought of ways to speed up my own classes.

Animated, Benford said, "I've got my guys building things so fast I don't have enough assignments to keep them busy the entire period! They just whip through anything I give 'em! So next time you see my guys sitting around outside, you'll know they worked their tails off and that I just gave them a well deserved break. You might want to try it with your players, too. I'll bet you can get your guys running twice as fast as they normally do."

That was enough to shake me back to reality as I looked at the possum grin plastered on Benford's face. "Uh-huh, so I suppose I'll be seeing your guys outside thirty minutes early *every day?*"

Mr. Frizzell shrugged and gave me a wink. "Who knows, Coach? I'm teaching faster every day!"

I burst out laughing and turned back to Mrs. Baker, who just rolled her eyes. She handed me my tray across the cafeteria line. "Don't you listen to Mr. Frizzell, but you can put us both down as loyal supporters of the team. I won't miss a game or a move you make out there."

I was still chuckling as I sat down, just in time to see Mrs. Baker making her way over to the table with a young man following behind her.

Coach Johnny Carter

"This is my son, Curtis, the *second* most loyal fan in Kennard. I'm still the first," she said laughingly. "I'm older, so I've managed to see a few more games than he has."

Curtis was a stocky kid. He had a pronounced jaw line and cheekbones, reminding me of a picture I'd seen of Chief Sitting Bull. It quickly became apparent that Curtis had the desire to be a coach and his passion for the game was palpable. He wasn't in college, but was seriously considering going back to Stephen F. Austin and getting his degree. That lunch passed quickly as we talked about the team's previous years, players, and tendencies. It was quite an education. As the bell rang, I realized I'd just made both a friend and an ally.

~~~

Period bells seemed to ring endlessly one after the other and I thought the first day of school was supposed to be tough on the students! Finally, it was time for seventh period and boys basketball practice. Realizing that would be my daily routine for the school year, I quickly began to recognize the importance of the assigned classroom duty. Nonetheless, that period was what I'd taken the job for, where my passion was.

My first day of practice at Kennard High School was about to begin. I had a practice plan in mind—complete with the basics and fundamentals to be covered which looked good on paper. In fact, it looked beautiful! It was the implementation that had me worried. One thing that I did notice was the fact that I had every player on the team in the gym the first day of practice. We didn't have football in our school so that meant that at each practice, every day, every player would be coached from Day One. That was why so many small schools had excellent basketball programs.

After warming up and shooting layups, I picked two teams to scrimmage. After watching each of the guys play, one thing was very clear to me: To my surprise, the five guys I was told would be my best players would indeed be my starters, at least if you went by that day's practice. Haywood was as athletic as he looked, moving up and down the court with ease and I watched in awe as Roy battled it out with Fred close to the net for rebounds. Herman was a range shooter and sunk shot after shot from anywhere on the floor. All the while, Nubbin was weaving in and out, a monster on defense, getting steals and confounding his opponents. I was even more surprised by Curtis's freshman picks. Lester had a mountain of heart on the floor and James turned out to be so quick that he reminded me of a hummingbird. He had the absolute quickest pair of hands I'd ever seen. He could take your watch off your wrist, reset the time, and slap it back on before you knew it was missing. There's a major difference in being quick and being fast—James was both. He could take a ball from you one-on-one, but if he missed on that steal attempt, he could beat you back to the paint in jet-like fashion. That school had some talent.

I blew my whistle and lined the guys up in pairs. "Let's get ready, sports fans! We're about to start our season-long journey of the joy that is fundamentals. You're about to go one-on-one, full court. This is a double dose of basics. I want the proper footwork on defense and just basic ball-handling skills on offense. If you notice, I've got some pieces of tape running parallel to the sideline. That tape is out-of-bounds for you on this drill, which significantly narrows the width of the playing court. Ball handlers, when you reach that tape, that's out-of-bounds. You have to change direction. Defenders, that line is your friend. If you beat the ball handler to that line, you force him to change direction every time. When you consistently and aggressively beat him to that line, you're playing the only type of defense I want to see. The more you make a ball handler change direction, the better the defense you're playing. What that means is that you're busting his butt!

"It's all about effort and I'm going to tell you right now, if you want to play for me, you're gonna have to give a *lot* of effort. When you play proper defense, you play with your feet, not your arms. It's all about body position. When somebody is about to get around you, you don't run along beside him and escort him to the other end. You don't just stay with him and start reaching for the ball—that's when you draw those cheap fouls. You turn and run as fast as you can and you beat him to the spot he's headed for. That way you just might draw the charge. You got that, Nubbin?"

With a smile, Nubbin looked at me. "Coach, you're talking my language. I love to play defense."

I grinned back. "You and I are going to get along real well. Now you guys handling the ball, listen up. I want you down low, protecting the ball. You're trying to take the ball baseline to baseline. When the defense beats you to that line, you've got to turn and zigzag to the other side. Any time you can go around the defender, burn him. Look, you've got to be ambidextrous and if you're not, the defense is going to eat your lunch."

Chuckling under his breath, Haywood looked at me and said, "What's that word you said? Ambi-what?"

"Ambidextrous. That means you use both hands. A good ball handler is only as good as his off-hand. Look, the good Lord gave us two hands and in basketball, he meant for us to use both of them. You show me a guy that uses only one hand and I'll show you a guy that I'll beat every time I face him! Okay, Roy, you're going to go against Haywood, so what are you going to do if he gets around you?"

Roy smiled, puffing out his chest. "I can't really say, Coach, because he's never *gonna* get around me!"

Haywood laughed. "Just give me the ball, Coach. I'm going to leave Roy in the dust."

I looked at Roy with a smirk. "Well, son, just tell me what you're supposed to do if someone *does* get around you?"

Roy was looking at Haywood, "I'm going to turn and run, Coach."

"You're going to turn and do what?"

"Run!"

I raised my voice, cupping my hand to my ear. "I can't hear you, Roy!"

"Run!"

The word bounced off the walls of the gym and I figured my point had been well made. Soon, everyone was going through the drill and although we were a long way from running it to perfection, the effort was definitely there. The Roy-versus-Haywood confrontation was highly competitive, both guys constantly trading being in control. As I watched those two guys battle it out, I was smiling, because I knew by what I was seeing that their level of play would improve daily.

The one thing that concerned me after watching my team for the first time was the apparent lack of depth. Evaluating the guys, there was a distinct difference in the five probable starters compared to the rest of the squad. Looking down the road, there would be no margin for error. No one could foul out, no one could get sick, and no one could flunk out. If any of those things happened, we could be in major trouble. Going through a basketball season without one or more of those happening—maybe even several times—would be virtually impossible, so my first order of business with the team would be to find someone, hopefully more than one person, to come off the bench with some quality minutes.

~~~

After a week of practice, several things were on my mind about the team. We had not great, but pretty good speed, our players had good attitudes, and they seemed to respond well to my coaching. But aside from depth, I could see us getting killed on the glass. I knew that we really needed to spend a lot of time working on rebounding. Doing some homework, I read as many magazines articles as I could get my hands on and read about players wearing weight vests to improve their vertical jumps. I found a catalogue and looked at the price. That was something the school couldn't afford. I visited with my mom at home that weekend and told her about the vests over lunch.

She looked over the catalog pictures I'd brought along. "I think I can make some of those for you. The only problem is gonna be getting some kind of weight and where to position it." Soon paper was on the table as my mother scribbled sketches as I looked on in awe. After much forethought and deliberation, we came up with the idea of using sandbags draped over the shoulders and in the pockets—six in all. When I headed out the door, she was still buried in the pictures. "Give me a week and I'll have some vests made for you."

Two days later, she had a prototype. Sure enough, the vest she had made was perfect. The next day at practice, I let Haywood try it on. He cocked an eyebrow and said, "Coach, I need more weight than *this*. It's way too light."

I just smiled and had him run through the exercise program I'd set up: touching the backboard twenty times with both hands and hopping up and the down the bleachers with both feet. Haywood started the exercises with ease, as if there was no resistance at all, but before finishing, he had slowed down considerably.

With a few bleachers to go, Haywood looked at me, sweat was pouring down his face and he was panting for breath. "Coach, this thing will work your butt off!.

Coach Johnny Carter

Indeed, we had something with those vests and shortly we had several more, giving my athletic player some much needed company in his drills. Slowly and surely, we were physically improving our jumping ability, but the biggest boon may have been psychologically because our guys were starting to think they could jump out of the gym!

3

Practice, Practice

It was late September in east Texas. Unlike the color change outside, no starting lineup change was imminent on the hardwood floor of the Kennard Tigers gym. In examining the starting lineup, I continued to be mystified that the starters would indeed be the five that were picked out for me that first day of school. Roy Harrison, actually five-foot-nine, was a scorer with very nice moves around the basket and a very good jumper. James "Nubbin" Pilkington was a short, quick, tough defender and a good ball handler. His brother, Fred, the only senior on the starting lineup, was a versatile post man that could shoot both inside and out, and more importantly, he was a silent leader by example. He gave more effort than I asked for and, in turn, pushed his fellow players to do the same. Haywood Henderson, with all the skills a team needs to keep the play in motion, was just an athlete—period. Herman Myers was a shooter with the range to rip the cords anywhere on the floor and an eye to move the ball up and down the floor. Those five guys had a balance that could develop into a successful team with continued improvement.

Gary Parrish, a sophomore, emerged as our sixth man. Other members of the squad were Danny Smith, a senior; juniors Walter Denman and Leeland Strban; Jerry Parrish and Eddie Pilkington representing the sophomore class. Lester Hutcherson was the only freshman. Over the next few weeks, we ran drill after drill and the payoff was apparent in more than fundamentals. A chemistry was slowly starting to develop among the starting five. There's something amazing about the camaraderie that develops between people who are pushed together. The harder I pushed the team, the more exhausted they became, the closer they seemed to bond, and the more they pulled each other onward. The fact that the team was slowly coming together was what I had envisioned and prayed for. Without teamwork, I knew that we would be mediocre, but with it, we had a chance at a lot more.

After almost a month of practicing in the athletic period during the normal school day, October 1 was fast approaching. It would be the first day of after-school practice as allowed by the University Interscholastic League, the governing body for all high school athletics in Texas. That day's practice would introduce our team to a new drill that I had come up with. I named it the "eleven break drill" because it took eleven players to execute. I explained it to the guys as a continuous three-on- two fast break. It turned out to be as fun for the players as it was good for them. It had them constantly on the run and getting in better shape every day. Almost everything about the running game was covered: the outlet pass, filling the lane, finding the open man for the quick jump shot, defending the break, blocking out, inbound pass pressure after a successful basket, and crashing the glass while defending half-court. When finishing with free throws after running the eleven break drill for an extended period of time, a game-like situation was created that the players really seemed to enjoy executing. Creating fun was something I soon learned was integral if I wanted my team's full effort.

At the end of practice, I took the guys to the side, "Look, after-school practice will be a very different timeline. We're looking at being up here for some very long practices. Look around at these walls." Their eyes moved across the fresh white paint. "This is your new home away from home. We'll be up here until dark many practices, starting Monday."

I noticed a few raised eyebrows. "Look, I took this job with a purpose and a goal in mind—to make this the best team humanly possible. You're not gonna get shortchanged by me. You'll get everything I have—that's a promise. In turn, I expect you to give me everything *you* have. Anything else is totally unacceptable. Whether you play a lot or very seldom, each of you has an important role on this team. For those of you who sit on the bench and don't get to play as much as you want, let me tell you something. I've been there and done that, so I can identify with you. Look, I've been a starter and a bench player, both have important roles. I expect you to accept whatever role you get and deal with it positively for the team."

I was finding that honesty was definitely the best policy. The faster I could get my team to accept the amount of effort needed to play the game-and play it well, the better off we'd be.

October 1st arrived and our first day of after-school practice began. That day, we were working on defense in general and guarding the baseline in particular. I pointed toward the end line. That line is your friend. It's like an additional sixth man on the floor for the defense. You do not let someone drive between you and that line."

I looked at the boys. "Haywood, I'm going to guard you." He stepped forward and stood where I pointed. "Okay, you just received a pass here in the corner. You now have three options: shoot, pass, or dribble. I want you to drive around me on the baseline side. I'm going to tell you right now, I'm not going to let you do it."

Haywood's mouth was slightly ajar, " Let me get this straight— you're telling me that you're *not* gonna let me dribble the ball between you and the baseline to the basket?

"That's right."

"Coach," he said with a big smile, "I know that you're pretty quick, I mean, I've seen you play with us. I don't mean to be disrespectful here, but there is no way that you're going to keep me from taking this ball around you."

Having coached Haywood for a few weeks, a sliver of doubt wedged itself in my mind. *Maybe I should have picked a different player.* I looked him over as he squared up. *I may have just set myself up to look* really *foolish. On the other hand, it's a basketball sin to let anybody drive the baseline on you. I'm only twenty-three and I'm in pretty good shape,* I thought, but I knew I wasn't in basketball shape. My mind was already trying to work out a lesson in case Haywood managed to get past me.

I got into a defensive position. "Are you ready?"

"Yes, sir."

"Okay, let's do it!"

With the whole team standing around waiting, the air was electric. Being the athlete that he was, Haywood exploded on the dribble toward the baseline. I took a quick, big step, planting my foot on the baseline.

Promptly, Haywood crashed into me, knocking me straight back on the seat of my pants and following me down to the floor with a thud. The gym rang with laughter. I got up, dusting myself off.

"Guess what, fellas? It's my ball. Haywood, that's a charge, an offensive foul. Nobody drives the baseline on you—*nobody*. You know why? Cause you're not going to let them, that's why. Is that understood?" They were still suppressing smiles, but the point was well made.

The majority of that first after-school practice had been devoted to defense in the hope that its importance would rub off on my players. We'd been emphasizing the big *D* during our seventh-period workouts since the first day of school; however, I was finding that the best way to make a point was to work it to exhaustion. The amount of time you spend practicing any particular phase of the game sends a message to your team. A team with defense as its backbone always has a chance of success because you can count on it to be there. Unlike offense, defense never has an off-night. It should become as natural for players as lacing up their sneakers—eventually it becomes a reflex. Every day, I was trying hard to keep my team focused on the basic premise that offense may sometimes win a game, but defense wins championships.

We were slowly approaching our first game and our training intensity was growing accordingly. Fred Pilkington's value on our team became clearer with each practice session. The soft-spoken senior post had an endless supply of energy. His training in long distance running gave him a level of stamina that was amazing to behold and he set the pace for the team to follow, pushing our guys' competitive spirits to the limit. Stamina was going to be a very important issue with our team, especially since it looked like our starters would have to be in the game almost in its entirety. My guys didn't need to be in good shape, they needed to be in *great* shape. In a thirty-two minute game, I needed them to be able to play just as hard the last two minutes as they had the first two. With Fred pushing them, we had a shot at getting there. The best part about him was his lack of ego. He didn't even realize he was leading his teammates; he just came every day ready to play the game hard. Every team needs a guy like Fred and I was just glad he was wearing the purple and white.

One particular practice, I'd ridden him hard about his position as post. With our double-post offense, I needed him to take a lot of high-post jump shots. I'd watched him carefully and I knew he could sink those baskets in high percentages. It was just a question of whether or not he would get the opportunity to try. I pounded into my players the necessity of crashing the glass after a shot. We weren't big so rebounding was going to have to be a team effort. I watched them, especially Fred, as they ran the drill. As he missed another opportunity, I blew my whistle, "Fred!" The ball stopped bouncing.

"Son, when you shoot that high-post jumper you've got to go to the glass hard after each shot. One of the most important, if not *the* most important facets of the game is offensive rebounding. Crashing the offensive boards for a rebound is like giving yourself an unassisted assist. You've got to be relentless. When your feet hit the floor after flipping that jumper, I want you to explode to the basket. I want it to become automatic. I want the other coaches to get on someone's butt because they didn't keep you off that backboard."

Fred nodded, biting the inside of his lip as I blew the whistle to resume play. True to form, Fred pushed himself hard and soon had become a terrific offensive rebounder, surging forward after each shot and planting himself in position. His value as our silent leader gradually rose to new heights as I watched my other players struggle to match his intensity. By the end of practice, we had a team attempting to out-rebound one another.

The next day in practice, we had a full scrimmage against our second string, along with some of the better junior high players. Jeff Myers and Donald Denman were practicing with us and when I coupled them with our freshmen, James Smith and Lester Hutcherson, I saw the nucleus of a possible special team for the future. They were young to be going against my starters, but that day they were holding their own.
One particular play, there was a breakaway layup by one of those youngsters. The layup was missed, but Donald Denman ran the floor hard, got the offensive rebound, and put the ball back in the bucket while my starting five stood and watched. I felt my face flush and suddenly that gym felt too hot to stand. The whistle was in my mouth before I could even blink. I let it shriek long and loud because it was better than screaming myself. The balls stopped bouncing. "A basketball

team doesn't *watch* the game when they're on the court—they *play* the game there! When it's time to run the floor, you don't walk, you don't jog, you *run* the floor! *Do you understand?"*

Haywood had his eyes cast down and Herman's mouth was slightly ajar as my voice rang off the bleachers for at least six seconds after I had closed my mouth. With that, I had the starting five benched, replacing them with a new five. As they sat watching the continuing scrimmage, I turned to them, "If you want to watch the game, *this* is where you sit. If I was playing on your team right now, I can promise you, I would never be sitting where you are right now. I don't care if you're dead tired. You will run the floor." By then, my anger had been given time to simmer, but I decided to give them some time to get the message across.

Instruction and correction are the ongoing business of a coach. How a team or a player reacts to criticism says a lot about the team's chemistry, which determines whether or not they will show improvement or become discouraged. Roy spoke up from behind me. "Coach, I can't speak for everyone, but you'll never have to get on me again for not running the floor."

The others chimed in their agreement. That was one of the things I loved about those guys—they weren't dummies. They understood what needed to be done, accepted constructive criticism, and pulled improvement out of even tough situations—and they did so as a team. That was the heart of my Tigers. They knew that I wouldn't accept mediocrity from them because I would never accept mediocrity from myself, especially when it came to hustle.

After letting them sit the bench for quite some time to mull it over, I turned to face them. "How hard is that bench?"

Nubbin rubbed his backside. "Pretty hard, Coach."

"Well, if you guys haven't got enough splinters in your butt, maybe you haven't been there long enough."

Roy shot up out of his seat. "Wait a minute, Coach, we've all got 'em, but I know I've got the most!"

Haywood pulled him back down to the bench. "Like heck you do. I've done a lot more squirming over here than you have!"

Continuing to watch three eighth graders and two freshmen do a number against our second team, I looked over to the bench, crossing my arms. "You know how to keep from getting splinters in your butt, don't you?"

Herman turned around like he was directing a choir and the starting five followed his conducting, shouting as one, *"Run the floor!"*

I jerked a thumb toward the floor and gave a sharp whistle to pull back the bench players. "Get back in there and show me."

Soon, they were back on the floor with a new intensity and desire. They showed the drive that I already knew was there. The young team that had been holding their own before continued to play their hearts out, but they didn't have a chance when the starting five played with fire in their bellies. It appeared as if our team had grown up a little. Only time would tell.

That proved to be the high point of pre-season practice thus far, but we still had many bridges to cross to reach the level of play that I envisioned. I looked over at the bleachers and noticed Curtis had come to sit in on the practice. I found a seat beside him.

"How's it going, Coach? They're looking good to me."

"You know, many nights I've gone home and second-guessed myself about a drill or the guidance I'm giving these boys. When you come to that fork in the river and you don't know if you should go left or right, you can only hope that you made the right choice. I'm making a lot of choices just on instinct right now. I really want this team to do well. I feel like we have so much potential! Do you know what I mean?"

Curtis nodded. "Yeah, potential, I know what that means. It means you ain't done nothin' yet." He cracked a smile and so did I. "If what I saw today was any indication of some of the decisions you've been making, I think you took the right bend. You did something today that a lot of coaches would have handled differently. I saw how you took them apart and put them back together for the better. I saw the response when they went back on the floor. If we can somehow reach that level consistently, then we'll really have something!"

I looked over my team still dominating the floor. "Yeah, but this is still practice. No uniforms, no fans raging in the stands, no referees, no cheerleaders jumping around in short skirts. When you have a game, it's just...different."

Coach Johnny Carter

"Coach, all I know is that those sons-of-guns couldn't wait to get back on the floor and show you that they could do exactly what you wanted them to do. That's what coaching is all about—motivating a team to do the job your way. I talked to Roy the other day and asked him about you. He said and I quote, 'This guy makes me want to be a better player every day.'" My eyebrows shot up and I couldn't help the smile that crept across my face.

He also said, "'Coach makes our team believe.'"

I looked at Roy and my other players out on the court, giving it their all. Needless to say, I bought Curtis his supper that day.

~~~

As the end of lunch sounded one day, Mrs. Nona Baker walked over to the table. "Coach, I've got something for you," she said.

With that she handed me a plate covered with aluminum foil. "Just something special I whipped up for you this morning." The intoxicating scent of fried pies set me to drooling. "They're apricot. I was told that was your favorite."

They were still warm as I took a bite and I just about cried. She was all smiles, her plump cheeks crinkling as she watched me wolf them down. "I'm glad you like them, Coach. It's the least I can do. You've taken such an interest in Curtis and he needs that right now. I think he's really considering going back to school because of you. He keeps telling me about how impressed he is with you, the sincere way that you go about your job and the example that you set for the team."

I had to stop her before I started blushing. "Mrs. Baker, I really appreciate you saying that. I just hope that you feel the same way after we've played, say, thirty games."

"Oh, Coach, this team has achieved a lot already and we haven't even played a game. Let me tell you something. There's a genuine caring for you by these guys. Whether you know it or not, this little school community is slowly falling in love with you." About that time, the bell rang and it was a good thing it did because I had no idea what to say. I just thanked her for the pies and headed to my next class, feeling a little taller than I had when I woke up that morning.

We were getting close to our first game of the season and our team wasn't ready—at least not in my eyes. Methodically, we were working our way there, but with only a week left, I was worried. At least we were in good shape physically. We had gradually been increasing our intensity level in practice until I began to worry that we would burn out before we even got a chance to play a real game. Pacing around my office, the worry growing in my mind, I eventually broke. Marching down the hall, I found Fred in his homeroom and called him outside, excusing myself to the teacher. When I explained my worries, he just laughed at me.

"Burning us out? Heck no, Coach. We need to keep doing just like we have been. I think I'm in the best shape of my life and that includes when I train for track. I think if you ask the rest of the guys, they'll tell you the same thing. I can't wait to play our first game because I know I'm going to be much better on the boards than any year before." His brow furrowed. "Coach, did somebody complain about our workouts being too tough? Who was it? I'll have a talk with them."

He had fire in his eyes, a deep disappointment waiting to be unleashed on whoever doubted our team's regimen and it was working on its intended target. "Well, I just... the guy asked me not to mention his name." I couldn't meet his eyes.

He shook his head, but gave me a big smile, "This is just the price you have to pay when you're trying to be the best you can be. Do me a favor, Coach. Don't change a thing. I think we have a chance to be a really good team this year. We're much further along right now than I ever thought we'd be. No one on the team wants to be ordinary. We all know ordinary is nowhere to be seen in you and we're willing to take the difficult road to get better."

I waved him back to his classes and thought about his words. That was my leader by example and he'd done more for my reassurance than I could tell him.

Our afternoon practice that day was focused on offense. I stressed from the start that our offense was broken down into two simple phases. The first and foremost was the fast break. If it wasn't there, we would immediately move right into phase two, which was our half-court offense. On one particular occasion when the fast break failed to materialize, I called for the blue set and sat back in disbelief as I watched my players attempt to run the set in slow motion. Their lack of ball movement had me about ready to explode. *Freeze!* Nobody move! We were supposedly running the *blue set.* That isn't the blue set, that *is* the blues."

I received several groans from my players—people just don't appreciate word play. "Fellas, really, our team has the ball right now— that's supposed to be called 'offense.' You're playing better defense than the guys guarding you! When you move the ball that slow, you make it easy for the slowest guy in America to guard you. The object of offense is to make the defense have to *work.* It's not a rest period for them. Let's try this again. This time I want to see some ball movement! You don't win games by slow dancing with each other, you win them with quick passes. The ball is supposed to be a hot potato. Don't hold it like a bag of potato chips!"

Driving home some nights after practice, I had to remind myself that they were sixteen and seventeen year-old kids. They were bound to make mistakes. With only a few days left until our first game of the season, I headed home to visit my parents. There's always something special about returning home and my anxiety about the upcoming match was lessened just being there. Not that my mother's home-cooking didn't help all the more. Our conversation inevitably turned toward the season and I was thankful to have some time to talk to my dad. He always managed to put things in the right perspective. My mom was clearing the plates when I confessed that I had no idea what I was doing, that I didn't think the team was ready, and that I was scared to death of the upcoming bout.

My dad placed a hand on my shoulder. "Son, every head coach had to start somewhere and probably had the same butterflies and nervousness that you're experiencing right now."

I gave him a weak smile. "In some respects, I feel more like I'm one of the guys than their coach."

My dad sat back in his chair, crossing his arms over his stomach. "Son, have you ever heard of on-the-job training? When your grandfather drowned, I was thirteen years old. I was devastated, as was our entire family. I realized that not only had I lost my father, I had lost my childhood in one night. I had to become the breadwinner in our family with a dump truck load of responsibility deposited right in my lap. I said to myself, 'How in the world can I deal with all of this?' I really had no other choice but to start working full-time to support the family. I was a little boy that had to become a man overnight. I was unsure, afraid, fearful, nervous, and to be completely honest, I didn't know if I could handle it."

Standing, he moved to the bookshelf and pulled the bible down, handing it to me. "Open up the Bible to 1 Timothy 4:12; it really helped me when I felt like a little fish in deep water."

I leafed through the pages until I came to the chapter and verse he'd indicated and read the selection out loud. "Don't let anyone think little of you because you are young. Be their example; let them follow the way you teach and live."

Dad was smiling. "Everybody is young and unsure at one time or another. It's not in the rule book that you have to be thirty, forty, or fifty years old before you can be a good coach or a good man. You just give it everything that you have, every day, and you'll be fine. Not that you won't make mistakes—everybody does, but that's just part of learning."

~~~

Leaving my parents' house, I felt stronger. I had my feet back under me. I still didn't feel prepared for what was ahead, but at least I felt secure in knowing that I would give it everything I had and that was all that could be expected of me.

Coach Johnny Carter

4

Opening Night

Monday morning, I met Herman before the bell and we chatted about the players' progress compared to last year. He seemed excited, giving everyone positive marks.

"Now, Fred, I think he's going to have a monster year! He's playing *way* better than he did last year, both shooting and in rebounding. Not bad for a guy with a heart murmur, huh, Coach?"

I felt as if a grapefruit had lodged itself in my now very dry throat. "Heart murmur? Didn't Fred go to State in the mile last year?"

Herman was bobbing his head. "Yeah, actually he's already working on that training as well. Fred and Nubbin live about twelve miles from the school and a lot of days they walk or jog it after practice, so he should be in great shape come time for track." I managed to swallow that grapefruit, but then there was a weight in the pit of my stomach.

"You mean to tell me that Fred and Nubbin have been jogging twelve miles to get home after practice?"

"Well..." Herman was shuffling nervously. "They get a ride occasionally and it doesn't take 'em too long when they run it."

My mouth dropped open. Herman was waving his hands trying to reassure me. "Coach, Fred and Nubbin want to play *real* bad and I honestly don't think they mind walking home."

I was quickly heading down the hall looking for Fred. I found him in his first-period class and called him out into the hall.

He had his arms crossed. "What is it, Coach? Did someone complain again? I swear..."

"Fred, Herman just told me you have a heart murmur."

With a sigh, he answered, "Yeah, I do. I've lived with it my whole life and yes, I did pass my physical. I expect to play as many minutes as you want me to and still plan on running the mile when the season is over."

I was probably overreacting; the kid had more stamina than anyone on the team. "Herman also told me that you and Nubbin have been walking home a lot of nights after practice. Is that true?"

Fred nodded his head in concession. "Yes, sir, but we don't mind, Coach. We just want to do whatever it takes to be on your team."

I looked at my lead-by-example post man and couldn't help but feel proud of him. "Fred, why didn't you guys tell me that you didn't have a ride home? I would have taken you any time."

Shrugging, he looked down at his feet. "We didn't want to bother you. You've got a lot more things to take care of with your own job. Getting home after practice is our responsibility."

I rested a hand on his shoulder. "Listen to me, Fred. It will be my pleasure to take you guys home today. In fact, any day that you don't have a ride home, you let me know. You and Nubbin work your butts off in practice every day. You shouldn't have to spend half the night just getting home." I let him head back to class and stared after him. Those kids were truly dedicated to the team. I hoped I'd be able to reward their efforts.

~~~

Our last practice prior to the opening game of the season went smoothly. After several weeks of hard-nosed fundamentals, I began to back off, incorporating a little more fun into the practice. My plan was to create a positive atmosphere. We would recap the basic fundamentals and sneak in important basics, but most important was just bringing the guys together in some game-like situations. It definitely created a fun atmosphere while continually reaffirming many of the things we had learned along the way. My whistles and constant harping began to gain a little more respect now that I could call out the problem in a normal play situation and bring up the solution in the drills we'd perfected. Slowly but surely, the many repetitions we had methodically worked through in practice started to pay dividends. There was no question in my mind that those guys had a hunger for excellence. The word "hustle" had already become synonymous with our practice and when you combine that with fundamentals, your team efficiency becomes a constant. In basketball, like everything else, if a tool isn't reliable, it's a liability.

We were near the end of our last round of free throws when I called everyone over. "I'm cutting practice just a little short today because we have something pretty important happening tomorrow night." I bit my lower lip in thought. "I know it's something... just what do we have going on tomorrow?"

Roy looked at me with a grin. " Aw, come on, Coach. You know we play our first game of the season tomorrow night."

I snapped my fingers. "Right! The season. I knew I was forgetting something." I looked my team over. "Well, do you think we're ready?"

Heads were nodding all around me as players exchanged smiles. Roy continued to be the spokesman. "As hard as you've been pushing us, it's time to put all that practice on display. I'm ready to play against somebody besides these slowpokes." Lester gave him a shove as the team chuckled.

"Fellas, we turned a page today and hopefully all the practices we've gone through have begun to prepare you for the games we're about to play. So phase one of our season is over. Phase two starts tomorrow night. Every game, every play, every decision will be criticized by the crowd. Don't listen to what the crowd says because most of them don't know what they're talking about. I promise you that I'm gonna know more about this team than anybody in the stands and there won't be anyone in those stands that will be a bigger fan than I already am. Keep this in mind and keep yourselves focused on what *I* say, not what those folks in the bleachers do."

I pointed towards the stands. "There will be a lot of people sitting right up there that love this game; I'm in that category, too. But how many of those fans *live* this game? Well, fellas, I do and I will be here for you every day at school, every practice, and every game we play. If you've got some problem in the early hours of the morning and no one to turn to, call me. I'm in the book and I'll be there for you then too. We're a family, we're gonna act like we're family and we're gonna play like we're family. I want every team we play to know from the start that they can't just take on one of us and get the job done. If they take on one of us then they take on all of us because we'll be playing as one unit.

"Look, things will be different starting tomorrow night. Everything we do will be under the microscope. The decisions that I make and the structure of our play will be analyzed, criticized, and sometimes chastised. In the upcoming games, how you respond to me and how I respond to you will go a long way in determining the degree of success we have. That being said, I want to make something very clear—something we've already talked about. There is no 'I' in the word team. Have you ever wondered why some teams have great players and still never manage to get very far? These teams usually win a lot of battles, but rarely win any wars. Why do you think that's the case?"

Haywood looked up. "They're selfish, Coach. They don't play as a team."

With a big smile, I looked at my muscular wingman. "Bingo! Basketball is a team sport and if you don't approach it in that manner, you will never come close to reaching your potential. The best teams are the ones that play together, unselfishly, with every individual member blending together as a close-knit unit." I grabbed my clipboard and started tracing as I continued talking. "Get this ingrained in your minds. We do not have stars on this team. The team is the star. When you draw a star, what do you see?" I raised my clipboard. "I see five points connected by lines with each point representing one of you out there on the floor. I've seen your connections growing stronger every day. You take away one of those points and..." I took my pen and scratched out one of them. "The star is lost. It takes five individuals working in unison, performing their roles—whatever they may be—for a team to scratch the surface of stardom. I don't want this to be your goal, I want it to be your duty. You guys on the bench never know when you'll be out there as one of the five points. That's why you always have to stay focused and be in the game mentally, even when you're not on the court physically. Tomorrow night will be the first of many games. I expect you to approach this game and every game this season in the manner that I just described. Let's do what it takes to make this star shine."

~~~

THE FIRST SEASON

It was game day and we were traveling on the school's soon-to-be familiar yellow dog, jammed into the brown naugahyde and cardboard bench seats. Benford Frizzell was behind the wheel and I was glad. I was totally lost in the backcountry roads of that pine forest. We were somewhere in the deepest of deep east Texas headed for Zavalla, a town I'd heard of, but whose name marked the extent of my knowledge. Schools in the B classification dotted the Texas map and I knew there would be many other small east Texas towns that I'd become very familiar with as the season progressed.

Our gym at Kennard wasn't exactly big, but that one was *tiny*. We were in the middle of October and about to play our first game while all the schools I was familiar with still had a month of football left before they even began practicing. Even if we were playing in the smallest gym I'd ever seen, we were about to get quite a head start in our season.

Nervously heading for the dressing room, a multitude of questions bounced through my mind. I'd rehearsed the mental notes for the pre-game speech of my life again and again and then suddenly, I found myself standing before my team. Their faces were intent, their eyes filled with determination, waiting—and the words were stuck in my throat. I must have blacked out because I have no idea what I said. Whatever it was must have been sufficient because the next thing I knew we'd put our hands together and were shouting, "1, 2, 3, let's go!" and were on the floor warming up.

Sitting alone on the bench while we went through our pre-game warm-up drills, I wondered just how we would respond to an actual game. I'd tried to make our practices as close to game conditions as I could, but having been around the sport all my life, I knew too well that practice and games were like night and day. Shortly afterwards, the horn sounded, sending both teams to their respective benches. With the team huddled up around me, my heart was pounding in my chest. I could tell it was the same for my players. Somehow I managed to force a much needed smile. I didn't feel like smiling. I had no desire to smile, but sometimes you do what you think is necessary because your gut instinct says to do it. I'll be the first to admit that my acting skills are limited, but my guys seemed to buy it. Secretly, I was thanking Zula Pearson, my professor from the one acting class I'd taken at Lon

Morris It seemed to ease the tension and I could see a few returned smiles around the huddle.

"Look, fellas, go out there and employ our game plan just like we worked on it. I've worked you guys hard every day preparing you for this moment. Now I want you to go out there and *enjoy* this game. This is what all the sweat, all the repetition, all the practice was for! Play the game the way I taught you and have fun doing it. Look, the practices we've had were your appetizer; this game is the main course. What's for dessert? Well..." I forced my smile wider, "you have to win to get it. Now let's see if you get yours!"

Our cheerleaders were going through an early pre-game cheer as the horn echoed in the background. With the opening tip, the mounting nervousness was released. My personal pressure gauge dropped back to normal as my pent-up energy found an outlet and soon I was lost in the game. Running our half-court offense, we got the ball to Fred for an opening free- throw-line, high-post jumper. Fred squared up, flicked his wrist, and ripped the cords. My lead-by-example senior had just given us the lead. Coming off the bench with a raised fist of approval, I experienced a feeling of exhilaration that I didn't know was possible. It was total affirmation that let me know that I had made the right choice at the University of Houston when I changed majors. A genuine lifetime love affair was conceived as I watched the net sway back and forth with the force of the ball.

I'd grown up with a passion for the sport which steadily increased through grade school, watching countless games with my dad. But that basket that Fred had just made fanned the ever-burning flame that I had for the game into a bonfire. I had no time to savor the moment. Roy got the ball down low and made a sensational post move after a nice feed from Herman. With an off-balance, fade-away shot, Roy's soft touch and wrist flip put two more on the board. We were off and running, at least early on, as we dominated the first quarter. Before the half was over, Herman, Nubbin, and Haywood had all joined the barrage of buckets with every starter officially joining the scoring parade, propelling us to a fourteen-point lead. We left the floor and headed for the dressing room in command of the game.

A halftime lead can be a double-edged sword. On the one hand, a lot of self-confidence could be seen in that positive expression shining on the young faces of my team. On the other hand, too much confidence can cause a team to forget just how hard they worked to get that lead in the first place. The end result of that cockiness has obliterated many a hard-earned lead, subsequently awarding an opponent an undeserved gift. Looking into the faces of my players at halftime, I was determined to get that point across.

"Look, you played very well and don't take this the wrong way because I'm very pleased with the way we played our first half, but this game is *far* from over. The question is 'Are you going to continue to play with the same aggressiveness and effort in the second half?

"When you have a team down, you don't toy around with them." I looked each of my team members in the eye. "You put them away when you have the chance. What I'm saying here is——you bury them. When you have somebody down, you don't wait to finish the job later. You finish the business there and then. You let them know that you are not about to let them get back in the game. Is that clear, sports fans?" A cheer let me know that I'd been heard loud and clear.

~~~

Soon the second half started and we continued right where we left off. I was particularly pleased because our team seemed to have taken to heart what I had stressed at halftime. We put them away, ending with a convincing 67-44 opening season win.

Walking off the floor toward the dressing room, my heart was racing with delight. The feeling within me was absolutely indescribable. It was the height of highs and I felt like I was walking on air as I reached the dressing room door. There was Benford, who grabbed my hand. "Great job, Coach and you've only had these guys for how long? That's what I call teaching fast!" Still laughing, I pulled open the door and walked in.

The atmosphere was ringing with emotion as an air of accomplishment engulfed the room. I had experienced that feeling as a player, but the energy in the room far exceeded anything I'd ever known. Walking around the dressing room, I congratulated every player, shaking each one's hand. A few minutes later, I had all of them sitting in front of me.

"Congratulations! We played very well. I'm proud of what we did tonight. Of course, I was watching and we made our share of mistakes, which we will correct as we go through the season. There are two very important things that I want to point out to you: One, I was very pleased with the fact that you had 100 percent hustle the entire game. Two, you played together as a unit. That's huge! This is what teamwork is all about and we reaped the benefits tonight. And, this is something... " My face fell into a stony stare. We're going to work to improve on every game and every practice."

Nubbin looked at me with a big smile. "Coach, is this smile on my face my dessert?"

I couldn't hold my serious face any longer. Laughing, I nodded and said, "You've got that right, son. In fact, look at Gary over there. You're supposed to smile when you win, even if you look like a possum when you do it."

Gary's smile vanished and he turned away, sulking. "What do you mean 'like a possum,' Coach?"

Everyone was laughing then and Herman pointed towards me. "Coach, I think you have one of those on yourself!" The dressing room erupted in laughter once again as the thrill of victory had everybody enjoying their just desserts.

The bus ride home passed much more quickly than the trip over, which is usually the case when you ride home with a win. I enjoyed the trip back as I pondered and replayed the game over and over in my mind. We had played a lot better than I thought we would and to a coach, that is what you are always striving for. The first game that I would ever coach in my life was now in the record books and my mind eased immensely. I gazed out the bus window into the night, watching the pine trees flow past in rapid succession until the lights of Kennard flickered into view and I knew we were home.

Walking up the stairs to my little apartment, I slumped down onto my porch, taking in the night air and savoring the moment. I knew that the minute I went upstairs the day would be over and with it would pass the feeling of triumph that tingled in every pore. I wanted to sit there forever.

5

A Hard Loss

I had a little extra bounce in my step as I walked down the deserted wooden floor toward our school cafeteria. It was a little after seven on a beautiful early bird Wednesday morning and the taste of coffee and cream seemed even better than usual. Sitting alone, I admired the early signs of fall beyond the window and barely noticed as our Ag teacher took a seat beside me.

"Good morning, Coach!" he said with his now familiar smile.

"After the way you guys played last night, that coffee ought to taste pretty darn good this morning."

I looked at him with a big smile, gently holding my cup aloft in a toast. "There's something special about the aroma of fresh-brewed morning coffee. I always wondered why it never managed to taste as good as it smelled. Well, I think I hit the jackpot this morning."

Benford was smiling. "It's the taste of the big V, Coach. You earned it."

"Big V?" Nona Baker stood just outside the kitchen, wide-eyed and staring at us. 'Coach! Benford, you didn't put vodka in his coffee, did you?" I sat back laughing as Mrs. Baker berated Benford while he stood waving his hands in defense.

"*Victory,* Nona, victory! You think the poor man would be driven to drink after just one game?"

Mrs. Baker's feathers seemed to be settling as she poured me a little more. "Well, you can be sure that the coffee's going to taste that good after *every* win, so you best keep it up, Johnny."

Coach Johnny Carter

In our practices over the next couple of weeks, as well as our games, we continued to show day-by-day, game-by-game improvement. We were a long way from being what I considered a good team, but after winning our first five games, my players were starting to think we were already there. It had me worried. When a team thinks they're better than they actually are, sooner or later— usually sooner—Old Man Reality raises his ugly head and steps out from the shadows.

We were paired up against Douglass, a team that we'd soundly defeated by sixteen points just a week before. Coach Tommy Murray, a Lon Morris classmate of mine, had his team fired up and ready for the challenge in their return engagement. The game was close from the opening tip. They were after us with a passion and our sloppy play was only making it worse. For the first time that year, I had to stand and watch our team get totally outhustled. My frustration overrode the reality of the moment. Without thinking, I came off the bench and planted a roundhouse punch straight into a steel beam behind me. The pain actually helped me regain some focus and I don't think anyone was more surprised than I was to find that my hand was miraculously unbroken. I overheard a raised whisper from the crowd, "Whatever you do, don't tee that guy off!" I never pulled a stunt that stupid again. I graduated to those much safer, ring-bending floor slaps and later to boot-loosening bench kicks. All classic coach moves, as I found out.

It was pretty hard for me to sit there and watch the game end in a 57-55 loss. As a player, as a fan, and as a coach, I may be one of the worst losers in the world. I hate losing with a passion. I was determined that the loss would be transformed into a motivational device for our team. I wanted it to ignite the same feelings of anger and frustration within them that smoldered deep within me. Losing should be something that gives you a burning desire to work harder. It should make the value of your practices much more meaningful. You'll always be able to say, "...if we had done this" or "if you had done that?" but it's what you do with the reality of your situation that matters. If you put a loss into the right perspective, it could improve your team over the long run. In my opinion, there is no greater teacher than a defeat at the right time.

My brother Billy and I were discussing that very issue when an interesting question was brought up. He asked me if I would rather have a player that loved to win or one that hated to lose. To me that was a given. I'll take the one that hates to lose any day. Everybody loves to win and everybody always seems to love a winner, but the guy that hates to lose is going to be a player that will go above and beyond the call of duty to prevent that loss. That's my kind of player.

Walking into the dressing room after our first defeat, I shared my sentiments with my team in no uncertain terms. "Everybody get over here and sit down. I want your undivided attention."

A couple of guys continued to jaw off in the back. For the first time in my life, I knew what it meant to bellow. "I don't want you guys saying a word when I'm talking! Matter of fact, I don't want you yawning; I don't want you untying your shoes; I don't want you scratching your butt; I don't want you blinking! What I do want is your eyes looking right at me, listening to every word I say, because this had better be the last time that I have to make this speech!"

There was dead silence. You could have heard a mouse walking on cotton balls. Truthfully, I felt sorry for the kids. Shoulders were drooping as they reluctantly made eye contact, but it was imperative that we pull a win from that loss. "Why do you think we lost that game?"

The silence continued. "You got outhustled and that's *inexcusable.* Look in my eyes, fellas. What do you see in there? Look real close, Roy. What do *you* see?"

"I see..." he looked at me hesitantly. "...green. Your eyes are green, Coach."

"Look closer, Roy, because apparently you don't see the fire in my eyes." I leaned in close. "Do you see it now?"

He nodded his head. "Yes, sir, I feel it a lot more than I see it."

"Good," I said, stalking around the room. "Let me tell you something, fellas. If you're going to play on this team, you're going to play *my* way. I can and will overlook a lot of things in this game, but if you think that I will ever overlook not hustling for the entirety of a game, you'd better wake up and open your eyes. I'm not talking hustling 99.9 percent of the time. That's how you managed to lose tonight. I don't mind getting out-talented; I don't mind getting out-shot. In fact, I don't mind getting beaten by a better team. What I do mind is getting beaten by a team that you take for granted just because you beat them by sixteen last week! What did you think...that they were going to roll over and play dead simply because you kicked their butts the first time? Every game is a brand-new ballgame. You think the referees give a dang who won the first game? Do you think they even *know?* You have to go out there on that floor every night and play your butt off. That's what I expect out of you."

As we drove home that night, I learned a valuable lesson in the coaching profession. Learning to move past the multitude of emotions that cloud one's judgment after a loss requires a tool set that I had not yet acquired. It was my inability to lay a loss easily to rest that had pushed me to be a coach in the first place. I somehow had to shut the door and start working on the next game and it was tough to move past the competitive spirit still in anguish within me. I could rage all I wanted about the loss, but it would accomplish nothing. A win would not erase it and all I could do was make sure that more would not follow *en suite.* As we slowly moved through the season, that was something on my mind constantly.

In our practices, I watched as my players pushed themselves harder than ever before. They grew closer together, learning to read one another while anticipating the next move. I could only hope that I'd instilled in them the motivation that I felt after a loss. All I knew was that despite everything I'd said and felt after our last game, I couldn't wait to get them back out on that floor again.

~~~

Tommy Ferguson, a former classmate, former teammate, very good friend, and first-year coach at Richards High School happened to be the next game on our schedule. Although I looked for-ward to seeing him, I wasn't exactly looking forward to going against his team in a game among best friends. We'd both approach the game as sentimentalists, remembering all those backyard one-on-one games of days gone by.

Tommy was always a fierce competitor on the floor and coached his team in that same manner. Although deadly serious every time he stepped on the court, off the floor Tommy was a practical joker. He had a little Eddie Haskell in him. Quick comeback lines came as naturally to him as bees to honey. I'll never forget that day when we stopped by the local barbershop for a shoe shine. The absolute best shoe shines anywhere could be had at this shop by a fellow named Joe Johnson.

Entering the shop, Tommy didn't see Joe at his post and asked the barber if Joe was in. Real sarcastically the guy rolled his eyes and asked Tommy, "Do you *see* a shine boy in here?"

Never at a loss for words, Tommy cut right back. "Nope, matter of fact, I don't see no barber in here either!"

The barber dropped his paper and bolted after Tommy, but only caught sight of the soles of his shoes as he hightailed it down the pavement. I think Tommy shined his own shoes for quite a while after that.

Looking at the other end of the gym, there he was, coming across the floor toward me. It was almost time for us to lock horns once again, only this time our reputations as young coaches were on the line. Going against each other in the backyard was one thing, putting our teams on display in that highly competitive arena was something that had me sweating. I could see that gleam in Tommy's eye as he approached, remembering it from my childhood. He was not about to back down that day. He'd come for a win. I hoped even as we faced up that we were still friends. Reaching out and grabbing Tommy's hand at mid-court, we exchanged a firm handshake. Looking at me, his mouth turned into a devilish grin, "How you doing? I'm Doc Hayes!"

I exhaled, my held breath, then laughed as relief flooded my system. "Nice to meet you. I'm Johnny Wooden." He chuckled as he returned to the bench. We were both ready to give it our all.

Since that was our team's first game after our big loss, I had much greater expectations for my team than our previous six matchups. A renewed high level of play coupled with a fierce competitive fervor had been showing through during practice; I could only hope it would emerge again here. It would have to if we wanted a win. That early in the season, it was hard to pull reliable stats on a team, but so far, Richards had been scoring lots of points. If we played like we did the previous game, there was no way we'd be able to take a win.

As the ball went up, I was glad to see that at the very least, our hustle was back. However, it was quickly becoming apparent that our offense was still MIA as shot after shot missed the mark. When the first quarter came to an end, it was a very low-scoring tie. I knew they thought they'd be doing much better, especially after the effort they'd been giving during practice. I figured that now was the time for encouragement.

"Great hustle out there! Fred, Roy, I want you to focus on rebounds and getting that ball out to Herman and Haywood. We seem to be having a little better luck when we have some air to breathe. I know it may not seem like it, but holding their offense this low, well, that's a pretty big deal. Keep up the D! Tigers on three!"

The second quarter went much better and it looked like my players had taken our talk about defense to heart, especially Nubbin and Haywood who blocked out better than I'd seen at any point previously. Thanks to the defense, the score remained low as we matched them point for point despite our continued poor shooting. Even Herman seemed to have caught the bug and as the time was ticking down, Richards got a breakaway. It looked like they would take the lead to the dressing room at the half. I caught Tommy's eye as he cheered on his player, racing down center court. Then out of nowhere, athlete that he was, Haywood stepped in the lane, planting his position just like we'd drilled, drawing the offensive charge for a turnover. I came off the bench, clapping and looking back at Tommy who was running his fingers through his hair as he shook his head in disbelief. Inbounding the ball, Roy shot a quick pass to Fred for a quick breakaway layup before the buzzer. The Tigers took a two-point lead to the lockers.

There was a feeling of building excitement in the dressing room. I could barely keep the guys in their seats to congratulate them on holding Richards to twenty-two at the half. Soon we were back on the floor and our Tiger personality emerged for the first time in the game. Our defense was on fire. Richards tried a quick down-court pass, but Nubbin was quicker. Snatching the ball out of the air, he fired it to Haywood as he raced down the court like a freight train. A quick pass back to Herman put two more on the board. I was out of my seat pumping my fist as my guys devoted themselves to the big *D* and Nubbin snagged yet another interception for an easy layup. Our shooting remained the same, but we refused to let that stand in the way as our tenacious defense denied attempt after attempt from Tommy's high-scoring team, culminating in a 52-40 win.

Shaking hands with Tommy after the game, he looked at me, forcing a smile. "You keep playing like that and you just might make a pretty good ball coach."

Obviously just glad to get a win, I said, "Your defense was good tonight, you pushed my guys *way* off their offensive game."

He glanced at me with that competitive look in his eye. "Just good enough to get my butt beat." He wagged his finger at me, sending a flashback through my mind as he walked off the court. "We'll be back, Johnny, and we'll have round two!"

As I headed for our dressing room after that very pleasing victory, there was a tap on my shoulder. It was Curtis. "Hold up, Coach! Great job! We were an entirely different team out there tonight. What did you *feed* those guys?"

I winked at him. "We ought to change our name to the Bears because offensively we were in hibernation tonight! I'm glad we managed to eke that one out."

Curtis just smiled and looked at me with a gleam in his eye. "Well, we were Tigers on defense!"

I felt a swelling of pride. I'd worked hard to burn that aspect into those guys and the effect was obvious to the fans. We'd managed to win a game almost totally on defense. I hoped my guys were seeing the truth in what I'd been telling them from day one. I didn't want to jinx it by saying it aloud, but that was proof that we had crossed one of those small bridges towards reaching the level of play that I envisioned for that team.

I walked through the doors to the dressing room and looked over my beaming team.

"That was, without question, the best defense I've seen you play all year. I've been telling you all along that good defense never takes a vacation because sometimes the offense takes a week off. You stepped above and beyond on defense tonight and guess what? If you hadn't done that, there's no way we'd have won this game."

Roy looked at me with a smile. "Aw, don't worry, Coach. Our offense didn't take the week, just a sick day. It'll be back Friday!"

"You played defense tonight with a lot of heart and I want you to understand that this is the kind of effort that I will expect out of you from now on, every night!"

Groans drifted to my ears and Haywood locked eyes with me.

"Coach, I'm beginning to think that this is going to be a never-ending process."

I nodded to my muscular junior wingman. "You've got that right, son. We're never going to reach a point where we can't improve, but as long as I'm your coach, we're never going to stop striving for it. This is what separates good teams from great teams. Good teams sometimes reach that point—knowing that they're good—and they forget to keep climbing the mountain. They get satisfied just being good. Good thus becomes the enemy of great."

Pulling a towel off his head, Roy spoke up. "Coach, what do we have to do to become a great team?"

I just shook my head. "Well, let's focus on becoming a *good* team first. Look fellas, even though you are knocking on the door to being a good team, you are not even close to being a great team."

Roy waved his hands. "All right, Coach, let me back up. What do we have to do to become a *good* team?"

The noise in the room grew quieter as I leaned in, looked my junior post man in the eye and said, "Practice."

Roy rolled his eyes.

"We need to keep our practice sessions at the same intensity level or higher than they were the last two or three days. Are we capable of doing this? You bet. Will we do this? Well, that's up to you. It all depends on just how bad you want it. I promise you this: I'm going to do my part, I'm gonna work you, I'm gonna drive you, and I'm gonna push you. But once again, the bottom line here is you."

Standing tall, I waited for silence. "We are what we repeatedly do; therefore, 'excellence is not an act, but a habit.' That was Aristotle. If you want me to recognize you as a good team, show me...every day...that you are one."

~~~

Our practices the remainder of that week continued to be intense. I was encouraged. I knew that was the only way that we would ever reach the higher ground that I envisioned beneath our feet before the season was over. Scouting other schools, I saw that talent-wise my starting five were adequate, but far from amazing. Relying on talent alone, we were ordinary. However, what I had seen the past week had sparked a glimmer of hope in my feeling for the team. They had the right mindset, believing in repetitive, relentless coaching and encouragement, and they had the drive, using each day to prove to themselves—and to me that they *were* a good team. Theodore Roosevelt once said, "It's not what we have that will make us a great nation, it's the way in which we use it." How I structured and used the talent that we had would be the deciding factor in determining just how far we climbed that semester. I'd known the task since day one, but putting all the pieces in the right place at the right time—that was the hard part!

Continuing our intensified approach, we played very well and defeated a good Chireno team in our next game, 50-43. More importantly, we showed improvement in all areas of the game, sending a few more positive vibes down to my toes. For the first time, I started to see significant changes in my team's overall approach to the game. We were really tightening up the cracks in our teamwork and in response our game was becoming unified...stronger. Looking them over from the sidelines, I began to reevaluate my potential-meter for the team.

~~~

With each pine tree I passed on my drive home for the weekend, thoughts about my team continued to encompass my every thought. Although we were a far cry from where I hoped we'd eventually be, for the first time since the start of the school year, I could literally feel our team's center migrating, redefining our "normal" level of play.

The following morning, I rose early and drove with Tommy Ferguson to Dallas to watch Jerry Levias lead SMU, our favorite team, to victory over A&M in the Cotton Bowl. It was Levias, along with John Westbrook playing for Baylor, who broke the color barrier by becoming the first black football players in a previously segregated Southwest Conference. I watched as whites and blacks cheered together as their team was led to the win by a man who would not have been allowed to play a year earlier. They cheered now, but I'd heard some of the things uttered about the man prior to the game, things I heard uttered in my own stands once in a while, and I thought back to what Mr. Bitner and I had talked about when I'd gotten the job. The undue pressure on our black players in that initial year of full integration weighed heavily on my mind. Yet the only idea I could come up with was to ignore it, not let the volatile nature of racism be an issue for our team. It was ironic that each day I drove to school, I passed by the home of the Grand Dragon of the KKK. In that time of change, unrest, and tension across the country, that house became a daily reminder of my duty to my team. The smoothness which had transpired so far was all I could have hoped for and I resolved to keep my kids as far away from the racism as I could.

~~~

The weekend was over, but by then I was used to the school's hours and they seemed to pass more quickly each day. The intensity of our practices had continued to be at levels close to our game the week before. With each succeeding practice and game, the personality of our team was becoming solidified. Our game successes reinforced our efforts in practice and good practice habits had begun to evolve into ingrained reflexes and better game decisions. A basic formula had developed.

That day's practice was going very well, and soon I found myself heavy into it, pushing my guys harder than I'd ever pushed them before. During a free throw break, Gary Parrish looked at me between breaths for air. "Coach, what are you trying to do, kill us?"

Looking at Gary, I had a sly smile as I gave him my best impersonation of that well-known character on The Gomer Pyle Show. "I can't hear you!"

Gary jabbed Haywood in the ribs. "Man, he even sounds like Sergeant Carter! Coach, why don't you give us a 'Surprise, surprise, surprise!' and tell us that practice is about over."

I looked over my breathless but determined group. They would go as long as I wanted them to and they were determined to give their all every minute. Finally I nodded at Gary and let my whistle shriek through the gym. Herman sunk his last free throw and the guys gathered around.

"Look, tomorrow night you play Chireno again. We did well against them last week, but remember the last time we thought we had a team just because we played well against them before."

I watched their faces and soon goose bumps were running down my spine as I saw that frustration, that anger on their faces as they thought about our last game against Douglas. I almost smiled.

"Listen to me, fellas. They gave us all we wanted and I feel sure they'll try something different this time, so be ready."

I was right, Chireno had come to *play*. They had a disciplined approach and weren't giving us any points this time. Seeing our running game before, they were determined to slow the game down, keep the score low and that's exactly what they did. The execution was beautiful to behold and it was obvious they'd spent a lot of time working it over. It was a great game plan. They made very few mistakes and in the end, it paid off for them—they defeated us 36-34. I could see the heartbreak in my guys' faces—one basket standing between them and a loss. Despite it all, we played hard and I wasn't disappointed at all in our effort. There was a forlorn mood hovering when I first got in the dressing room; however, I had to show my team the other important aspect of losing. It should frustrate you, it should get you angry, but not even a loss should overshadow the acknowledgment of a game well played.

After informing the young team of my thoughts, there was a gradual shift from sadness to determination on the faces of those young men. They knew that I hated losing with a passion, but when they realized that my belief in the team had strengthened with that game, there was an air of confidence, almost as if we had won. I grew up a little as a coach that night. I realized that being hard to please was an asset to a coach because it made your praise mean that much more.

"I can't wait to practice tomorrow because I can see and feel that we're getting better every time we play. Fellas, this is how good teams are made! I'm gonna tell you right now, you're becoming a *good* team."

The bus ride home wasn't exuberant, but neither was it grim. We thought about the game as a failure of tactic and understood as a team that we still had a lot to learn.

The next day, I was home for the weekend in Madisonville, visiting with my parents. We'd just finished dinner, homemade by my mother, when my dad sat back in his seat. "That was a tough loss to Chireno. They were determined to keep the score down. They made you play their game."

I couldn't deny it. "They did a great job with that game plan. That's probably the only way that they're ever going to beat us."

"I thought for a minute you were playing Snook."

I let out a laugh. I'd thought the same thing as I stood on the sidelines watching their strategy develop.

47

"Oh, one more thing—something your mother mentioned. We noticed one more thing about that Chireno game." Both my parents know the game and since I was still lacking my assistant coach, my parents and Curtis were as close as I could get. "You are in desperate need of a new game-day wardrobe."

I laughed, but the next day I bought a brand-new blazer from Jack Viser's Department Store.

6

A Good Team

The following week, wearing my new blue blazer, we played quite a bit better, winning the next three games with double-digit differences. Next on our schedule would be an all-Houston-County shootout against Coach Monte Jack Driskell's Crockett Bulldogs. I had known Coach Driskell since my sophomore year in high school when he coached the Groveton Indians and had a tremendous amount of respect for him. I knew that Coach Driskell was a very serious competitor, having a real passion for the coaching profession.

That day's game would be our first game against one of the so-called larger schools. I was convinced that we would have a distinct advantage, having twelve games under our belt, not to mention two-and-a-half months of practice. Meanwhile, Coach Driskell's team was just coming out of football and would probably take a while to get their basketball legs beneath them.

There was a brisk breeze rippling through the trees on that overcast Monday morning. After entering the school building, I was soon walking down that hallway leading to the cafeteria. Sitting at one of the tables were Curtis and his mom.

"Good morning, Coach." Mrs. Baker wore that good- natured smile that always seemed to accompany her. "Have a seat. I'll pour you a hot, steaming cup of fresh-brewed coffee."

"I'm not helpless, Mrs. Baker. I certainly don't mind getting it myself."

Mrs. Baker's ever-present smile disappeared. "If you don't beat Crockett tonight, *then* I'll let you get your own coffee."

Curtis chuckled. "I'll go along with that. This is the *Crockett* game and some of the people around here would rather beat Crockett than win District."

I didn't need coffee to wake me up after that. "Why's it so important?"

Curtis shrugged, "You watched the SMU and A&M game a couple of weeks ago, but that doesn't hold a candle to the A&M versus Texas Thanksgiving Day battle. Well, Crockett's mascot is the bulldog, but around here, they're the 'big dogs.' The rest of the schools in our county are tiny compared to them, but every one of 'em wants to take down Crockett."

Mrs. Baker had gone back to the kitchen a few minutes earlier and was now returning to our table with a covered plate. "A surprise for you, Coach." Taking the cover off the plate, the warm aroma of fried pie got me salivating. As she walked back toward the kitchen, she stopped and turned around, catching me stuffing one almost whole into my mouth.

"Well, I'm glad you like them." She fixed me with a stare. If you ever plan on eating any more, beat Crockett tonight!"

~~~

Going for our fourth straight win in my new blue blazer, I soon found out that Curtis had been right on the money in his assessment of that night's game. Our guys were practically exploding to get out of the dressing room. I was barely able to get my pre-game speech over with before they were on the floor, playing hard-nosed, determined basketball with, by far, our highest intensity level of the year. Our players weren't the only ones. The stands were packed and I came off the bench numerous times with that double-clutch fist pump as we sunk basket after basket. The experience factor weighed heavily in the outcome and it was pretty obvious that Crockett was still thinking in football terms. Obviously, the Bulldogs would need much more practice before they could get their engines cranked up and running at full throttle. Our play rose on the cheers of our fans as we convincingly beat the Bulldogs, rolling to our fourth consecutive victory.

My dad was all smiles as he found me in the crowd. He had to shout just so I could hear him. "That was the hardest your guys have played all year. Did you do something different in practice? Whatever you did, keep at it!" he said, flashing me a thumbs up.

Looking at my loyal, but very biased father, I wished I knew what I could do to get my guys to play that way every game. They were more determined to win that game than any other game we'd played all year. If we could continue to play like that, we could beat a lot of teams—a lot of really good teams.

Smiling as I headed to the dressing room, I almost careened into Mrs. Baker. She caught me in a hug. "Congratulations, Coach! How about those Tigers?"

I laughed. "How about those fried pies?"

Playfully, she slapped my chest and made her way back into the crowd.

~~~

It was hard to think that twelve young men in the dressing room could be louder than the crowd outside the door, but somehow they managed it. As I entered our dressing room, the positive vibes in the atmosphere were in abundance.

"Great job, fellas! That's what I'm talking about! Everybody get over here and listen up. This was one heck of an effort. You totally outplayed them with, by far, the most determination that I've seen out of you guys all year! Hold on before you get too wound up because I've got something very important that I need to ask you. If you can play with that kind of effort against Crockett, then why can't we do that every time we take the floor? Look, fellas, I've got news for you, it's gonna take this kind of effort and then some, day in and day out, with consistency, for you to be the kind of team I think you can become."

Herman looked up, scratching his head. "Aw Coach, this was Crockett. We're just a little extra motivated."

I looked into Herman's eyes. "Well, we've got another game tomorrow night. Does that mean that your level of play, which was way up here," I said, extending my hand above my head, "Is it gonna be somewhere down here tomorrow night?"

I nodded towards Roy. "Two or three weeks ago you asked me what we had to do to become a good team. We've played about six or seven games since then. You guys have definitely improved, but listen up, here's the news. You showed me tonight that you are capable of playing a whole lot better than you've been playing so far, so guess what? I'm going to expect that same kind of effort tomorrow night and every night after this one."

Now each player was looking at another teammate.

"What's the matter, fellas? If you can play that way once, you can play that way again. This is how good teams are made. They decide that they want to get better, they walk on that floor every day, and they execute that mindset on a consistent basis. If you really want to become a better team, it starts right up here," I said, tapping my head. "Congratulations, fellas! I'm proud of what you did tonight, but I'm going to be even more proud of what you do tomorrow. Now go home and enjoy this big win and come back tomorrow night ready to do it all over again!"

~~~

The next day, as the first period tardy bell rang, I found myself on the other side of Mr. Bitner's desk. He'd asked me to come by his office earlier. I wasn't sure if it was about my coaching or my teaching, so I decided to spread my apprehension and anxiety between the two. Mr. Bitner, a no-nonsense, stern taskmaster, had been the superintendent of schools at Kennard for twenty years. He looked me over, teeth still gnashing at his omnipresent gum, "Close that door, Johnny, and sit down."

He stood, popped a new piece of gum into his mouth, and turning his back to me, looked out the window. "Coach, what kind of a job do you think you're doing?" He turned, wearing that same serious look as the day I interviewed.

There were a hundred options to choose from, but since honesty had gotten me this far, I decided to stick with it.

"I really don't know, sir. Sometimes I wonder about my inexperience and the fact that I'm not but a few years older than my players. I guess all I can say in answer to your question is that I'm doing the best I can."

Mr. Bitner looked at me with an ever-so-slight smile. "Coach, I just wanted to share something with you about your teaching. One of my favorite quotes comes from Harry Adams. 'A teacher affects eternity. He can never tell when his influence stops.' That being said, I wanted to tell you that you are doing a good job, both in the classroom and on the court. I'm pleased with the way your team has been playing—particularly last night."

A big surge of relief rushed through me.

"Tell me something," he said. "You got these guys playing together pretty well. I know this season is still young and we've got a whole lot of games to go. I also know that teamwork is the name of the game and we're headed in the right direction in that department." He took off his glasses and rubbed his eyes. "I've also been around this game long enough to realize that things can change abruptly and without notice. Whatever you do, Coach, don't let up on these guys. Keep them headed in the direction that you've got them going."

~~~

Later that afternoon, we were going over our opponent for the night, Maydelle. After walking through some of our offensive sets and shooting free throws, I clapped my hands together. " Listen up. This is the same situation that we didn't fare too well with the last two times."

Herman looked at me and said, "Believe me, Coach, we'll never take any team for granted ever again."

I raised an eyebrow. "That's good to hear, now prove it tonight."

Nubbin grimaced. "Coach, do you really expect us to go out there and be as fired up tonight as we were last night? That was Crockett, this is Maydelle."

"Look, I saw what you did last night and tonight had better be a continuation of that effort. I'm not talking about what's on the scoreboard. I'm talking about whether we get the same all-out big 'E' as in effort that I saw last night. That's what you guys need to show me tonight."

In the locker room, everyone was suited up as I entered.

"Listen up! Everybody in this room knows that earlier we let two teams beat us even though we were better than them. That ought to be enough motivation within itself for you to play your butts off tonight. Look, we're eleven wins and two losses and what that means, I don't know, but what I do know is that those two losses could have been two wins if we had played with the same passion that you played with last night."

I walked around the dressing room, cleared my throat, and then continued. "Look, I've been around this game long enough to know what it takes to become a good team. And even though you're knocking on the door to achieving that status, you've got to do this on a consistent basis to get there."

I tried to make eye contact with as many of them as I could. "Last night you were a good team. *You* are the only thing standing in the way of being one again."

~~~

In our second game in as many nights, we indeed continued our Crockett game effort by soundly beating Maydelle by twenty-five points. Actually, there appeared to be very little, if any, drop-off in our level of play from the night before. That was more than just another victory. It was a high-water mark for the year and for our team. It was my job to convince my players that we could indeed keep the flow of our game headed in the right direction. What we could not do was sit back and rest on our laurels because that would mean losing our desire to improve. Once a team loses that fire, it spells the death of the team. Even if they continue to win, they have lost the very heart of the game, the personal challenge to excel. We had the river flowing in the right direction and it certainly was no time to start treading water. The ride would not be smooth, but seeing what our team had accomplished the last two games had me totally believing that we were about to tackle the rapids and see just how far we could go.

"Super job, fellas, this is what it takes to become a good team."

Roy looked up at me with a grin on his face. "Coach, I think we're definitely ready to be called a good team, particularly after the way we played the last two nights. What do you think?"

Looking at Roy with a big smile, I said, "If I answer that question based on the way you played the last two nights, I'd have to say yes." It was hard to cut him down when that grin was coming to fruition. "But if I based my answer on the way we played for the whole year, I'd have to say no. Look, this is not meant to be a negative answer. There's no comparison between our first eleven games and our last two. You've been a different team these last two nights. The big question is

'Can we continue to play like this?' I think we can and if indeed we do, we can surpass the so-called "good team" label and jump right to being a *very* good team."

Roy's smile hadn't gone away. "Mark it down then, Coach, we're going to be a very good team. There's no doubt in my mind."

"Well, we may very well find out this weekend because we're going to the Madisonville Tournament and it's loaded with really good teams this year."

Haywood took up the call. "Good, I can't wait Coach! We're ready!"

"You'd better be because there are at least sixteen teams on the bracket, mostly much larger schools. You just played your two best games of the year back-to-hack, but I can promise you that if we don't play at that level or higher this weekend, we're going to get blown right out of the water."

~~~

Driving through the shadows of the pine forest on that late November night, the short trip back home seemed to take even less time than after the other wins. We had played much better than I'd thought we would with virtually the same intensity we had displayed in the Crockett game. It had taken my team fourteen games to reach that level and I was absolutely thrilled. Until the game that night, I really wasn't sure where the team stood, despite the very good won-lost record that we had compiled. Sure, we had won a lot of games and to the ordinary fan we looked like world beaters, but I knew differently—at least until the last two games. One thought continued to captivate my mind. *What can I do as a coach to convince my team that they can continue this higher level of play?* I had only coached a little over a dozen games in my young career, but I knew it to be a fact that the longer a team played at a higher performance level, the sooner it would become the norm, and the sooner we would reach an even higher level. The luck of the schedule was about to become a huge asset in attempting to achieve that because we were about to experience a lot of competition in the upcoming tournament.

~~~

Walking down the hall with a smile on my face, I was feeling great. The newfound energy and execution that my team had exhibited the past two nights had suddenly given me a new perspective on our season. Although I feared that it might just be a temporary high, I knew then just what we were capable of doing. I wasn't about to let my team forget how they'd played and they were about to be drilled with that in mind during practice that day.

As Herman popped a fifteen-footer near the end of practice, I decided to conclude our workout right then and there. I was once told by a veteran coach that he always tried to finish practice on a high note, if possible, because he wanted his team to leave the gym in a good frame of mind. I'd done my best to follow his advice and the effect was a positive outlook by my players. Any team, despite their talent, will be beaten if they are sure they are going to lose. For the most part, that day had been a very good practice. Calling my players over after we shot free throws, I was trying to sort through all the information I had on the tournament. I probably knew more about the Madisonville Tournament than most, having played in it four times and having watched my brothers play the past five years. Until our most recent two games, I really didn't think we'd be able to compete there, but then I knew that we could go to that tournament and compete with anybody over there, including the high-flying Snook Bluejays.

Under the leadership and direction of Jimmy Horn, Snook had yet another stellar year going. They were a favorite to win their third straight State Championship, not to mention the tournament. During a two-year span, at one point the Bluejays had won an amazing ninety straight games. Their dominance in Class B basketball was legendary. The reaction on the faces of my players said it all when the word "Snook" was mentioned.

"My plan for this tournament is going to be a little different than you might have expected. We will play Thursday, Friday, and possibly two games on Saturday. I don't know how you're going to feel about what I'm about to say, but nevertheless, here goes. We're going to spend the night in Madisonville on Friday. Does anyone have a problem with that?"

Nubbin looked at me with raised eyebrows. "Coach, you mean to tell me that the school is going to pay for a motel? I don't believe it."

"Sure they are, Nubbin," I said with a smile. "They're gonna spend that kind of money on us the same way they bought you guys new tennis shoes."

Roy slumped back in the bleachers. "Coach, if the school isn't going to pay for our rooms, who is? I can't speak for everybody in here, but I'm broke, so I guess I can't go."

Fred looked at me as the elder spokesman. "Coach, there's no way we could pay our way, at least not me and Nubbin."

"What would you say if I told you that I already got you a place to stay, absolutely free?"

Haywood clapped his hands together. "Now you're talking my language! That's about the only way that I could afford to do this."

Herman had shifty eyes and a hushed voice. "Coach, is this *legal?*"

I burst out laughing. "Yes, it's legal if you stay at my parents' house."

Roy's eyes were big as saucers. "You mean your mom and dad agreed to let us stay at their home?"

I noticed t h a t he looked around the room, locking eyes with Haywood, Lester, and Walter—all the black kids. I didn't know what to say. *Should I address it? Ignore it?*

I looked at Roy and let my eyes fall to the floor. "Well, there is one problem. There's not enough room in the house for everyone, so the white guys will stay in the house and the black guys will stay in the garage."

Suddenly, there was dead silence as my players looked at each other. Amazingly, I had managed to keep a straight face and had everyone believing what I was saying. Unable to hold it any longer, I burst out laughing. "Just kidding, Roy! We'll make room for everyone!"

The tension broke. Roy was probably laughing the hardest of all.

"Look, fellas, my mom has it all figured out and there's plenty of room for everybody."

Fun was fun, but there had been an acorn of truth in that silence. It was something I had to address—not just as a coach, but as a teacher.

"Fellas, we're a team. Either all of us are going to do this together, as one, or not at all. This is the way it's been up to now, this is the way it is today, and this is the way I certainly want it to be tomorrow.

That isn't the way the world always works, but it's the way it should work."

7

The Madisonville Tournament

Thursday, the first day of the tournament, had breezed by and late Friday afternoon our bus rumbled down Highway 21 to Madisonville for the second time in as many days. Having won our first-round game in the tournament the day before, we'd continued to display our upgraded level of play.

The Madisonville Tournament was one of the oldest continuously-running school tournaments in the state with a lot of history in its many years of existence. Many State qualifiers and champions had fought their way through the lower rounds of that tournament to battle for the trophy. Playing at the same high performance level for the fourth straight game, we soundly beat a pretty good Trinity team and with that win, we advanced to the semi-final round of the tournament. We had watched the surging Snook Bluejays crush their second round opponent earlier, thus propelling them into the semi-finals. A very strange thing had now developed on our side of the bracket, as the two smallest schools in this very large tournament had just seen their teams reach the doorstep of the championship. Everyone knew that Snook would be there, but we were considered a dark horse and the longest of long shots against the reigning State Champions. The talk in our dressing room after the game centered on our next opponent.

"Coach, just how good is Snook?" Haywood had on maybe the most serious face I'd ever seen on him.

"You watched part of their game today, what do you think?"

"Coach," he said with the mindset of a student of the game, "they're disciplined and they make very few mistakes, but I don't think they're any more talented than we are."

I smiled. "Haywood, you're right on target. Two years in a row they've won the State Championship doing just what you said. Their game-by-game execution is almost flawless. Are they good? You bet they are. Snook is very good. Can we beat them? Well, that all depends on us. I've seen them play many times the last couple of years and they follow the same strategy. If it's a close game and they get a lead, they usually put the game on ice as good as anybody I've ever seen. What they do can be mind-bending and if you don't keep yourself focused on the job at hand, they can literally frustrate you right into a loss. Snook centers their game plan on the high percentage shots, great defense, and patience.

"Right now they have a ton of tradition going for them. I'm not saying that we can't beat them, we're very capable, but there is a catch. In order for you to achieve this, the level of play that you've been performing at the last four games—which has been exactly what I asked of you—needs to be stepped up to an even higher level of play. The question of the day is: Do you think that you are capable of stepping up?"

Haywood narrowed his eyes, nodding, " I don't have any doubt in my mind. We can step it up a lot more."

Herman stood shoulder-to-shoulder or at least to mid-arm, with Haywood. "So you're saying you think we *can* beat them, but do you think we will?"

"I don't think you can do this...I *know* you can."

The silence that hung after my words was broken by a smiling Roy.

"Hey guys, we played pretty good for the last four games, right?" There was general agreement around the room. "Well, what do you think?" Shrugging his shoulders, Roy now had that look in his eyes.

I smiled. "Roy, son, there's no doubt in my mind anymore. We're definitely a *good* team." Reacting like he was posing for a photograph,

Roy displayed a huge, cheesy smile, revealing all his pearly whites. "But just like I told you before, fellas, you'd better *never, ever* be satisfied with just being a *good* team because if we aren't more than just a good team tomorrow against Snook, we'll never beat them."

~~~

With a little work later that evening, my parents' home was trans-formed into a makeshift hotel. My mom had everything organized. My players were working like bees, moving furniture around and bringing in mattresses, placing them side by side on the floor. We'd gotten most of them from my grandmother's house. In no time, we had twelve ready-made beds neatly arranged like army bunks.

"Fellas, this isn't the Hilton, but you can't beat the price!"

Nubbin looked over the completed work. "Coach, does this meet the guidelines of the Kennard Tigers' basketball budget?"

I rolled my eyes. "What budget?"

My players were laughing as I watched Fred thank my mother for helping our team, a call that was quickly echoed by the rest until there was a chorus of "Thank you!" coming from every member of my team.

My mother just flapped her hands at them. "Having my son at home, with you all here, is special. I'm honored to have you spend the night at my house. I feel like you're family anyway. This weekend, my house is your house."

Suddenly Herman perked up. "Mrs. Carter, are you baking a cake?"

My mother beamed. "How about a big piece of warm cake and a glass of milk before you go to bed?" Now it was Herman's turn to beam.

"It'll be ready in about ten minutes. Why don't you get everything situated in the bedroom and by the time you finish, the cake will be ready."

Ten minutes later, we were all sitting around a couple of tables that my mom had arranged in the kitchen.

"Mrs. Carter, it's delicious! What kind of cake is this?"

"It's called pound cake, Herman," I assured him. "You know why they call it pound cake, don't you? After you eat one piece..." I poked him in the stomach for emphasis.

Roy was laughing between bites. "What he's really saying here, Herman, is that you can't afford to have two pieces!"

"No!" my mom stepped in. "Now just a minute. I've got plenty of cake. I've got enough cake for everybody to have at least two pieces."

"Come on, Coach," Herman said. "Look at Lester over there. His mouth is watering for another piece of cake! We've got to build him up. He's way too skinny!"

There was a unanimous consensus that for Lester's sake, we all needed to have another slice. I narrowed my eyes at my team of comedians. "Just remember, tomorrow we're playing Snook and I'd better not look out there on that court and even *suspect* that you're not running hard. If I even think for one second that this second piece of cake slowed you down in the least, the next practice you know I'll get you back."

Herman met my hard-eyed stare. " Coach, that cake is amazing. I'll take the risk! Besides, I'm sure I'm going to run it off quick tomorrow!"

Later in the evening, my father and I sat in the kitchen after my team had bedded down. The clatter of dishes could be heard in the back as my mother worked in the kitchen. He looked at me, leaning in and talking low so as not to disturb the team. "What kind of a chance do we have against Snook?"

Around the team, I constantly had their morale on my mind, but with my father, I let the uncertainty come. "A week ago, I would have said no chance, but the way we've played since the Crockett game, we've got a shot. We're playing on a different level right now. I don't know if it's enough, but Dad, it's close. If we can bring it up just a tad tomorrow, who knows?" He was nodding, frowning at the ceiling.

"I do know this—we'll definitely be competitive. Whether we can get over the top tomorrow, we'll just have to wait and see. Regardless, we need this right now. We need to play someone of this caliber to show them that there's always another challenge waiting for them. I'm scared they're starting to think they're the big fish."

"I watched Snook play their first two games of the tournament. They're a typical Snook team. They're gonna be tough to beat. They seem to be playing the same style they've played the last two years."

I laughed. "Yeah and they won it all both years. We've played their style before against Chireno—maybe that's something."

"Maybe," he nodded.

With a hug, we turned in. If anything could raise our already high level of play, it would be playing a two-time defending State Champion.

~~~

I was awakened the next morning by the captivating aroma of hot coffee. Making my way to the kitchen, I was greeted by my mom, who handed me a cup with a smile. There are few better ways to start a day.

"Has Dad already gone to work?"

She nodded. "He's been gone a good while. You said you wanted your guys to eat at 8:00 a.m., didn't you?" She'd already been hard at work and it looked like the mountain of pancakes would soon be complete. We were to play at 11:30 a.m., giving us three hours to digest our food and be ready to go. "Breakfast will be ready shortly. I've just got a few pancakes left to go. Why don't you go sit down and read the paper and enjoy your coffee?"

The paper was full of news about our opponent, the Snook Bluejays. I was about halfway through the article when I looked up at Fred coming into the kitchen.

"Good morning. Whatcha reading, Coach?"

"Oh, it's just an article about the Jays, about the tradition they're building down there. Their basketball team has put their little town on the map."

Fred craned his neck above my shoulder. "How'd they manage to do that?"

"That's a hard question. They have a coach with a philosophy and he's completely sold his team on it. Jimmy Horn has built quite a name for himself starting that program. My senior year we played for the Regional Championship against the undefeated Buna Cougars, losing in a real close game to Coach Cotton Robinson's legendary team. Robinson's teams won seven State Championships there. Well, Jimmy Horn is a disciple of Cotton. A lot of what we'll see Snook do on the floor has been directly influenced by that team. They've got tradition, which means that kids go to school every day *knowing* that they'll play on a State Championship team." I tapped my head. "That state of mind carries with them through every practice and game. When you think like that, it's much easier to win. If you believe it, you can achieve it."

~~~

The pancakes were placed on the table and one by one, they lured my players out of bed and to the table like a magnet. It was about eight in the morning, some three-and-a-half hours before we would hit the floor for the semi-final clash against Snook. The "few" pancakes had been piled to the ceiling. My players crowded around the table. Herman and Haywood were arguing about the priorities of the day. Haywood was firmly set on playing the Bluejays, while true to form, Herman found the mountain of flapjacks to be the true test of skill. As the silence of full mouths fell over us, I decided it was as good a time as any to talk about our opponent.

"Fellas, this is not Crockett. Crockett was the big dog, but there are a lot of big dogs in Texas. There's only one top dog and that's Snook. You're gonna go out there and play the hardest game you've played all year. And you know what guys? I'm *excited!* This is gonna be the beginning of a new level of play for our team. Can we beat these guys? You'd better believe it. Will we beat them today? We'll just have to play the game and see. Regardless, we're about to play a higher level of play, starting today. I could see smiles and looks of determination spreading through their young faces, and I returned my own mask of confidence, but deep down, I knew that our chance to pull that off was remote.

~~~

With the crowd still coming in, the gym was nowhere near full, but it was Saturday morning. Tournaments of that size have no other choice but to have the final four play two games on the same day. This would be something new for my team. In a matter of hours, we would play two games. Not for the first time since the season began, I was thankful for the endurance drills we'd worked on. I'd figured early on that I needed to approach those two games differently and look for times that I could sub my starters. We still didn't have a lot of depth and if I wasn't careful I'd exhaust my players, coaching my team into a loss in the second round if I pushed them too hard for the morning win. The problem was that we would need to give it all we had to stand a chance against Snook.

I watched apprehensively as the ball went up and play began. Snook showed their expertise in playing so many high-profile games, taking the early lead on our team. We managed to keep up, showing an intensity level that was the highest I'd seen for the season. I was thrilled with the effort of our team going to the dressing room at the half. We were behind, but we were within striking distance for a possible upset.

The delay tactic that I had warned my team about was in full force in the second half and since we were behind, it was our time to make some small changes defensively. Playing Chireno gave my guys an eye for their ball movement, but Snook ran their delay game to perfection, methodically increasing their lead. Our fans didn't appreciate in the least this perfectly legal but very unpopular strategy as those ball-control experts slowly but surely froze the game into a win.

The two teams had already shaken hands and were heading for the dressing room when Herman's father, Harley Myers, stood in Jimmy Horn's way. "That was pitiful!" Jimmy just stared at the man.

"I drove all the way over here to watch a basketball game, not keep-away! What's the matter—are you guys afraid to play the game?"

Jimmy Horn had a smile on his face as he headed into the dressing room, fully knowing that the strategy he had employed many times had just paid off again.

After a game of this significance, there's downtime, particularly when you lose. My players seemed to be more angry than hurt. We had played those guys tough and my team knew it. Taking away a couple of very correctable defensive lapses, we might well have had a different game. Several players had their heads in their hands when I walked into the dressing room.

"Look up here, get your heads up, and listen. We didn't win this game today but you accomplished a lot. You definitely raised your level of play considerably this morning. That's much more important to me at this juncture than winning." It just about broke my heart to see my guys' heads continue to hang.

"Hey, guys, do you believe what I'm saying?"

Haywood raised his head to meet my eyes. "Coach, I always believe everything you tell me, but dang it, I wanted to *win* this game!'"

Heads nodded in general agreement and I looked into Haywood's dark eyes. "Not any more than I did, I promise you that. They may have won the battle, that's true, but in the long run, we may eventually win the war."

A few heads perked up.

"The war ain't over, fellas—not unless you intend to let it be. Snook brought out something in you today that amazed me. Today was by far the best you've played all year and you did it against the number one ranked, so-called best team in the state! Who do you think benefitted the most from this game today? Herman?"

Herman glanced at me. "Coach, games are judged by the scoreboard. The final score says we lost."

"Snook played the way they *always* do and today it just happened to be good enough for a win. On the other hand, we played *much* better than we've ever played. This is the second time this week that I've been able to make that statement. Do you know how important that is? Some coaches go a whole season and are never able to say it even once and here I've seen you up your level of play considerably *twice* in the same week. You're way ahead of schedule and I feel great! In my opinion, that accomplishment totally overshadows today's loss. Today, your level of play far exceeded that Crockett game when you told me that only Crockett could get you so excited."

Positive looks and smiles were emerging out of the gloom. Somehow I was pulling the right strings. "We're loaded guys, now we just need to find the trigger. We're really learning to play this game. I'm watching you out there and I'm seeing the fundamentals we've worked on. I'm seeing our drills, but I'm also seeing natural synergy and creativity. You're beginning to consistently apply your knowledge and really *play* this game. So far we've played five games this week and I can tell you right now that in that short period of time, we have grown up a lot as a team, especially today. Fellas, we're about to get a whole lot better. So I'll ask you again, Herman, ' who benefitted the most from this game today?"

Herman was now smiling from ear to ear. "Well, Coach, when you put it that way—we did!"

Haywood stood and thrust his hand forward. "Everybody get a hand in here."

THE FIRST SEASON

As my team chanted and cheered, I had one more reason to feel proud of our school. Making a win out of a loss is something that can be difficult to achieve. Walking out of our dressing room with a big smile on my face, it appeared to me that had just been accomplished. In that stage of my inexperienced young team's season, achieving that was an absolute necessity, not only for their morale, but more importantly for their very delicate, very impressionable frame of mind.

Will Rogers once said, "Live your life so that whenever you lose, you are ahead." Even though Snook had beaten us, I already felt like we had come away from that game winners in the long run and I couldn't wait to use that experience the rest of our season.

~~~

When we returned to my parents' house, my mom had prepared enough spaghetti to feed an army. Several loaves of French bread warming in the oven softened the spicy smell of tomato sauce as the team gravitated to the table. The loss to Snook suddenly took a backseat to our now fully awakened taste buds. The decision to spend the night, unfortunately, hadn't resulted in us defeating Snook, but it brought about something much more significant. These guys had been building ongoing, developing friendships dating back to the beginning of practice, but as they passed food and jokes across the table, it seemed more pronounced than ever before. I'd seen the bond both on a n d o f f the court and each part was feeding the other. Successful teams have that smooth chemistry that carries them through thick and thin. It can maximize the productivity of the good times while largely minimizing the bad ones. If for no other reason, spending the night had been worth it just for that closeness.

Noticing that Haywood had been unusually quiet during the meal, I asked him to go with me for a walk after dinner. The small talk slowly died away as we strolled down the street adjacent to our house.

"So, what's on your mind, son? You were pretty quiet during dinner."

He scuffed a rock by the roadside, "Aw, Coach, that game just got to me. I wanted to beat those guys, especially for you." His eyes watched his feet as we strolled down the sidewalk.

"Haywood, I have a feeling that the whole team wanted that win just as much as I did. You don't owe me any more than anyone else."

He shook his head. "Naw, Coach, the way you've gone out of the way for us in this tournament, letting us stay here in your parents' house. I don't know if you realize it, Coach, but this is a really big deal for Roy and me—as far as that goes, for Lester and Walter too. You know, being the first black players ever to play on this team is a pretty big thing for all of us, but spending the night in your home—to me, that means even more. It makes me want to play extra hard for you. I'm sorry we didn't get this win for you today."

I tried to speak, but the words caught in my throat.

He stopped and faced me with a look of fire in his eyes. "Coach, we can beat Snook."

"Haywood!" He looked at me, eyes wide. "Enough!" I let out a laugh that I hoped wasn't too shaky. "I love the competitive spirit in you, but you don't owe me an apology. You played your butt off out there. You played harder than I'd ever seen you play before—we all did. Snook is hard to beat, especially when they get a lead. And about you guys staying at my parents' house, I never gave it a second thought. You're on my *team* and I brought my team to spend the night—not *some* of my team, my *whole* team—black, white, and any other color that might be wearing Kennard purple."

As we continued to walk down the street, I couldn't believe that spending the night at my parents' house had such an impact on Haywood and by his words, on Roy, Walter, and Lester, too. A great, perhaps ironic quote by Carl W. Buecher says, "They will forget what you said, but they will never forget how you made them feel."

When I discussed having my team spend the night here, my mom and dad both thought it was a great idea. The fact that I had four black guys wasn't even mentioned, but for Haywood it was huge. It dawned on me that I was much more than a coach to those guys; I was something that many of them had never experienced in the Deep South. I never thought there had been a coach-to-player, black-to-white issue with my team, but if there was, that weekend had erased it.

~~~

After a very relaxed, lazy afternoon, my players were refreshed and ready to play our second game of the day. Our opponent would be the Fairfield Eagles, a school that over the past few years had begun to develop some very good teams. In fact, they had been a Regional finalist just a few years before. They'd lost to my alma mater, the Madisonville Mustangs in the semi-finals and now would meet us in the third place game.

Motivating a team to play its best in a game of that nature can be difficult. Playing for third, it was hard to make the game sound like it counted. Yet the mood in the locker room hadn't dipped at all. They were ready to show me again that same fighting spirit they'd gained playing Snook. Showing little, if any, effect from our earlier loss, we blew right past a very good Fairfield team, handily pulling a double-digit lead, but it became apparent at halftime that my team was slowing down. Inevitably, fatigue set in and the game slowed, despite their best efforts. This was particularly disturbing to me because I thought we were in great shape. In reality we were and I noticed the Eagles slowing their game as well, stressing to me all over again the importance of stamina. We'd spent too much energy in our all-out effort trying to beat Snook. My starters had played virtually nonstop. The fatigue factor could have very well cost us the Fairfield game as well if we hadn't taken care of business early. We ended the game with a win and I grew up a little bit more as a coach.

Sitting in the stands with my players, watching the finals before a packed house, I pulled for Madisonville to beat Snook. There was a small blessing in that had we won, we would then be facing Coach Jerry Dyer's Mustangs and my brother James Otis—a family feud I hadn't been looking forward to. The Mustangs gave a valiant effort and James Otis played his heart out, but the Bluejays rolled on to another championship.

Near the end of the game, Haywood came over and sat down beside me. "Coach, after watching Snook play again, I feel stronger than ever that we can beat those guys."

I looked at him with a smile. "That may be, but it just wasn't meant to be today."

"I know that, Coach, and we're a better team because of it." His juices were flowing. "But I want to play those guys again!"

"Well, we won't manage that unless both of us advance a long way in the playoffs...and you really can't count on that happening."

Inside, I wanted the same thing as Haywood and I had to be careful not to mention the words "State Tournament" but if indeed we were to meet Snook again this year, that's where it will be.

Monday morning came early as I once again headed down Highway 7. Erasing the darkness of the previous night, the birth of a new day was about to put yesterday to bed forever. As I drove, I watched the sun gradually light up the eastern sky above the National Forest, sunbeams repainting the night's azure background. Seeing the beauty of those sunrises, it almost felt like the good Lord was speaking to me and I took those moments to give thanks for my life and ask for guidance in the day to come. By the time I got to school each morning, I felt like I was charged up and ready for anything.

We would have another game that night and I was looking forward to it. My good friend from Jacksonville, Robert Loper, would be bringing his very good Neches team to Kennard. While attending Lon Morris, we had become good friends the summer I spent working baseball play-by-play for KEBE, the local radio station in Jacksonville.

Memories raced through my mind as Robert Loper walked into the Tiger gym with his team. Meeting him at the door, we shook hands. "Man, it's good to see you, Robert."

He gave me a smile. "I've been hearing some really good things about your team. You've got to take it easy on me tonight." He shook his head sadly. "I'm afraid we're not very good."

I laughed at the coaching idiom, "That's the same thing your friend Tommy Murray at Douglass told me right before he beat us."

He shrugged, smiling. "All I can say is I hope you haven't taught those guys to shoot like you did back when we played that outlaw tournament in Rusk."

I rolled my eyes. "If I knew how to do that, I'd be playing with Jerry West tonight."

Watching my team warm up, I caught sight of my brother, James Otis, taking his usual seat on the front row of the stage. It was his favorite because from that spot you were close enough to touch the official while they were calling the game. I winced, remembering the animated words my brother usually liked to use when evaluating a referee's calls. Our official had noticed his entrance too and his mood darkened visibly. The ref stalked towards my brother and from my brother's face, I could tell this was another warning about being kicked out. I hoped he'd manage at least a quarter before his spirit got the best of him.

Neches gave us exactly the challenge I was hoping for, but it looked like my guys were taking a while to kick it into gear. James Otis actually held back much better than I'd thought he would, even ignoring a few questionable calls, but he still fell short of the first quarter as I heard his voice hollering across the gym, "You're missing a *pretty* good game, ref! You wanna borrow my handkerchief to wipe off your glasses?"

I lost track of the ball, just about choking as I looked at my little brother. But true to the profession, our official shrugged it off. Officials are just human beings and the really good ones learn to turn their ears off. Lesser referees get so worried about the crowd's reaction that they lose concentration on the game itself. That kind of guy doesn't last very long in the business because like coaches, officials are employed to be criticized. Neither will please everybody all the time and each has to accept criticism because it comes with the territory.

We managed to gain control near the end of the first half, pulling away from the close game played so far. Up by sixteen late in the third quarter, a timeout was called by Neches. I'd subbed my sixth man in for Roy earlier in the game and I took a moment to pull him aside.

"Gary, I need to see some rebounds out of you, son. Go to the glass, battle for position, and block out anybody in your area. I need to see you grab the ball aggressively—not with one hand like you've been trying to do, but with both hands. *Rip* it out of the air. That last rebound you tried to get with one hand ended up out of bounds. Remember, you have two hands—use 'em. Do you savvy?" Gary gave a sharp nod.

"When you come down, bring that ball down hard to your chest with your elbows out. You've got to play with authority, son. Send a message to everybody in the gym when you come down with the ball. Tell everybody it belongs to *you.*"

"Yes, sir! You watch me the next time I get a rebound. Everybody's gonna know who that ball belongs to!"

Play resumed and it wasn't three minutes later that Gary ripped the ball out of the air with a textbook rebound. Bringing the ball down forcefully into his chest with his elbows out, he hit the floor. Unfortunately, while his body stopped, the ball kept going straight down, out of his grip, and bounced straight back up, catching a very surprised Gary in the worst place. He promptly crumpled to the floor.

I ran to check him out. "Gary, are you okay?"

His groan had me fighting back an oncoming smile. Looking in his face I could tell he was more embarrassed than anything. Completely red-faced, Gary looked at me and then around at the response of the fans.

"Coach, I made a complete fool out of myself."

Unable to hide my smile any longer, it spread across my face. "This isn't choir class, son, so why are you singing soprano?"

I followed his baleful looks to the second row where I saw some girls cracking up. "Coach, they'll be teasing me about this the rest of my life."

Helping him to his feet, I said, "I can get some athletic tape and tape them up if you want."

He looked at me with a very sarcastic smile. "Coach, you're all heart, you know that?"

With the encouragement of a large, enthusiastic crowd, we managed to run to a 67-46 victory. Shaking hands with Robert after the game, he shook his head. "Johnny, you guys did a great job tonight. You've shown a lot of improvement from last time I saw you play."

"Robert, you weren't scouting us, were you?"

He shrugged. "Not like it did a lot of good now, did it?"

I looked at him with a slight smile. "We've been playing progressively better almost every game. We played really well in our loss to Snook in the Madisonville Tournament."

"I like your team, Johnny. They play well together. For a team made up predominantly of juniors, they really seem to have knowledge of the game. Johnny, I hate to risk the kiss of death, but if you can keep this team improving, down the road I think you just might have a shot."

I had to take a step back, looking at him in bewilderment. Robert just laughed. "Hey, I'm no expert; I'm just a rookie coach like you, but your guys are doing a lot of things right. Look, you've got good guard play and that point guard can shoot. Your inside game isn't bad either and they go to the boards hard. They're quick and aggressive on defense. I like that number 22, what's his name?"

I smiled as I looked at the back of my athletic player. "Haywood Henderson," I said with a smile.

"Johnny, that guy is an athlete! It all boils down to how much you improve the second half of the season." He grinned, shaking my hand one more time. "Or you could just teach 'em to shoot like you did back at Rusk and bag that trophy today!"

~~~

With rapid-fire repetition we clawed straight through all our opponents. Not only did we travel to Crockett and soundly beat a fast-improving Bulldog team again, we returned to the same site and won their tournament with three straight, convincing weekend wins. Bringing home the first place trophy from Crockett on Saturday night was a particularly rewarding experience. It marked the first time that this team had won any kind of a championship. The words "hustle," "determination," "execution," and "togetherness" were evolving into the description of this young team's ever-growing personality.

Arriving back in Crockett after the championship game, I pulled into a filling station and asked the attendant to top her off.

"Do you guys still have the cheapest gas in town?" I asked him.

"Yes, sir," he said. "Twenty-nine cents a gallon!"

Still savoring winning the tournament, I walked into the empty restroom and closed a stall door. I heard two people enter.

"Hey, did you go to the game tonight?"

A different voice, closer to me, answered. "No, I missed it."

"You should have gone, man, that Kennard team is *good*. They won the tournament."

The second kid scoffed. "Man, I ain't gonna go waste my time watching a bunch of dang niggers run up and down a court."

The high I'd been riding disappeared and my sobriety was fueled by fire. I came out of the stall, letting the metal slam against the cement wall and stalked up to the kid. His eyes were wide as apples.

"Son, I coach that team and I don't care if they're black, white, or green! I play the guys that perform the best!" I let my voice get quiet. "And you know what? I'm very pleased with every player on our team."

He managed to stutter a few syllables, none of which managed to form any sort of coherent words. The other kid was standing there,

73

almost smiling and enjoying the fact that I was giving his buddy a dose of medicine.

I stood up to my full height, shaking my head, "It's not so much about what you said, it's what's in your heart right now. And what's in your heart is screwed up. In this moment, you know what it means to be ignorant, son. I promise you that's something you don't want to be forever. Think about what you said. You owe it to yourself and you owe it to my players."

I never knew if what I said registered in that scared kid's mind, but for one fleeting moment, he got some much needed feedback from the other side of the street. Hopefully in some small way it made him think about it and maybe that was enough.

I rolled down the windows, letting the night air fill the car as I finished the drive home. It's a strange feeling to realize the significance of your time. I felt detached from my body as I thought about the number of hearts and minds embodied in what that young kid had said. I thought about my team and how they came together perfectly, despite the fact that several of their parents were known to have racist views. It gave me hope that people could change—without bloodshed and without even discomfort, given the right circumstances and encouragement. The ever-developing relationship between that team and their young coach was something I'd come to treasure. We were playing much better than I'd thought we were capable of and now a new fear had grown inside me. Perhaps we were peaking too early and would become relaxed, losing the hunger for improvement. That was something I would have to make sure didn't happen.

It was incredible how much fun coaching that team was becoming for me. I found myself literally counting the hours to the bell for seventh period and I couldn't wait to get to the gym. I wasn't exactly minimizing the importance of the first six classes, but seventh period had become my daily dessert. Using the aftereffects of the previous week's loss to Snook as our new starting point, we had come out of the blocks full speed ahead and had now reeled off six consecutive victories. As a rookie coach, I obviously had a lot to learn and seemed to do so with every breath I took. I knew how a tough loss to a really good team affected me a few years back, and I was thrilled that my team seemed to have a similar heartbeat.

Motivation has many faces and no boundaries or guidelines. We were reaping the reward of losing to the top-ranked team in the state and appeared to be out to prove that we should be right there with them. I doubted that we could ever get to *that* point, but the way we were working, coupled with the improvement we were showing, you never knew—even the skies might not be the limit.

Coach Johnny Carter

8

Christmas Break

A few days later, we returned home from Richards after winning a hard fought, 42-32 defensive game over Tommy Ferguson's much-improved team. Congratulating my team on our seventh straight victory, I wished everyone a Merry Christmas. With the Kennard School in my rearview mirror, I was happily headed home for the Holidays. Even as I looked forward to the holidays, I almost hated to stop playing, even for a short period of time. We were on a roll and I didn't want to lose that momentum. Worse, our schedule was set so that we would have only one day of practice before our first match in the Centerville Tournament. With Christmas music in the background, I headed down Highway 7 with a smile on my face as Gene Autry floated over the air waves. It was hard to be too concerned with the singing cowboy lighting up the radio dial with "Rudolph the Red-Nosed Reindeer."

The Christmas season was not only on the air this night, it was clearly visible as I drove through the moonlit shadows of the pines. The beautiful array of colored lights brightened the scene even more with each passing house as I made my way through the countryside. Thoughts of childhood brought an unbidden smile to my face.

The holiday break was short, but it was great to spend a few days at home with my family. Visiting with my two brothers, even for only a couple of days, was pretty special. I hadn't realized how tense I was becoming until I had a break. My muscles all tried to unwind at once and I was sure that well-deserved break in the middle of the furious pace of the season was as good for the kids as it was for me. It wasn't until I got back to work setting up a practice schedule of drills that I felt those muscles begin to tighten up again.

Our practice had arrived and thankfully no one was detained by vacation; however, there was a slight problem. The school was locked- and I didn't have my key.

Roy looked at me with that usual smile. "Coach, I thought you never made mistakes."

I hung my head. "I don't. This is the first mistake I've made all year! I really thought I was going to make it with a perfect record, but no!" I held my thumb and index finger about two inches apart. "Missed it by that much."

The kids were laughing, but I had to figure out a way to get into that gym or we would hit the tournament after having gone almost a week without practice. Nubbin reminded me of a high window at the back of the gym that was usually left slightly open. The troops walked around the back and sure enough, it was maybe four or five inches ajar.

Haywood stepped forward. "Let me get up there and I'll get that thing open."

We watched him clamber up and take a grip. His muscles flexed and soon he was baring his teeth. He took a deep breath and reset his footing; a long groan later, he was shaking his head and puffing for air.

"Coach, I don't think this window has been touched for about twenty years! It's totally sealed."

Gary had been eyeballing the crack for some time and was biting his lip. Finally he nodded, reaching some mental calculation. "Wait a minute, I've got an idea. Walter, I bet you can squeeze through that somehow, shimmy-shake your body through."

Walter went bug-eyed. "No way!"

Gary was persistent. "Give it a try, Walter. I've seen you do something like that before. You're the most limber guy I've ever seen. How many times have I seen you win money off those suckers who bet you couldn't scratch your ear behind your own back?"

Walter smiled, eyeing his shoes. "A lot."

There seemed to be some group approval of Gary's plan and reluctantly Walter began the climb. We stood watching this wiry kid haul his bones up to the window as I did my own calculations. As he stuck his leg through, I called out, "Before we get you stuck up there, Houdini, check and see if your head will fit."

Roy was laughing. "It's not about his head; it's whether or not those big ears of his will scrape off!"

Walter cast a withering glance at Roy and tried his head. "It's gonna be real tight, but I think I just might be able to do it."

Walter began to meticulously work his way through. Changing the contour of his body like a snake, slowly and methodically he eased through. The last glimpse of his leg was followed by the thud of feet on wood and a slow whistle from Roy.

"Guess I owe him an apology."

Walter reappeared, opening the gym door with an ear-to-ear smile to the applause and cheering of our team.

My back-up guard had saved the day. With a smile, I slapped his shoulder. "How does it feel to be the hero? Guys, if we win the Centerville Tournament, Walter here will be the main reason."

Gary and Nubbin wrapped their arms around his shoulders. "Son, you the man. No, no, you the main man!"

A few minutes later, we started the practice that almost wasn't. At the conclusion, I had all the guys sit down to go over our plans for the upcoming tournament. "I trust each of you had an enjoyable holiday?" I poked at Herman. "Didn't eat too much turkey, I hope." They were laughing and that's exactly what I wanted—to recapture that feeling of ease, power, and togetherness that we'd had before the break.

Herman looked at me with that familiar sneaking smile and said, "Aw, Coach, we'll have that worked out of our system before the first half is over."

"Well you'd better have it worked out before that because sometimes games are decided in that first half. More importantly, we play Elkhart first."

A couple of the guys exchanged looks.

"I know, I know, that's where Wesley Taylor, your old coach, moved to."

Fred nodded his head. "I think he's in administration now."

"Well, I'll bet you he'll be at this game to check you guys out, so you'd better go out there and bust your butts."

Coach Johnny Carter

"Yeah," Nubbin said putting his hands on his hips. "We've got to show him what a mistake he made by leaving us!"

~~~

Sitting on the bench, watching my team the first three or four minutes of the game, it became pretty obvious that we were nowhere close to our before-the-holidays level of play. With the score yo-yoing back and forth early in the first quarter, I called a quick timeout. My words seethed with the frustration I was feeling.

"So you're gonna get that holiday turkey and dressing out of your system early, eh, fellas? Well, I'm ready for that to happen, right now! Do some of you guys need a shot of Ex-Lax? Because you guys are all clogged up! I don't see any movement out there at all. That's *not* the way our offense works." You're standing around out there, looking at each other, waiting on someone else to do something. Every one of you guys, smell your thumb. No really, do it." I waited for each of them to raise their hands to their faces. "When you stand around out there on the floor with your thumbs up your butt, that's the way it's supposed to smell!" I could see the embarrassment in their eyes; the time for brimstone was over. "You didn't win twenty-four games this year by standing around. You won all those games because you kept moving on offense and out-hustled your opponents!"

As my starters returned to the floor, Walter leaned over from the seat beside me. "Coach, they're a little out of sync right now—rusty— but there's one thing that hasn't changed a bit—you're still coaching with the same fire you did our last game. Coach, every time you get on their butts like you just did, they always play a whole lot better. You'll see."

Sure enough, I had riled up our Tigers. The next three minutes our team played like someone had just put a torch beneath them, went on a fourteen-point run, and dominated the floor.

The first convincing win carried us the next two nights as we defeated Coldspring 65-49 in the semi-finals and soundly beat a pretty good Rosebud team 69-48 in the finals to win the championship. Mr. Bitner was particularly pleased with our play as he got to showcase our team for his brother Bill, the superintendent of Centerville Schools, who had gotten me my job. They met me by the door and Bill shook my hand.

"Looks like you've got your team playing hard. They were pretty impressive.

I finally saw what it was like for Mr. Bitner to really smile.

"Yeah, Johnny's working their butts off and they're improving every day. He's already got them playing much better than I thought was possible and we're talking about a coach here that's just a few years older than the guys he's coaching. So much for the theory that experience is everything in the coaching profession! I keep holding my breath hoping the balloon doesn't burst. So far, so good—knock on wood."

Bill stuffed his hands in his pockets. "Well, I'll tell you this. They look much better to me than a month ago. Anytime you want to start thanking me, I suppose I'll let you. Just remember, I single-handedly delivered Johnny to your doorstep. You'd better be thankful I didn't have an opening here in Centerville because if I had, he'd be on *my* coaching staff right now."

Mr. Bitner actually laughed. "Your loss is our gain and he's on my side now! Thanks, brother, you did your good deed for me and I will forever be grateful." Mr. Bitner slowly walked away with a big smile on his face and the first place trophy in his hand.

Herman and Fred were voted to the all-Tournament team for the second tournament in a row. However, after the game in the dressing room, I made a special effort to make a point to my team. "Look, I'm proud that Herman and Fred made all-Tournament, but our *team* won this together. That being said, they don't give an MVP prize, but our team certainly has one. I don't have a game ball, but if I did, I would give it to our Centerville Tournament MVP!"

My team exchanged glances and Haywood laughed, wearing a big smile. "I know who it was, Coach and I'm surprised everyone else doesn't. It's my man Walter here! If he didn't get through the window, we wouldn't have even practiced for this tournament!"

"Right on target! Congratulations, Walter! You are our unsung hero and as of now, officially the MVP of the Centerville Tournament." The team descended on our hapless wireframe, cheering on a wide-eyed Walter.

We had one game left the next week on the road and then our all-important District schedule would make all our games up until that seem like warm-ups. District was the real test of a team. Our record would not be the deciding factor of our abilities and team consistency would be more key than ever. We had just finished the year with a 24-3 won-lost record and that strong wind of confidence was still thrusting our sails smoothly onward. A blue northern had arrived and the temperature had dropped significantly as we left the gym headed for the bus.

"Brrr..." Herman's teeth chattered. "Man, it's getting cold." The kids were hustling toward the yellow dog. The north wind was howling, swirling through the trees. Soon we were traveling through the cold night, making our way through the darkness as we headed east. The heater seemed to take forever to warm up and we huddled together as best we could. Even so, my breath continued to puff little plumes of vapor before my eyes.

Herman plunked down beside me. "Coach, where do we stand right now in our level of play compared to before Christmas?"

"Let me put it this way: We are much closer to that level of play than I thought we would be after a break...much closer."

Herman was quiet as the bus rumbled down the highway, but finally he spoke. "Coach, a lot of games are behind us now and we've got a pretty good record to show for it. I guess it's all right that we took a small step back because something tells me that you're going to push us even harder when those District games start. Keep pushing us, Coach. We don't just expect this from you, we *want* this from you."

That surging, pine-penetrating wind had all the needles quivering in the breeze as I quickly walked down the sidewalk toward my car. That frostbite feeling in the air could be felt all the way down my spine. Before I opened the door, Curtis pulled up and rolled down his window. "We played a lot better than I thought we would after that layoff."

With a shivering smile, I nodded. "The true test comes next week when the District schedule starts."

"Coach, I know it's cold out there so I won't keep you long...just one more question. It's about a really important game. Can the Cowboys beat the Packers tomorrow?"

I laughed. "It's all about the new guy on the block trying to upset the favorite. Green Bay has all that tradition. They've already won nine NFL championships and will be going for their second straight tomorrow. The Cowboys, well they're the team of the future. They're gonna have to play way beyond their youth and inexperience to win."

A grin cracked across Curtis's face. "Are you sure you're talking about the NFL? It sounds to me like you're talking about Snook versus Kennard."

As he drove away into the night, my mouth was open. He was the second person who'd just told me that they thought we were going to the State finals. If they didn't stop, I'd start believing it myself.

~~~

It was New Year's Day and I'd driven home to watch the NFL Championship game with my family. The Dallas Cowboys had finally reached that elite game after suffering many years of mediocrity. Tom Landry was quickly be-coming that one special coach that I admired, respected, and looked up to. He epitomized the word "class" in the coaching profession. This was the seventh season for the Cowboys and their first winning record since entering the league in 1960. I had followed them passionately from their inception as they innovatively and skillfully built their franchise from the ground up. Attempting to unseat the legendary Vince Lombardi in their first try, they faced an almost impossible task. Despite my prayers and cheers, they couldn't pull off the upset and Green Bay won 34-27. Led by Don Meredith, one of my SMU heroes, they just couldn't overcome all that Packer tradition. My dad clamped a hand on my shoulder. "Any fan worth his salt understands how hard it is to overcome a champion."

I was still smarting from that frustrating Cowboy loss, but I had to put that in the back of my mind because we were about to play our last regular season game in Neches. It turned out to be close right to the final minute. We'd played very well and managed to keep the lead for the majority of the game. With only one minute left on the clock, we had possession and a two-point lead. Robert Loper's much improved team had played this return game better than the previous one. They were prepared and had matched us basket for basket in attempting to pull off the upset. During a timeout, I got my guys huddled.

"Fellas, it's time to show some poise, discipline, and concentration with our delay game. Remember, when you have the ball you're looking for that easy pass, that sure thing. This isn't the time to get fancy or experiment. This has got to be plain vanilla. There's got to be no doubt in your mind that your pass will be successful. If you have a doubt *at all*, then fake the pass and look for the backdoor. If you get in trouble, don't take any chances, don't make a prayer pass, just call a timeout. That's what I saved them for."

Fred, our quiet leader, looked at me. "Coach, we worked on this over and over; now it's time to put these guys away."

Back on the floor, we executed our delay game with perfection. Herman initiated the backdoor cut for Roy and made a picture perfect bounce pass for an easy layup. We won the game by five in a hard-fought, close finish. That was a great way to end our last regular season game while using a seldom seen tactic of our game. Robert had coached his team well and they were prepared to take us on, but the delay game tactic had proven that we were more versatile than expected.

In the dressing room, I congratulated my team. "Great job, fellas! You executed the way a real good team is supposed to."

Roy looked at me with a big smile. "Coach, does this mean that we have now moved up from a *good* team to a *really* good team?"

All eyes were all on me. The time was right. I looked at Roy and the rest of the team. "There's no doubt in my mind anymore, fellas. We are, as of this moment, a really good team."

"Coach," Herman was on his feet. "We're 25-3. That's a *really good* record in any league. Why'd you have to take so long to say it?" A couple of the guys were laughing.

I nodded my head. "Yes, it took me a while to say it, but I wasn't about to let you guys get big heads about it. Guess what? This doesn't mean that we've reached the top. We haven't even come close to reaching our full potential. Besides, we haven't even won a District game yet."

Haywood looked at me with a big smile. "That's only because we haven't *played* one yet, Coach. Just you wait!"

With an inordinate amount of confidence, we had reeled off eleven consecutive impressive victories. More importantly, we had continued to consistently improve on virtually every phase of our game. With the winner-takes-all District games now upon us, we began to add new dimensions to the overall game plan. Having worked on a half-court trapping defense for several days, we were hoping that it would be another surprise asset in our arsenal for the District schedule. However, as I watched my guys run it back and forth down the court, I was wary of using a defense we weren't used to.

In practice on Thursday, the day before our first District game, I was stressing the importance of player rotation in order for this defense to be effective. I had Roy playing the back of our 2-2-1 half-court zone defense. When the trap was made at mid-court by Haywood and Herman, it was Roy's job to intercept that down-the-sideline pass. We had a great trap situation, but the pass was made to a wide-open receiver in the corner. My whistle trilled out.

Stop in your tracks! Nobody move!" I pointed at Roy. "Roy, where were you? That pass down the sideline was yours! I could have picked off that pass myself in my street clothes! Let me see that ball, Lester." I caught the pass. "Look at this ball, Roy." He craned in to look at it. "Do you see this right here? On the side of the ball it says 'Roy Harrison.'"

He pointed feebly at Walter, "Coach, I was guarding..."

I whipped out my pen and slowly wrote "Roy" on the ball. "See, there it is right there."

Roy threw up his hands. "Coach, that's not exactly fair."

"That's right," I gave him a look. "It's not fair for your team if you don't do your job. That was your ball, son, and you stood there and watched it go straight down the sideline. The first pass out of that trap is *always* going to be yours."

Roy pointed back to Walter, whom he'd been guarding. "Coach, what about this guy right here, wide open under the basket. I'm supposed to just *leave* him here wide open?"

I looked at Roy with fire in my eyes. *"That* guy is not your responsibility. I want *that* guy to look like he's wide open so *Fred* can pick it off from the other side. This is the rotation that happens when you go for that sideline pass. I expect to see you anticipate and intercept every pass down that sideline. Do you understand? I mean *every* pass!" My worries were growing about our new tactic.

~~~

It was eleven at night and I had been attempting off and on for about two hours to make out a biology test for the next day. A fifteen to twenty-minute job had turned into a very lengthy ordeal. My mind kept drifting to thoughts about the next night. The importance of the outcome of that game was magnified by it being my first District game as a coach. Getting off on the right foot in District consumed me, because if we got off on the wrong one, there would be no second step. The importance of an opening victory in that game was imperative and that thought had totally obliterated everything else in my mind. Somehow, two of our three losses for the year kept easing into the picture. Yes, Snook had beaten us, but realistically, losing to the reigning State Champions was no big deal. It was the other two losses that kept popping into my mind. We had been defeated in those two games by teams that I knew in my heart we were better than. The word "upset" was definitely ingrained in my mind.

Finally finishing the biology test in the wee hours of the morning, I tried to fall asleep, but to no avail. All of my life I had more or less pulled for the underdog and yet here I was, hours away from our most important game of the year and I was now worried about the downside of that possibility. The sheer thought of an upset gave me the shivers. I don't remember falling asleep, but I do remember the next morning, driving east down Highway 7 on that all-too-familiar road to work, feeling drained and worried.

BOOK TWO

A Rising Star

Coach Johnny Carter

9

Best Coach in the Room

The school day zipped by and before I knew it, I was looking into the young faces of my team in the huddle prior to the opening tip. Looking across the floor at a full house, I took a deep breath. "This is it. We've worked all year for this moment and now it's here. You are more than ready to go out there, right now, and get the job done. Don't forget how we got to where we are: hustle, teamwork, and tact." I pointed to the playing court. "You're about to go out there on that floor and play the hardest and the best you've played all year."

With an overflow crowd packing the home court, the friendly confines of the Tigers Den, we snagged the opening tip and took the ball quickly down the court. Our offense then reversed the ball from the right wing to the top of the key to a wide-open Herman. His fifteen-footer arched perfectly toward the rim and ripped the cords to a roar from a highly partisan home crowd. That basket seemed to set the trend for the rest of the game as we sprinted from a 31-16 halftime lead to a 70-36, very convincing first-game District win. Particularly pleasing was the fact that although my team seemed to know early that we would win the game, they never backed off in their determination, effort, and execution.

Walking off the floor, obviously elated by what we had accomplished that night, I was met in the hallway by an obviously very pleased Curtis Baker.

"Well, Coach, it's always good to get that first District win. It looked to me—like there was never a doubt."

"Well, I had plenty of doubts last night. I'm just happy I stayed awake through the game! I hardly got any sleep last night."

Curtis raised an eyebrow. "Aw, Coach, you've got to have more faith in your team than that! Besides, the only team that bothers me in our district is Apple Springs. They're pretty good."

I nodded. "They're *real* good. I saw them play a couple of times in the Palestine Tournament two weeks ago. They got a couple of players that were really impressive."

"That would be Eugene Brooks and Paul Cook. Both of those guys can *play!*

As we walked toward the dressing room, I stopped. "Curtis, I could really use your help next Friday night."

"What do you need, Coach?"

"The good news about this is that you just might be able to help us win the District Championship. The bad news is that you'll miss our game Tuesday. You've got the eye and you know the game. I need you to go scout Apple Springs for me."

~~~

Continuing to perform at an unusually high level of play against Latexo, we raced to a lopsided 72-45 road win, setting up the District showdown for first place against Apple Springs.

With both teams being 2-0 after the first week of District play, that game would determine the undisputed leader in our district. We were slated for a road game on Apple Springs' turf. Wednesday morning, I met with Curtis to go over the team. Mrs. Baker dropped off some coffee for us, listening in as much as she could.

"Coach, they're much better than I thought they'd be, but I don't think they can beat us—unless we're having a real poor game."

I rested my chin on my knuckles. "Sometimes that happens, but you judge a team's real worth when they have their worst days and still manage to pull out the win."

Curtis sipped his coffee, nodding his head. "Coach, have you heard about the Apple Springs gym? It's different. Their floor...it's tile."

"Tile?" I'd never heard of such a thing. "How can a player get footing on a tile floor?"

Curtis gave a wry laugh. "Not very well. The traction is terrible. I saw more than a few slips and slides last night, so be ready. They have an advantage. They practice on it every day. Our boys will be unsteady on their feet."

"Well, that's just great."

Curtis went back to drinking his coffee. "I'm telling you, Coach, they're tough to beat over there, but something tells me you'll find a way."

"I sure hope you're right."

~~~

Our Thursday practice was very upbeat, to say the least. The team seemed to completely understand the significance of this game and our intensity level reflected it. The feeling in the air in our gym that chilly January afternoon was one of cautious, but growing optimism. Near the end of practice, we were going through our consecutive free throw drill.

Walking over to the bleachers, I sat down by Curtis as we watched the contest. I patted my chief scout on the shoulder. "You know, Curtis, this game is far more important for Apple Springs than us."

"You're right about that. It's their best chance to beat us on their own court, but Coach, I just can't see that happening. We're just playing too good for us to lose now."

"I'm still young at this, but I've been around long enough to know that strange things sometimes happen, even to those highly-seasoned veteran teams. We're talking about a very inexperienced team here, led by a young, inexperienced coach."

"Coach," he said with a raised eyebrow, "just wait a minute. This team, including you, was young in October, but that's come and gone. So have November and December, as a matter of fact. This is January and this team isn't green anymore. You may have been a rookie coach when this season started, but if you judge this team in terms of what it's accomplished so far, then you already have two or three years' experience under your belt."

I hoped he was right. Either way, it felt great to hear. "Yeah, well you might just be a little bit prejudiced." He nodded his head, chuckling as we watched the continuous rain of buckets. I blew the whistle. "Time's up!"

Herman flapped his arms at his sides."It's overtime, Coach!"

I sighed. "Okay, who's next for you guys, Herman?"

"Roy is our next shooter."

"How about your team, Fred?"

"It's Haywood."

"Okay then, Roy, it's your shot."

With a roar of approval from his team, Roy hit his free throw and spun to face his friend Haywood. " It's your turn, son, don't blow it!"

With Haywood now at the line, he calmly arched the ball toward the rim. *Swish*. It split the cords amid cheers from his team.

I waved them over. "Everybody over here and fill in the bleachers."

Herman staunchly refused to leave the court. " Coach, we had a tie at nine. Can't we find out who wins?"

"We have a winner." Looking at Curtis with a smile, I said, "The team won this game and you know what that means? There's no running." I quieted the cheers and continued. "Besides, when you shoot free throws like that tomorrow night, we're going to put Apple Springs in second place! It's time to call it a day and go home. Great practice, fellas! Get a good night's sleep and I'll see you tomorrow."

~~~

The Apple Springs bleachers were jammed to the rafters. People were sitting two or three deep on the floor and down both sidelines. Even the end lines were packed, with standing room now at a premium. Administrators were herding fans closer together and from beyond the door, the flood of people continued in as space was made. The home team was just as aware as we were that whoever won here tonight would probably move on to sweep past the lesser teams to win District. With the pressure mounting, both teams were soon making their way to their respective benches. I could almost feel the waves of sound and energy emanating from the crowd, sending shock waves of support from baseline to baseline.

I looked into the faces of my team, trying to block out the walls of sound around me. "Fellas, this is what it's all about. This is what all those hours of work we've done are for. You know what to do. Now's the time to go out and do it. These people..." I waved a hand around me, "...they're here to see you. Don't forget to have fun." Nervous laughter followed my words, and I stuck my hand out for our chant. As our hands went up with a shout, I felt the energy that had been restored in my team. I was glad to see it and tried to dry my palms against my pant leg.

The ball went up and I lost all remembrance of my case of nerves.

With the Apple Springs home crowd anticipating a victory for their beloved Eagles, we quickly gave them something to worry about. Herman received a quick pass in the far right corner and squared up. Bending his knees from a balanced position, he jumped in the air and with a fingertip release, launched a long-range spinner. With the gentle touch, it softly circled the rim's perimeter before gracefully ruffling the crisscrossed strings below.

Instantly, we transitioned to our 2-2-1 half court trap and quickly got a steal as Roy picked off a pass and managed to shoot off a pass before he slipped, hitting the floor hard. Scrambling back to his feet, he gave me thumbs up and was back in the game. That floor was a hazard, but my players seemed to take note and adjust accordingly. With our feet beneath us, we were off to the races. We overwhelmingly out-ran, out-shot, and out-jumped the home team. Then with Fred and Roy joining Herman, we scored several more unanswered early baskets. Thanks to Haywood and Nubbin's determined, aggressive defense, we were holding them scoreless at 9-0 and forced an early timeout for the Eagles.

I pulled my guys in. "Remember what I preached to you. When you get somebody down, you don't give them a chance to recover." I looked at Nubbin wiping his brow with a purple towel. "What do we do, son?"

He tossed the towel on the bench. "We up the pressure and bury them!"

"Now you're talking, son! Let's make them pay for that bad start." With the shell-shocked Eagles in disarray, we managed to cruise to a twelve-point halftime lead.

Walking into the dressing room, I looked into the elated faces of a confident basketball team. Whatever nervousness was there at the start of the game was gone for good now.

"Great first half," I said with a smile. "You took it right to them. Right now, their coach is in their dressing room, trying to tell them that they can catch up. They're looking up a mountain, wondering if they can get up here and meet us. Are you going to let them or are you going to slam the door in their face while we have the chance? Our defense was superb the first half, particularly the half-court trap. Losing the ball like that did more than just earn points, it hit 'em mentally. They were second-guessing each pass after that. As sure as I'm standing here, they're going to be better prepared for us. They're going to play better in the second half, so we had better too!" I looked my guys over as they nodded along. "Are we going to take care of business? Are we going to put 'em away?"

The dressing room rang out with, *"Yes, sir!"*

~~~

Sure enough, Apple Springs played much better the second half, but just like I'd predicted, so did we. Managing to match us basket for basket in the second half, it was a great game. At the foul line, they hit an outstanding twelve out of fourteen. That was the good news for the Eagles. The bad news was that we shot the lights out from the charity stripe ourselves. With that constant sound of sweet music fine-tuning the chords, we stroked the strings for a blistering eighteen for twenty-two. That's great shooting for the NBA, let alone Class B basketball. Running our delay game with precision late in the fourth quarter caused the Eagles a lot of problems, leaving them little choice but to foul and hope for rebounds. That only gave us more chances to shine, passing the free throw test with an eye-popping 82 percent. It was money in the bank. It was like practice all over again, watching my guys standing at the line sinking free throw after free throw.

All in all, it was a highly competitive, well-played, very good high school basketball game. With a 58-46 hard-fought, much deserved victory under our belt, we moved into sole possession of first place. Walking off the floor, I was met by Curtis greeting me with a hearty handshake and his now well-known smile.

"What did I tell you, Coach? Never a doubt! I'm beginning to think that the blue blazer that you're wearing is definitely a good luck charm. What's our record since you started wearing it?"

I shook my head. "No idea, but I know we lost to Snook in it." Curtis's finger poked my chest. "The way we're playing right now, I better not see you walk into the gym unless you're wearing that blazer! And just for your information, we're twelve wins, one loss since you started wearing it and we're not even going to count that Snook loss because since playing those guys we seem to be on a different playing field."

Before I got to the dressing room, my mom and dad stopped me and both gave me a big hug. With joy on his face, my dad said, "Man, I'm proud of you, son! When a team spots you nine points that early in the game, they know they're in trouble. They never recovered from that poor start and your guys never let them get out of the hole that you put them in."

The sight, sound, and feel in our dressing room was one of total warmth. When I entered, Gary Parrish looked at me with that possum grin and said, "Let's hear it for the best basketball coach in the state of Texas!" A rousing chorus of cheers hit me and I had to fight the pressure behind my eyes.

"The state of Texas? I don't think so, but I'm probably the best coach in the room right now!" Anyone will laugh at a good joke, but your friends will laugh at your bad ones and I was glad to be in a room full of friends.

Herman tossed his towel aside. "We know that you're not one to blow your own horn, but we're glad that you're our coach. We couldn't be doing any of this without you."

I cleared my throat. "Well thanks, Herman, I appreciate it, but I didn't score a point, I didn't get one rebound, and I didn't play a lick of defense out there tonight."

The team was beaming, but Gary spoke up. "I sit beside you almost every game and even though you haven't got a uniform on, believe me you're doing all that stuff." He put his finger to his head. "The difference is you're playing beside us up here."

As my eye scanned over my team, the warmth in their twelve young faces made me feel more content than I could remember feeling.

"Everyone have a seat. This was a special win and I'm very proud of how you played tonight. You stepped up your game to a new level once again, fellas. Nothing excites me more than seeing you do that. This is the best we've played all year—but guess what?"

Haywood slightly rolled his eyes. "We can play a lot better."

"Bingo! Haywood, you just get smarter every day."

"We hear it every day, Coach, but I think you've really convinced us. I know you have me because we're never going to stop working as long as you're our coach."

My twelve were nodding their heads and I added my voice to the chorus. "Get your hands in here!"

10

Apple Springs

Three weeks went by as my grueling work ethic caused me to fear peaking too early, but that fear was blown away as we got our second wind and sprinted past our next four opponents. To my amazement, our team continued to improve from practice to practice and game to game. Our winning streak had reached eighteen and we were really starting to think we were unbeatable. With a rippling wind of self-confidence at our back, I was growing increasingly worried each day at the attitude I was seeing. It's hard to tell the difference between cockiness and natural gym-floor bravado, but I was beginning to see inklings breaking the surface and my warnings seemed to be going unheeded.

When I caught myself bragging about our team to the faculty, talking about our 32-3 record, it was a wake-up call. I was the one who'd told my team that records didn't win games. I got my head back on straight and tried to think of a way to get the guys to see it too.

The worst part was the news that Apple Springs had also won their last four games. We were on a collision course and they would arrive at our gym in two days with fire in their bellies and a legitimate chance to tie the race.

Curtis waved me over after a practice, his new Apple Springs scouting report in his hands. "Okay, give me the bad news, how did they look?"

Curtis nodded as he looked over his notepad. "Well, they've definitely improved since last we saw them, but so have we. They'll have to have a *great* game to beat us and I don't think our defense will allow that to happen. Our defense is probably the main reason that we've won thirty-two games. As long as we have that as our backbone, I'm not sure how much damage they can do to us."

I smiled. "Curtis, you're talking more and more like a coach every time I see you! Our defense is way ahead of our offense right now."

Curtis leaned back in the bleachers. "Well, that's not a really bad thing, is it, Coach? These last games, our offense has been pretty darn good."

The morning's rain heralded another game day and our cozy gym was overflowing. Our stands were jammed to capacity with our ever-growing following. The stage on the far end of the gym was lined with several rows of chairs at the front and behind them people perched against the wall, shoulder to shoulder, straining to get a look as the fans continued to find their places. Standing room was becoming limited well before we even started our pre-game warm-up, yet people were still worming their way inside, hoping to find some place to watch what might possibly be the playoff-deciding game. It had been labeled the marquee game of our district since the previous encounter. With every second that ticked off the clock in the pregame warm-up, the tension continued to mount, particularly for our opponent. Sitting on our bench, fully aware of the importance of this game, I glanced down to the other end of the floor, watching Apple Springs warm up. There was a look of determination, but I could also see the uneasiness on their faces. It was do-or-die time for that very good team and if they slipped up, it was over.

I was wondering when I'd started smiling. If we could get off to another cat-quick start like we got the first time we played, that would be all it would take. If we came off the starting block with a sprint, that defeatist attitude in their eyes would be assured. We had them against the ropes after winning at their place and now their backs were to the wall. With only two games remaining after tonight, Apple Springs had to beat us on our own floor or the race was over and we would be the District 45 representatives for the upcoming State playoffs. Our team had always performed its best during the biggest games and I prayed it would be that way again. With a win tonight, we could open that door to a brand-new season of nothing but big games.

THE FIRST SEASON

I stood in the huddle looking into the now familiar faces of a very confident basketball team. "Fellas," I said, glancing toward the Apple Springs huddle, "that team doesn't really think that they can beat you. I could see it in their eyes as they warmed up. They remember us and it still stings. We can beat them in the first few minutes of this game. It's up to you to go out there and show them. Send that message loud and clear. I want you to reinforce that negative feeling that they already have. If you don't take control early, they're going to start believing they can beat us and our battle is going to get a lot tougher. You let them know that they're not going to come into our house and have their way. Right now they think they can't beat you. I want them to *know* they can't beat you! Is that clear, sports fans?" The shout that came from my team was the roar I was hoping for.

I watched my starting five Tigers head to the center circle and the massive crowd surged to its feet with a roof-lifting cheer. Goosebumps ran up and down my body as I returned the wide-eyed stares of Gary and Lester who were sitting beside me on our bench.

With the explosive home crowd applauding our every move, we took control early, sending the exact message I asked for in the huddle. Fred's picture-perfect wrist flip and follow-through arched the ball skyward, spinning toward the goal. There was a thunderous ovation as the shot put two on the board. Coming back with the aggressive defense which had become the trademark for our team, we forced a turnover as Nubbin got the steal and ripped a pass to Haywood on the run. Seeing Herman squared up in the far right corner, Haywood sent a bullet his way. Herman's fifteen-foot rainbow found its pot of gold in the bottom of the net. I came off the bench with the knee-jerking, double-fist pump that had become my personal symbol of elation. The crowd was standing, sensing the building of our early game momentum and they were not disappointed. All that simply paved the way for a ferocious first quarter finish resulting in a 22-10 lead. Coming off the floor at the end of the first quarter, our team could sense it, and most importantly, Apple Springs could sense it. This game was ours for the taking.

In our fired-up huddle between quarters, I looked at my business-like team. They were obviously thrilled by what had just transpired, but absolutely not surprised. They'd fully expected to do what they had just done. With a smile of approval, I looked into the faces of every member of my team. "That's what I call sending a message. You beat them in every phase of the game and right now they're reeling! They're wondering when the knockout punch is coming. Let's give it to them right now. You blitz them this quarter and you can probably stick a fork in them! Listen to me, fellas. All year long I've been preaching to you that when you have a team down, you don't let them get back up...so what do we do?"

With beads of sweat pouring off his forehead, Haywood put his hand in the center, "Bury them, on three!" Our team was smiling and I was sure our shout was heard by Apple Springs across the court.

Soon we were back on the floor, determined to finalize the job right then. With the crowd in a frenzy, we upped the pressure on defense while continuing to double our point production offensively. With Fred and Herman ripping the cords, we outplayed them again in the second quarter. We ran off the floor at halftime with a 40-19, almost insurmountable lead. We had all but sealed the tomb psychologically and with a twenty-one-point lead, we were looking good to seal it in the record books.

The Eagles managed to rally in the second half, but our level never faltered and we matched them basket for basket. They gave it all they had, but our superb first-half blitz was too much to overcome. The second half quickly became a formality, and we played just well enough to maintain our lead.

This capacity crowd continued to send us rippling waves of approval every time we scored and with our huge Tiger following encouraging our every move, we soundly defeated a well-coached team by twenty-two. For the second time in as many meetings, we had overcome the team we had to beat to win District. When we beat them two-and-a-half weeks before, we had played our best game of the season. However, that night, we crushed that measuring stick beneath our feet. Our defense had always been there, but tonight our offense was right there with them, side-by-side. This was the type of togetherness that had been gradually developing with this team. They were starting to respond to each other automatically without a word being said. Players were feeding off each other and the phases of the game were gradually becoming one. When players react to a situation just by the look of one to the other, synergy develops. With the playoffs right around the corner, the timing appeared to be perfect.

Looking into the faces of twelve very positive young men, I shook my head, "I'm almost at a loss for words. I'm proud of you guys and what you have accomplished this year! But right now, what I am most proud of is what you did tonight. I know I've made this statement before...okay, I've been making it a lot lately, but tonight was by far the *best* you have played." I pointed back toward the playing court. "You were *awesome* out there tonight. This was the most pumped up I've been all year."

The dressing room exploded as my team whooped and hollered. Raising my fist triumphantly above their heads, I couldn't help but join in. Haywood caught my hand in his vise-like grip and shook it. "Coach, aren't you forgetting something?"

I stared dumbly at him for a second before remembering. "Right!" I gave him a wink. "Remember, this is just another step on the path. We are going to work harder and get better!"

Roy was looking at me with that devious half-smile and I could almost sense what he was going to say before he even opened his mouth. "Coach, you said we played by far the best we've played all year. I think we played *great* tonight, how about you?"

My eyes panned the room. There was a sudden quiet as they waited. I made eye contact with each member of the team. I smiled. "I totally agree with you, Roy. We never let those guys have a chance. We were in control from the tip to the last shot. You'd better believe it, Roy, we played *great* tonight...and it's a giant step towards becoming a great team. You played your best in a game of importance, but if you wanna say that we're a *great* team, well we still have two District games left and two warm-up games the week after that. Time will show if tonight was a fluke or if you guys are the real thing."

Fred spoke up. "Coach, for the warm-up game, let's play Grapeland. They're one of the best teams around."

"I couldn't agree more and that's exactly who I'm trying to get. Our next four games will be setting the table for our first playoff game because that's where we're headed. Fellas, there are a lot of very good teams about to begin the playoffs. Some will step it up and keep playing, some will step aside and bow out. Tonight, you stepped it up. Let's keep stepping it up right into the playoffs. We've already had two very good seasons. We played twenty-eight non-District games, which was the first season, and you basically finished the second season tonight. First place earns you a third and that season is here. I'm talking about the playoff season. It's here, fellas, and we start working on phase three tomorrow."

A few minutes later, one by one, each member of my team left the dressing room. Although heading outside into the cold February night air, I never saw any of them flinch against it. Each player walked with his head high, the warmth of our win staying with us. I was hoping and praying that the feeling would carry over into the upcoming playoff schedule.

~~~

The playoff season arrived and even though we had two District games remaining, my practices centered around the first playoff game of my coaching career. Our confidence level was soaring as we approached our last two District games. In fact, that cockiness that I was picking up was becoming more and more apparent and it showed in our performance the last two District games. There was a considerable reduction in our level of play as we went through the motions. We managed a win against Lovelady 51-40, but allowed their star, Jack Newbauer, to score twenty-six of the team's points. In our last home game, Centerville-Groveton, who we had soundly beaten on the road by twenty-three, gave us all we wanted, actually leading by a point starting the fourth quarter. We eventually managed to pull the game out, winning a squeaker by four, in a game that we should have easily dominated. We'd taken those two games for granted and it showed.

In the dressing room after our last home game, I looked at my team with a very concerned look. "Fellas, we were lucky to win that game. You were lazing around out there like tomatoes on a vine—— when they get ripe, they get picked. You were ripe for the taking and if you were playing a playoff game tonight, you would've gotten picked clean."

Herman shrugged noncommittally. "The game didn't really mean a whole lot. I mean, we already won District."

My eyes narrowed and I could feel the heat beneath my collar. "It has a direct influence on your level of play in your upcoming games. Look, we worked hard to get to that high level of play. You all thought you were becoming a great team. Well, in the last two games, you were *ordinary.*" I stalked the room and thought about kicking one of the benches. "A team is based on how it performs and ordinary just won't cut it. We have two warm-up games on our schedule and I promise you, if you play those like you did tonight, you'll get kicked twice!"

My players' heads were downcast as I exited. Just as there can be victory in defeat, the opposite can be true if the victory wasn't earned and I left the dressing room as uncertain as I felt at the start of the season. Walking into the chill of the night air I was trying to think about how to jolt my team back on their feet, give them a wake-up call, anything to get us back on track. Maybe a loss was what we needed to re-ignite our determination. Time was short and the playoffs were near. If we didn't quickly turn that thing around, our first playoff game would likely be our team's last.

~~~~

My prognostication turned out to be correct. In our first warm-up game the following week, playing in Lufkin, we lost a heartbreaker to Coach Jim Foreman's well-coached, fundamentally sound Hudson Hornets by a score of 51-50. When the buzzer sounded, there was a look of astonishment on my players' faces and a grim smile on my own. To our credit, we had played better than the previous two games, but our level of play still wasn't close to where we had been at our peak.

I was upset about the loss, but not nearly as upset as I was about our level of play. I gave a talk to my kids full of "I-told-you-so" and about reaping what you sow. Truthfully, I don't think they needed me in their faces to help them understand that this was the result of thinking of any game as meaningless. We had one more game left before we played Anderson in the playoffs and that was with Grapeland. Three of their starters were in the six-foot-five range and would maul us if we didn't wake up.

Coach Johnny Carter

11

Proud of the Purple

It was a cold February morning as I got out of my car in the school parking lot. If the temperature had dropped any more, that ever-so-soft mist in the air just might have turned to snow. Turning my collar up, I held the *Dallas Morning News* over my head as I hurried up the sidewalk. The previous night's eyelash loss made it seem a lot colder to me than the actual temperature. That previous warm feeling that I had enjoyed for so long had dropped away and the winter chill was taking advantage of my vulnerable state. Just four games before, I was thinking that we had a good chance to advance into the playoffs, but our level of play had nosedived toward mediocrity. Even a few of our die-hard fans had vilified us, saying we'd seen our best play and that it was time to put us out to pasture. I couldn't blame them, they were entitled to think that way.

Walking down the hall, the smell was different and my nose wrinkled in defense. That was the first time in a little over two months that I was going to get a cup of coffee after a loss. I had been spoiled by our success just like the team and without it, everything was unfamiliar and abrasive. As I poured a cup of coffee and slumped into a seat, Mrs. Nona Baker walked over and stood in front of me. I didn't want to look up, but I met her eyes.

"Coach, don't you want some cream with that?"

I smiled at her and something within me felt lighter. "I probably should drink it straight black today, to match my team's performance last night—bitter and hard to swallow.

She waved a dishrag at me. "Now don't get down on the boys. They've risen to the occasion like clockwork whenever we've had a big game. People can think what they like, but last night was *not* a big game."

I grimaced as I took a swig. Mrs. Baker made her coffee strong and as I chewed it, it bit back. "The way we look right now, there's no way we can play with Grapeland."

She smiled, handing me the cream. "I think our guys will surprise you... and speaking of surprises, I have one for you." She disappeared into the kitchen and reappeared with a foil-wrapped package of hot apricot fried pies. Looking at me with big smile, she coaxed one into my hand.

"I thought this morning in particular you might need more than just a coffee pick-me-up, so I came up here early. Coach, we still love you, win or lose." I couldn't help but smile. I stood up and wrapped her in a big hug. Like the great lady and mother she was, she returned it harder and walked away smiling.

~~~

Walking on the floor for that day's workout, I was met by my five starters. I blew the whistle and called to start our warm-up, but the five stayed in place. Fred stepped forward, apparently the designated spokesman.

"Coach, we realize that our game hasn't been where it should be the last few games and we're really not sure why, but we wanted to let you know that we're ready to do whatever you think it's gonna take to get us back on track."

With a smile, I looked into the faces of this special group of players. The gates had been opened. "That's music to my ears. I can show you where we've gotten bumpy and I can show you how to smooth out the path, but it's up to you to do what it takes to keep it that way. We've lost our focus. I can see it in the dressing room before we go out and here in practice too. We don't have a particular team to beat and we don't have a record to defend. The playoffs will be a different thing, but they are the toughest games we have yet faced and the most important. I don't think that you let up on purpose, but subconsciously, you looked back on your season and said, 'Hey, we've done pretty good.' Well, what were you comparing to? Kennard's other teams? Your last seasons? Compare it to yourselves, because I can tell you that this team has a lot of potential and if you aren't striving to meet yours every day, then you've already been beaten. I think you've been going through the motions, you've been shadowboxing. You've forgotten how we reached the level of play that propelled us to that District Championship.

"When you win and you do it consistently, you become thought of as a leader—proven winner. Guess what, fellas? It's much tougher to maintain that status than it is to reach it. Look, I'm in total control of your physical condition. I've been working your butts off." I tapped the side of my head. "But most of this game is up here. You didn't lose this last game because you were tired, you *let* an inferior team beat you. How does that make you feel? I remember there was a time when losing got this team angry. What happened to that feeling?"

Haywood had been shaking his head, "Oh, it's there, Coach. I'm angry. It makes me sick to my stomach."

Fred gripped his shoulder and turned to the team. "I think we all feel like Haywood does and this is going to be the last time we let this happen, *right?*" I watched as Haywood and Fred eyed the rest of the team.

The atmosphere in the room changed almost immediately. My players seemed to be antsy, ready to play and prove themselves before one another. Once again, a loss looked like it had pushed us harder than my lecturing and carrying on ever could have. Judging by the rest of the day's practice, our eyes were open and we were determined to find our way back on the path.

Toward the end of practice, we worked the full-court press defense. That was something that admittedly I knew very little about, but I was intrigued with the style of play. We'd used it occasionally through our second season, but it was new territory for me and I didn't have enough confidence in its use to totally depend on it. The philosophy of an all-out, start-to-finish, pressing defense fit me like a glove, but I wasn't sure when to implement it in a game. I loved the fact that you could force your opponent to earn every inch of the floor before they ever had a chance to get in scoring range, but it felt dangerous and risked more fouls. As I watched my guys on the floor, the more I experimented with it, the more positive I became about it.

Coach Johnny Carter

We needed something to combat those Grapeland Giants that weekend. They had us completely outmanned on the boards and it looked like the press was it. We just had to play smart defense.

"Fellas, you're about to face the best rebounding team you've faced this year. This is a true test. These guys are capable of dominating you on the boards, but I'm telling you right now, that's not gonna happen." I paced before my benched team. "You're going to block out the man in your area, *every* time. I didn't say every other time, I didn't say sometimes, I said *every* time, and that's what I mean. I don't care how big those suckers are, you do this and we'll get our share of the rebounds. We are probably going to press much more in this particular game because we're quicker than they are and we want to establish a faster tempo. Remember, whether we win this game or not doesn't mean squat. Now the game we have next Tuesday, that's a different story."

~~~

Walking into the gym, I heard my name shouted out and looked up the bleachers. I was surprised to see my good friend, John McGilvra, who was then the head coach at Warren High School. Making his way down, we shook hands. As we talked, the opposite dressing room sprang open and Grapeland took the court. I saw John's jaw drop. "Look at the *size* of those guys. They make my whole team look like a squad of midgets!"

I laughed as I followed his gaze. "Your team? I promise you my team has a lot more midgets than yours."

With a sarcastic smile, he said, "Yeah, but at least your midgets are 35-4!" We were both chuckling as I turned my attention back to our guys warming up. He jerked his head back toward Grapeland. Their coach had them in a huddle. "Hey, Carter, what would you be saying to those guys over there?"

I shrugged, "I guess about the same thing I tell my team: Go over our strategy, hit the high points...why?"

"Because if I were the one surrounded by guys that big, all I'd say was, 'Fellas, whatever I do, don't ever let me piss you off!'"

I almost couldn't call my team in because I was laughing so hard.

THE FIRST SEASON

Just as I anticipated, the game at Grapeland turned out to be a low-scoring contest. Their size superiority gave us fits, but we blocked out extremely well and though we were slightly outrebounded, we held our own. With our team showing a new spark after three straight mediocre performances, we led most of the game. Though not totally back, our level of play had some of the old fire in it. With the score tied and no time left on the clock, Fred was at the foul line. With an overflow house full of apprehensive eyes fixated on the flight of the ball, his shot sliced the strings with a soft swish. Fred had just nailed the game-winning free throw, sending our ecstatic fans into a frenzy while leaving the home crowd in shock. We had just defeated the best rebounding team we had faced all year—and on their own floor at that! Although that was our best performance in our past four games, we were still well below our previous level of play. However, winning a game of that nature against one of the top teams in the state would hopefully help us turn the corner. Obviously our team was not all the way back, but that night we took a giant step toward getting there.

~~~

It was late February in Houston County as winter slowly evolved into spring. Inside the Tigers' Den, preparations were in full force for our first playoff game with the Anderson Owls. I looked at my players.

"Now, the Owls are 20-16 on the record, but they did play a very difficult schedule this season and they have a good coach, Warren Wood. Their starting five are Glen Shaeffer, James Baldwin, and three other guys. I'll try to give their names, but will probably butcher the pronunciation." I stuttered over the list. "Raymond Secheiski, Leonard Szymczak, and Joe Kitkoski." I finished feebly and looked into the puzzled eyes of my players.

"Coach, where did they get those guys from—Russia?"

Herman laughed. "With those names, we should be playing in the Olympics!"

Fred stepped up next to Herman. "Tell us what we have to do to beat them. We got to this point last year and Magnolia whipped us pretty good—sent us right back home."

Nubbin nodded in agreement. "Yeah, Fred, but that was last year. We're a bit better this year."

Herman scoffed. "A bit better? Come on, Nubbin, we're a lot better!"

Resting a ball on his hip, Roy nodded to Fred. "Just tell us what we've got to do tomorrow night, Coach."

"Well, first of all, I want you to know I pushed for this game to be played at Madisonville. We've played four games there and we know that gym well. It took some tricky negotiations to get there. They knew that we'd played there, but I finally convinced them that this was the best place for the game. We shot the ball and played very well in the Mustang gym, so the advantage is ours to lose. Also, I can guarantee the crowd will be for us."

My guys looked positive and as we went through the game plan, our practice came to a close. It had been a very good workout, much shorter than usual. I wanted the freshest legs and highest energy level possible. Despite our lull in the previous four games, our team had played too well the past couple of months to finish the season now. As we shot free throws, dropping bucket after bucket, Fred came and sat by me. "The guys are excited, Coach. This was a good practice. I say bring on the Owls."

Blowing the whistle, I called everyone over. "Get some rest tonight. Tomorrow we start a brand-new season—a season of nothing but big games. If we don't step up to the occasion, the occasion will walk all over us."

Despite my admonition, sleep wouldn't come. In less than twenty-four hours, I would be coaching the most important game of my young coaching life. My team did seem to play their best in the biggest games and if we continued in our normal pattern, we had a chance to move past our first game of the playoffs. Every coach, every team begins each season with dreams, aspirations, and desires, hoping that their team reaches that point. I had tried not to pressure my guys with talk about the playoffs, but we had worked diligently, striving for that very moment. It was the culmination of six months of an ever-developing special relationship between a first-year coach and a team of twelve young believers.

Each of our four losses that year had triggered us to a higher performance level. We came back like gangbusters after that Snook game and it was my hope that a new winning streak had started with our eyelash win at Grapeland. I had been to that point many times as a player, so I knew all too well that we had reached those bittersweet games of the season, never knowing which game would be our last.

Approaching the Madisonville city limit sign, we turned off the highway and into my parents' driveway. I had worked it out with my mom for our team to stop by before going to the gym.

"Come on, fellas, everybody out." Walking up to the back door, I was greeted by my mom's smiling face.

"Come in. Make yourselves at home." One by one, my players entered the house.

I glanced towards the kitchen. "Is it about ready?"

"All I've got to do is pour it into the cups."

I turned to my team, clapping my hands together. "My mom has graciously agreed to have us stop by for a very special, extra energy drink for the game. I don't know if you care for hot tea or not, but today you're going to drink it. We have plenty of honey for you to sweeten it with. This is the best energy boost that I know of. Drink it down so we can go take care of the Owls." There was some reluctance, but every player had a cup.

"Will this really make us play better?" Roy asked, pushing his empty cup away.

"Roy, you're gonna have so much energy tonight, I doubt if you'll even sweat!"

"Coach, you run us so much now in practice that I really never get tired in the game anyway. I'm so fast now I can almost fly!"

"Well, I'll tell you what. There are scientists who, as we speak, are working to send a man to the moon in the next couple of years. If those guys happen to see you flying down the floor tonight, they just might decide to send you to the moon instead. You could save the country a whole lot of money because you won't even need a rocket ship!" Everyone was really laughing, especially Mom.

With a slight smile, Roy said, "I kinda like that idea, Coach."

Roy struck a pose. "I'd be the first man on the moon—that ought to get a few headlines!"

Haywood was chuckling, "The real headline would be 'First *Black* man sent to the moon!' Don't worry about comin' back though, Roy.

Once they get one of us up there, just a matter of time before they send the rest of us black guys up there with you!

Roy was cracking up. "Coach, if they sent you up there with us, we would have a heck of a team. It could be the NBA's first moon division." With laughter ringing through Mama's kitchen, the pressure of the task at hand had been reduced significantly. Soon we were saying our goodbyes and loading onto the bus, waving and thanking her for all she had done. It was far more than a cup of tea, but how much more, I doubted she would ever know.

The pregame shoot around was going just as expected as we went through the rhythms of spot shooting. With the exception of that drumbeat echo of balls bouncing and an occasional ricochet off the rim, sober silence described the atmosphere. That would change shortly as hundreds of fans packed the gymnasium for the bi-District clash. Soon it was time to rack up the balls and head to the dressing room for our usual pre-game chalk talk.

The dressing room before a game, particularly a playoff game, is usually not without its share of pre-game jitters. We went over the game plan once again, focusing their minds on something proactive.

"Okay, you know what your roles are and you know what we have to do. Remember how you felt after that Hudson game? Remember how you felt after that Snook game? That Snook game propelled you to a long winning streak. Now Hudson has lit the fire once again and it's time for winning streak number two."

As I stood before that very close-knit group, I looked into the eyes of each player and felt a special warmth in my heart. Regardless of how the rest of the season played out, the camaraderie of the team continued to amaze me. Every time I thought they had reached the highest plateau possible, they defied the odds, climbing to an even higher one. That night would definitely be a true test of their teamwork and ability because it was far and away our most important game of the year. We prayed and put our hands in the middle. "Okay, guys, any questions? If you have one, ask it now. No questions?" A smile spread across my face. "Okay, then winning streak number two continues right now!"

~~~

THE FIRST SEASON

The gym was near capacity as we took the floor to a deafening roar from our fans. It was pretty obvious that the vast majority of fans were pulling for the Tigers. It was a really unique feeling sitting down on the bench for a game of that importance in my hometown. I always enjoyed going home anyway, but coming home to coach my first ever playoff game, well that was something special.

My dad came by the bench with my brother James Otis to wish me luck. He shook my hand. "You've already had a great year, regardless of what happens here on out. I'm proud of what your team has done this year. So, just how good is this Anderson bunch?"

"They're good, but I think we're ready. If we play our game like I know we can, we should be okay."

With the center jump, the game between the two District champions was underway. It was playoff basketball and it didn't take long in observing the reaction of the huge crowd to let you know how important the games had become. With an enthusiastic roar on just about every play, the fans sent shock waves of support for both teams. When James Baldwin hit a shot to tie the game at two, though not quite as loud as ours, the Anderson crowd showed their approval. Our offense and defense answered with a vengeance, beginning with Fred when he took the ball at the high post. With a quick square up, rocker step, pump fake, he put up a quick jumper. The spinning one-hander hit the back of the goal with a forceful thud. The rotation of the ball caused a sudden reverse action. With a rim-riveting *rat-a-tat-tat,* it went right through the net. Fred's jumper triggered a chain reaction of Tigers twos. The crowd was on their feet as Roy hit a post turnaround jumper, followed by Herman popping a long-range high flyer. Sensing we were about to grasp the first taste of momentum in the early stages of this do-or-die match, I again came off the bench with an enthusiastic clutched fist, double pump.

I had been pretty animated all year in the way I coached every game, but that one was what we had worked for all year. I wasn't trying to hide the enthusiasm that rushed through every fiber of my body. We had opened the game with a vengeance, and I was thrilled. With an emotional raised fist of approval, I barely had time to enjoy those three baskets when Nubbin stole the ball. He then hit Haywood on the run and with a burst of athletic speed, he shot past and around the surprised Owl defense, sprinting full force for an unopposed layup.

Our offense was scintillating as we had scorched the cords for four straight baskets. With the crowd stomping and cheering behind us, it felt like an earthquake. In response, we rewarded them once again with the after effect of yet another forced turnover. The ball shot to Herman, who canned another fifteen-footer. We had just scored ten unanswered points in a very short period. The board read 12-2. I was shouting to my players at the top of my lungs just to be heard over the crowd. With each basket, they got louder and louder and louder. When Anderson called timeout, they cheered us right into our huddle on a cloud of energy that was truly electric.

"*Yes!* That's what I'm talking about," I said, screaming words of encouragement. I could barely even hear myself. "Take it right to them!"

It wasn't an ostentatious display, it was just good basketball. Whatever doubts I had about this team's ability were erased by that amazing run. We'd scrambled up and over our highest levels of play during the second season. Our huddle was as high as a kite, sensing a possible blowout. We had the Owls on the ropes, but to their credit, they didn't give up. They came back after our run to trail by only seven at the end of the quarter. They played even better in the second quarter, scoring nineteen points, attempting to cut into our lead. Scoring was not their problem, it was keeping us from doing the same. Herman had a monster first half, single-handedly scoring eighteen points, leading us to a twenty-three-point second quarter and propelling us to an eleven-point lead at halftime. We left the floor with a totally positive attitude and a standing ovation of our now very confident following. Walking off the floor to the roar of approval, we headed for the dressing room in what we thought to be in total control.

Sensing that we were about to move to the next round of the playoffs, our dressing room was alive with emotion. I had to remind them that even though we had pretty much dominated the first half, leading 42-31, we still had work to do. An eleven-point lead can evaporate in a flash. I waved the team into silence.

"You played really well offensively, maybe as well as we've played all year, but we let them score thirty-one points and a lot of those were cheapies! If you had played as well defensively as you did on the offensive end, we could pack it up right now and go home because this game would be over. The first half you worked to outscore them. You know as well as I do that it takes more than that. It takes balance to win games." I was getting a lot of nods, and that level of elation was turning back into focus, particularly in Fred and Roy's eyes.

"I want to see the kind of defense that I know you can play in the third quarter! Move your feet, cheat toward the ball, and step into position to take the charge when the time comes! You step up the defense in this quarter and this game is history."

~~~

The third quarter brought on the complete game that I wanted to see. With a stingy, intensified defense, we held a very good offensive team to a mere six points while putting twenty-three of our own on the board. Our energy had been focused, our play tamed, and everyone flowed seamlessly into their job. It seemed that our team had grown up in the third quarter and the Owls couldn't keep up with our new level of maturity. Herman continued to shoot the lights out, hitting an incredible eleven of fourteen from the field. With that big lead, I took him out starting the fourth quarter as I began to clear the bench. One by one, I took out our starting five. They were playing harder than I'd ever seen them play. Now wasn't the time to risk an injury and our well-rested bench players were more than happy to get a piece of the action. By the end of the game, I had played every player on our team as we sailed to a very convincing 79-55 playoff victory. There could be no argument—the biggest game of the year had been our best game of the year. A bubbling thought kept rising in my mind, asking me just how far we could go in our third season.

As a young coach, I had just found out that my team was capable of playing a lot better than I had ever dreamed. Our timing was perfect. Never in my wildest dreams did I think we were capable of playing with that kind of domination in a game of that significance. Everything seemed to come together that third quarter in Madisonville. Passing our test there, we were about to go to the Regional Tournament with a new frame of mind and a confidence level beyond even my highest expectations.

On the way to the dressing room, my mom and dad gave me two monster hugs. "Wow!" my dad said. "You guys came to play tonight! I didn't know they could play that good."

I was laughing. "Neither did I." Scratching my head enigmatically, I said, "It's hard to believe that this is the same team that lost to Hudson a week ago. I can't explain it. They just play better in big games."

Smiling profusely, Curtis slapped me on the back. "That's what you want them to do, isn't it?"

~~~~~

Inside the locker room, it was hard for me to get my words together. "In the last three weeks, we've had six games, two of which were the most important games of the year." Their smiling faces were locked with mine. "In both of those big games, we stepped up to the challenge and leapt past it!" Cheers echoed through the locker room. "With Apple Springs, we played the best game of the year and tonight we were on a different planet all together!"

Haywood playfully punched Roy's shoulder, "I guess you did make it to the moon, son."

Roy shook his head. "We all made it to the moon tonight, right Coach?"

Nubbin jumped on the bench. "Forget about being the first black guys in space, I think we'll be the only tigers to *ever* leave orbit!"

As the laughter died, I pulled them all in. "I'll save you the trouble of asking today, Roy. We were great tonight, particularly in the third quarter. It was beautiful. You were awesome. I don't think that there's a Class B team in this state that could have beat you tonight. You were totally focused on what you had to do. Right now, let's enjoy tonight because our next game will be in the Regionals!"

~~~~~

Driving home, I looked over at a purple towel sitting on the passenger seat. I'd accidentally carried it out with me after the game. I had to admit that at the start of the season purple had not been my favorite color. I'd been happier playing in my Mustang red and blue, but as I looked at that towel and thought about my guys playing their hearts out on the floor, a smile crept over my face. In ancient times, purple was the symbol of royalty, the dye being extremely difficult to make. Back in those times, in order to wear it you either had a lot of money or had received it as a special gift. That team...that school was definitely lacking in the money department, which left me with the only other option. My Tigers were a gift and I was thankful for them. The sheer beauty of the color purple had shone brightly in the darkness that February evening and I was comforted even more knowing that if you mixed my old school colors—Mustang red and blue—they blended into a deep purple. I would wear it with pride for both my team and my history.

Coach Johnny Carter

12

A Little Help

It wasn't daybreak yet as I sped through the early morning darkness. With my headlights illuminating the highway in front of me, the pines became a slideshow, whisking past on the side of the highway. It was Wednesday morning and I was headed toward the historic, east Texas oil field city of Kilgore. I was one of seven hopeful coaches headed for Kilgore Junior College to meet with legendary coach and athletic director Joe Turner to determine the pairings for the Regional IV Tournament, the winner of which would be headed for the state capitol the following week to participate in the prestigious Texas State Tournament. The fact that my team was even mentioned in the same breath as those other teams had my head spinning. Despite the obscurity of our advancing past that point, we had a chance, be it ever so slight, to take a team to Austin.

~~~

Sitting behind the desk, absolutely burning up her typewriter was a very attractive young secretary. I rapped my knuckles lightly against the tabletop. "Excuse me, I'm looking for Coach Turner."

Looking up from her typewriter, she looked me over with an inquisitive and very pleasing-smile. "Do you play for Coach Turner? I thought I knew all our players."

I smiled. "I'm the coach at Kennard High School and I'm here for the Regional meeting."

She did a double take and her eyes narrowed. "You've got to be kidding me. Did someone put you up to this?"

119

Coach Johnny Carter

I struggled to keep my smile plastered on. "I may not look it, but I'm twenty-three years old and I assure you, I'm Johnny Carter, coach of the Kennard High School Tigers...and if you don't let me into that room, my team is going to have a *really* hard time winning their Regional game."

She took a second, looking into my eyes before her facadé disappeared and she started blushing. "I am *so* sorry. It's just that all the head basketball coaches I've known were really old guys."

"Actually most of them are only a few years older than I am; but it's the nature of the work that does that to them. I have yet to finish a year and I feel like I should have had seven birthdays." Rising quickly, she flashed me another smile and motioned for me to follow. "Come on, I'll walk you down to the meeting room."

I wasn't going to object—she was tall, blonde, and wore a pin of the nationally famous Kilgore Rangerettes. She continued her apologies as she led me down the hall and stopped at a door. "Good luck. Why don't you drop by the front office after your meeting and let me know how it comes out. I'd love to see your team play." As she walked away, all I could think was, *So far, so good.*

One by one, the other six coaches assembled in the meeting room, eagerly awaiting the proceedings. Not knowing who you were going to play or when you were going to play had us all a little edgy, and it was difficult to partake in small talk with my possible competition. Mercifully, Coach Turner didn't make us wait long.

"First, I would like to congratulate each of you on winning your bi-District games last night. As you know, we are now down to seven teams representing the fourteen districts of Region IV. Now, with an uneven number of teams, some lucky team will get a *bye* in Friday's first-round game of the tournament."

We shifted glances. A bye. Some lucky team would only have to win one game to get into the finals, while the others would have double the chance for elimination. Of course they would be a game behind in the competition as well and I knew what even a short break in competition could do to a team's focus.

Turner continued. "In this cap, I have seven pieces of paper with a number on each piece." Pointing to the wall, he said, "There's the bracket with the numbers and times that will be determined by whatever number you draw.

In the back of the room, one of the older coaches cleared his throat, "Carter, since you're obviously the youngest, you've got to draw first."

I knew it was about luck, that a blind draw gave me an equal chance to draw anything, but suddenly a lump crawled into my throat and my heart was racing full tilt. I nervously walked to the front of the room and reached into the hat. I flicked past a couple papers, feeling somehow as if that put me in control of the situation. My fingers came to rest on a slip and I closed my grip. Slowly opening the neatly folded piece of paper, my jaw dropped.

Looking over my shoulder, Turner nodded. "Lucky number seven. Well, looks like we have a winner; Tigers get the bye." Trying not to jump out of my shoes, I walked back to my seat. The other coaches' faces varied from laughter to looks that burned the back of my neck for the rest of the meeting.

Walking down the hall after the meeting, I was riding a wave of emotion. I stopped by the office to see the young secretary one more time. She took one look at the big smile spread across my face.

"I guess the meeting went the way that you wanted it to go," she said.

I tried to keep my voice even. "It was perfect. It absolutely could not have gone any better for our team. We advance to Saturday's semi-finals without even playing."

Her face dropped a little. "Great! Though I was actually hoping that you'd be playing on Friday because I could watch you play. I can't on Saturday because we're gonna be out of town for a performance, but I wish you the best of luck."

She shot me another smile and I couldn't help myself—my endorphins were pumping. "If I wanted to let you know how we did in our game, is there a number I might call?"

She blushed, but her smile got a little bigger as she slid a slip of paper across the desk.

That earlier soft breeze was now a howling wind, piercing the trees and rustling the leaves on that late February morning. With a feeling of sheer elation flowing through my veins, I was soon headed back through the east Texas oil fields toward home. When oil was discovered there in

1930, history was rewritten as a staggering twenty-six-mile stretch of land became the greatest concentration of oil wells in the world. I was hoping that my team could make some history of its own because a lot of things were starting to fall into place and that day's meeting was more than just icing on the cake—it could be the biggest break we had all year. When I coupled it with the fact that we had played great the night before, well, it all just seemed too good to be true. We needed one less victory than any of the other teams in the tournament to win it. *Wow,* I thought. *Just two more wins and we'll be in Austin.*

~~~

My drive back was much quicker than my early morning trip up. It was almost seventh period when I pulled into the school parking lot. Swiftly walking down the hallway, I headed for Mr. Bitner's office. He leapt out of his chair with a clenched fist. I couldn't help but laugh; it was the most animated I'd ever seen my superintendent.

"Coach, you must be living right! I can't believe it. You go up there, draw first, and literally steal a victory! I wonder what the odds are of that happening."

"Oh, I'd say they're about the same as us winning the State Championship." Now we were both laughing.

"Coach, you know what? This just may be our time because a lot of things are starting to fall our way. We play our best game of the year and then get a bye. It doesn't get any better than that." But it could and I knew it. It could get a lot better if we managed to win two more games.

~~~

As I walked into practice, the balls stopped bouncing and I was swamped by my players. I had to silence them before I could get a word in. As I told them about our automatic first round victory, there were shouts of joy from our entire team. It felt like the previous night's game all over again. I looked over my team after my news of our doubleheader victory.

"Congratulations, guys, we're in the semi-finals before we even shoot layups today. But remember, this means that those guys get another taste of tournament play when we don't. So our practices are going to be intense to make up for our loss."

With the adrenaline in our system feeding our thought process, we did go with the flow, having an intense practice, the best of the year.

THE FIRST SEASON

Things were going so well it was almost scary. The way we were executing, I almost wished that we'd had a first-round game. We would be playing the winner of Frankston and Big Sandy on Saturday morning. Having seen both of those teams play, I felt confident that Frankston would be our opponent and spent time preparing accordingly. One of my best friends and teammates at Lon Morris was Mike Cook, a Frankston native, and we spent a good amount of time talking about the team's established tradition under Coach Bo Osley. They'd already won State once and were consistently in the Regional Tournament. From my own scouting, I knew they were a solid team and had two excellent players in David Coker and Cole Pugh. It would take a great effort on our part to beat them, but we had three things in our favor: We were quicker; we had no established tradition, which might make us harder to prepare for and we would have an extra day of practice after I scouted them again in Kilgore on Friday.

~~~

The Regional Tournament was upon us and at that moment we were sitting in the best position of all the teams there. That is what I was continuously telling my players because I wanted them to firmly believe it. I wanted them to take the floor on Saturday morning in Kilgore with a completely positive frame of mind, sure that we would win. Kilgore wasn't a long drive and I decided that it would be best for us to drive up on Saturday morning, allowing each player to sleep in his own bed the night before the game. Some motel rooms were reserved for the afternoon for the players to rest between games. I'd learned the importance of not overtaxing my players and was going to do everything possible to make sure that they were ready to play. The fact that we would be playing the first game Saturday morning was yet another positive. We would have an extra couple of hours of rest, more than the two teams playing the second game behind us. Since the depth of our team was still a problem, the extra rest would be welcome. With all the good fortune falling our way, all we had to do was win the two hardest, most pressure-packed games we'd ever played. Hopefully our incredible bi-District performance had ignited a higher level of play for our young team.

Even now, as close as we had come, I wasn't even mentioning the State Tournament around my players. Two wins away from that coveted trip to Austin, I needed my players focused on the game they were playing, not the one down the road. There was enough pressure at the Regional Tournament without adding more.

13

The Regional Tournament

We were just minutes away from the start of the Regional IV Tournament. With a Dr. Pepper in one hand and a clipboard in the other, Curtis and I were ready to scout the Frankston versus Big Sandy game, knowing full well that we would play the winner the next morning.

"Look at these fans, Coach. You'd think we were at the State Tournament." Curtis was craning his neck and looking over the serious faces of the spectators around us.

I nodded, "Well, in many ways, these games have even more pressure in them than the State Tournament. Just qualifying for State is what it's all about, even if you don't win it. The teams that make it there are the best of the best and it can come down to luck as to who wins there, but here in the Regionals, it's almost always who draws the hot hand."

As Frankston and Big Sandy started their game, I watched keenly as two former State Champions with rich traditions began their battle. My team was still in the baby steps of trying to establish the kind of tradition that both of those schools already had. The game progressed and my feeling about the outcome proved correct. Frankston pulled away in the third quarter and held their lead, winning the game 62-54. Frankston would be our first round opponent on Saturday morning. They would definitely be the favorite and that was fine with me. I'd always liked pulling for the underdog.

It was going be a long night; we had two more games to scout before we drove home.

After watching Woden the first half, I turned to Curtis. "I don't think we want any part of them. Coach Keith Lowry has this team playing on all cylinders right now." As I said it, a lightning triple pass ended in a clean shot for two. "Curtis, these guys are good. They may be the best team I've seen all year."

Curtis nodded with a frown; our pencils had stopped their eternal crawl across the clipboards. "Well, we wouldn't see them until the finals anyway. Besides, we've got to get by Frankston first." Woden won the game by twelve, 79-67.

Avinger then played Carlisle in the final game of the day. Led by six-foot-five all-Stater, Charles Herren, the Indians went on the warpath during the second half for a convincing eleven- point victory. Coach David Murphy's well-coached team had reached the Regional finals the past year and they were just one win away from being there again.

It was very late when I dropped Curtis off. "I enjoyed it, Coach. Do we have a big day tomorrow or what?"

I glanced at my watch, "Well, we've certainly got a big one *today*."

Curtis's face was ashen. "Coach, you need to get back to Crockett. Get some sleep."

I put the car into gear and headed back down Highway 7 toward Crockett, fully knowing that getting a good night's sleep was questionable.

~~~

The morning did come early and soon I was driving back to Kennard. Saturday, February 25th, was a cool, crisp, late winter morning in east Texas. Arriving at the school well before daylight, I packed the necessary equipment for two games, hoping that caution wouldn't prove to be over-confidence. The whole thing felt surreal. What business did I have, at my young age, to be there? I shook myself. Maybe it was just the lack of sleep. One by one, my team members started arriving as we prepared to head for Kilgore. I tried real hard to act like it was just like any other game in front of them and informed the team that I had indeed guessed right. We would be playing Frankston.

"Look, this team is very beatable, but it won't be easy. They're seasoned, they're well coached, they're confident, and they've been here many times before. I really think they very well may look right past us. It's gonna be a big mistake if they do because I'm gonna tell you right now that we're a better team than they are. If we can get the upper hand at the beginning and make them play catch-up, I think we can deal them a lot of misery. Get after those guys from the start. Let them know that we mean business. *We* know we're better, we need to plant that idea in *their* heads." I tried hard to project a positive mindset all the way to Kilgore. I began to realize that my team was already a lot more sure of themselves than I was and they were instilling confidence in their coach. My team was a diamond in the rough and I could only hope we'd been polished enough to shine.

The backdrop of emerging oil derricks coupled with the wintry look of east Texas pines silhouetted the sky as we approached historic downtown Kilgore. Four teams were left, three of which would go home with shattered dreams and the other would be on their way to Austin, dreaming of a State Championship. One team would get on a roll, have the day of their lives, sweep two games, and then start making hotel reservations at the state capitol. We were the only team left that didn't have a history of being there. The general consensus was that if we hadn't drawn the bye we wouldn't be there at all. With a little luck, we could use that attitude to surprise them and ram that idea right back down their throats. We were primed and ready to pull off the upset. When you reach that point, anything can happen.

Stopping at a local restaurant for our pre-game pick-me-up, I smiled at my players. "Guess what, sports fans? It's time to fill up the tank with some super, shot-scoring juice." I flagged the waitress and ordered a hot tea and honey for everyone. Despite the fact that we had this prior to the Anderson game on Tuesday, there were still two or three that groaned at having to drink it again. With a slight smile, I said, "Get used to it, we're gonna be drinking this stuff several more times this year."

Herman looked at me with a smile. "Coach, would you pass the honey? Heck, the way I shot the ball against Anderson, I think I'm gonna add another shot of this sweet stuff." Watching my ace shooter double up on the honey, I leaned back in my chair. "Have you ever heard of the song, 'Tea for Two'?" Herman nodded. "You know, it was written by a basketball coach. He believed, just like I do, that this stuff just makes you a better player, particularly a better shooter."

Herman looked at me and rolled his eyes. "Come on, Coach, another one of your stories?"

I sipped my tea with one hand and flicked my wrists with the other, imitating a shot. "Drink the tea and get two points, son." Herman just stirred his tea, shaking his head. "Yup, the story supposedly was that the coach's best shooter went from eighteen points a game to thirty almost overnight after he started drinking this stuff!"

Listening intently, Nubbin leaned in, his eyes bugging out. "Wow, thirty points a game? Herman, you better get a bigger dose of this stuff!" With Herman and I both laughing, Nubbin continued to squeeze honey into his mug.

Arriving at Masters Gym a little over an hour before the game, I had my players lace up their Converse All-Stars to shoot for fifteen or twenty minutes even though they were still in their street clothes. I had told our players that they would like the floor, trying to emit yet more positive vibes before they saw our opponent. A loose ball rolled toward me, followed quickly by Herman. "Coach, I like this gym. The floor is a little different, but I like it."

"Pass that word along to your teammates," I said. "Never a better time than now to start thinking positive." I continued to walk around, watching my players go through their very business-like approach of spot shooting.

"What do you think, Fred?" He flicked his wrists, landing a fifteen-footer, before answering. "Great day for a game—even better day for two!" Receiving a pass from inside, he put up another patented free throw line jumper.

Roy stepped up behind him, "Somebody's gonna sweep two games today—might as well be the Tigers."

~~~

A dressing room before a big game can have all kinds of atmospheres. I wanted to make sure that ours was upbeat, positive, and relaxed. There would be enough tension and pressure when the game started. Soon all the players were dressed and it was time to go over the game plan. With every eye staring me right in the face, I said, "Remember, Frankston is not *just* a two-man team, but Coker and Pugh are their two main scorers. They're gonna get their points, but we can't let them get more than their share. We can't afford to let either one of those guys have a monster game. The other three—Westbrook, Tarrant, and Wilson—have got to be controlled. If you hold these three guys to twenty points or less, there's no doubt in my mind that we're gonna win this game. Get up and down the floor. Transition baskets may very well be the difference in this game. One more thing, at any time during the game, we might go into our delay game—not to stall, but to get that real easy basket. We run that very well and it's worked for us before. Okay, bow your heads and let's have our prayer."

~~~

With the crowd still coming in, it was time to throw it up and play ball. Early in the first quarter it became apparent that we had an edge with the overall speed of our team. With the crowd roaring on virtually every play, we managed a narrow, five-point lead at the end of the first quarter. Between the quarters, our huddle was positive and a feeling was building that we were indeed the better team. With Herman, Fred, and Roy consistently getting baskets in the second quarter, we slowly began to take control and our confidence began to soar. Our crowd rose to their feet, exploding with emotion as we left the floor to a thunderous ovation. It was halftime and we were headed to the dressing room with a ten-point lead over the favored Frankston team.

There was complete elation in the dressing room as I high-fived my players. When the excitement died down, I said, "Fellas, you act like we've already won the game. Look, this is far from over. Frankston has won thirty-five games this year. They didn't do that by giving up at the half."

Fred was nodding. "We're only ten points up, guys. That can be gone in a heartbeat, as we've proved before."

"We're not gonna allow that to happen. We're gonna start the second half in our delay game. This should be a complete surprise for the Indians. It will limit the number of possessions they get and at the same time, we'll be working for our high percentage shots. I don't want to give them a chance to get on a roll. Look, run this offense like we've worked it and we'll get some real good shots that we can put in. Force them to come and get us, which will make our speed an even greater advantage."

~~~

The second-half buzzer sounded and it was time to put our halftime strategy to work. We started the third quarter with a one-eighty and a much more disciplined approach. There is always danger when you change up your style of play, particularly when it was working, but slowing down the pace just might give us more energy for the finals in the evening. Remembering how the Snook game in the semi-finals of the Madisonville Tournament took its toll on our energy, I was hoping that this decision would keep that from happening again. When the third quarter ended, Frankston had only gained a couple of points.

In the huddle at the end of the third quarter, I had another big change in mind. "We've got them thinking we're gonna continue the rest of the game the way we played the third quarter. I think we've got a great chance right now to put this game away. They won't be ready for what we're gonna do. I want you to go out there and run the break like crazy. Let's make that quick outlet pass, fill the lanes, and run the floor hard. I promise you, if I was coaching against you guys right now this would be the last thing I would expect. We have a major advantage in speed and the fact that we conditioned them with this conservative third quarter is gonna make you look even faster the first couple of minutes of this quarter. All we need to do is to get two or three fast break baskets and this game is over."

We started the fourth quarter with a furious rush and our plan indeed started to pay dividends as we got a quick fast break basket by Roy. This radical change from conservative to frenzied attack caught Frankston off guard as a second fast break bucket by Herman came shortly after the first. To a thunderous ovation, we found ourselves up twelve in the fourth quarter with a ton of momentum on our side. They quickly called timeout. Our huddle was ecstatic. Out of the corner of my eye, I caught my dad standing up on the first row with his hat in his hand facing the Kennard fans, waving his arms wildly upward in a whirlybird motion. It seemed like the entire Kennard faithful rose to their feet in unison and their roar was deafening. I wasn't even sure if Frankston's timeout would do any good when the players couldn't even hear their coach. You could feel the electricity generated as we returned to the floor. We ended up winning 71-53. It was a monumental victory over a very sound, well-known team with a successful playoff history. Standing in line, shaking hands with the Frankston players, we had completed the first part of our mission.

As I shook hands with Coach Osley, I could see the pain in his eyes as he complimented my team. This was one coach with a tremendous amount of class and I couldn't help but feel for him. I had yet to experience what he was going through, but I knew it was only a matter of time. Every coach, sooner or later, will reach that low. You work your tail off trying to postpone it as long as possible, but inevitably, inexorably, it comes. When it does, it tears your heart out. The worst part is that the harder you work to stave it off, the more it hurts, and I knew that look on his face would linger judging by the amount of effort his team played with. Knowing that your own time is coming tempers your own celebration. In the Bible, Proverbs 24:17 states, "Do not gloat when your enemy falls, when he stumbles do not let your heart rejoice."

However, handshakes, kisses, hugs, and tears of joy were in abundance among the fans of the Kennard Tigers. My mom and dad came over to give me a big hug. My brother gave me a handshake. "Man, you guys played a smart game."

About that time, Curtis Baker came by. "Great job, Coach! What did I tell you? We are a better team than Frankston and this game pretty much proved it."

"Well, we both know that the best team doesn't always win."

The bottom line is that we played better *today* than they did, so it really makes no difference who the best team is. All that really matters is that we play again at 8:00 p.m. in the championship game."

My dad waved his hat in the air again. "And that we're one game away from Austin!"

Before I got off the floor, I was mobbed by our cheerleaders, having just finished doing the same to our players. My hair was not quite long enough to be with the Beatles, but I then knew why Ringo smiled a lot!

It was all smiles in the dressing room too."Man, I'm proud of you guys. This was a huge challenge, and you met it with flying colors. We flat outplayed them and your execution, particularly in the third quarter, was awesome. It set up the deciding fourth quarter. That's the second big game you've had this week and the second time you've amazed me. You soundly beat a well-established, tradition-laden, state-ranked basketball team today. So just keep your mind focused on the job at hand because you've got to do it all over again tonight. Congratulations again, fellas. We'll watch the next game and then go check into the motel and get some lunch."

As I left the dressing room, my head was in the clouds. This team was playing much better than I thought they ever could and seemed to be peaking at absolutely the right time. Sooner or later, teams that go very far in the playoffs have to win a close one. We hadn't faced that challenge yet, but hopefully, if that game came tonight, we were ready to handle the pressure. It was hard for me to believe that we were one game away from going to the State Tournament. It was my first year. State was my *long-range* goal, yet here we were, knocking on the door.

As I worked my way up the bleachers to Curtis, he was wearing that same, emotionally exhausted face as I was. Slowly his eyes met mine. "Coach, can you believe we're scouting this game?"

I shook my head. "No, can you believe we're one win away from going to the State Tournament? I keep thinking I'm going to wake up and this will all have just been a dream."

Curtis was laughing, "You're not dreaming, Coach. We've got work to do."

"Right!" I slapped my face a few times and got my clipboard ready. "Now let's just hope for some overtimes."

"How's that?" he asked, handing me some popcorn.

"Well, anytime you have a game pretty much decided early in the fourth quarter, you don't expend near as much energy as you do in a down-to-the-wire nail-biter. Playing two games of this significance the same day is hard enough anyway. A close game forces you to use a lot more energy to finish it and clinch that win."

Curtis pursed his lips, "So we're hoping for two, maybe three, overtimes here?"

We were laughing as the ball went up. Woden did take the early lead, but Avinger refused to let them take total control. With Meador, Hammack, Woodsen, and King all scoring in double figures, Woden held the lead, but Avinger answered with high scores by Herren, Qualls, Ball, and Neal. Woden had the ball and a lead of one point with seconds on the clock. I began scribbling my notes about our next opponent when Randall Wilson broke Woden's heart as he stole the ball and drove for the winning basket, ensuring his place as Avinger's hero.

Curtis let out a long, low whistle. "Well, it wasn't overtime, but it was a heck of a pressure cooker. Avinger's a much better team than I'd thought. Hey, Coach, how you feelin'?"

I cleared my throat. I thought just about the same as he had just said. "Charles Herren is a player and at six-foot-five, he'll give us problems, but their supporting cast worries me the most. They got here last year, too so they're going to be gunning for the win. They're hungry. We were the underdogs this morning and it looks like we will be again tonight." I shot him a smile. "I'm beginning to really like that position."

Heading back to the motel, our team was a few hours away from playing the biggest game in the history of Kennard High School. My young players probably didn't realize it, but those would be some of the biggest moments of their lives and memories they would remember forever. When you're young, you almost never realize that those are the moments that one day you will relate back to your grandchildren. One team would emerge in all the Regional final games as the eventual State Champion. If we won there, we put ourselves in that drawing.

We had a very informal, casual team meeting at the motel.

Looking at the young faces of my team I again congratulated them on the Frankston victory. "Fellas, we have a ton of momentum going for us right now. We're playing by far our best basketball and the fun is just beginning. Enjoy it. The rest of the afternoon I want you to get off your feet, lay around the room, take a nap, watch TV, and just rest." It wasn't difficult to project that positive feeling to my team as I talked. We had increased our level of play to new heights and with greater intensity. Like they say, "the proof is in the pudding." You always want the team chemistry to bind your team closer together when the hardest games come. That closeness showed as my kids lounged together— laughing, watching TV, and resting. We definitely had momentum on our side at that moment. The only problem was that our opponent did too. Avinger had just knocked off what looked like the best team I had seen all year. I wondered if the grueling, come-from-behind, eyelash victory had taken its toll on the Indians. I hoped so. They would definitely be the favorite.

Two teams had scratched and clawed their way to the base of the mountaintop and only one would reach the peak. Two teams with momentum, two teams on a mission, and two teams with major upset victories. The difference would be in the drive home. Which team would be smiling and which would have that solemn, far-off look in their eyes? I wasn't ready to be thinking about what might have been.

The time frame between the morning semi-final games and the night final of any Regional basketball tournament will pass slowly. As my players sat around the motel rooms, I watched the pressure slowly mounting, building to a crescendo. Their nervous energy showed through the cracks of their passive facade as legs pumped rhythms against the floor and fingers tapped against table tops, each player wondering how they would do in the biggest game of their young lives. Many a coach spends his entire career working and living for that moment, yet there I was, twenty-three years of age, in my first year of coaching, right in the mix. It was hard to believe we were one win from the State Tournament, something I *still* hadn't mentioned.

Later that afternoon, after our pre-game meal, we had a team meeting to discuss the Avinger Indians, the only team left in our way. "Charles Herren," I said, "is a very good player and by far their best one. At six-foot-five, he's a definite all-State candidate. He's the foundation of their team. He's going to get his points; however, he's foul-prone. We're not gonna make this a major priority, but if he *does* get into foul trouble, we're going to take the ball right to him. We've done a great job all year long at drawing the offensive foul. You hustle to get into position so you can take the big step and take the charge. Remember, you square up and fall back in the same direction the ball handler is going."

It felt good to be back in the game. Having something to focus all that energy into was helping the team as much as it was me. I could see their faces focusing, losing that nervous energy that had plagued us since the lunch ended. "Okay, let's look at Avinger's supporting cast. They're not a one-man team, which is why I said he wasn't our main priority. Herren scored nineteen points in the last game, including seven free throws. It was the four other guys who scored forty-eight of their sixty-seven points. We've got to guard them all. We can't back off of anybody. Look, they won a real tight, hard-fought, come- from-behind game against a very good team. They think they just knocked off the best team and right now, they're feeling sky high. They're probably thinking that beating us is just a formality. That's the mistake that Frankston made. We're gonna give them all they want and then some. Look, we just knocked off one Indian tribe this morning; we might as well take care of another tribe tonight!"

You never know what inner feelings each player has or a team has overall after a team meeting. Many a game has been decided by the reaction of a team, a player, or a coach in a particular moment, decision, or the result of second-guessing. A young, inexperienced coach could spell disaster for those kids who'd worked so hard to get there. The pressure was starting to take its toll. The butterflies, the uneasiness, and the tension were building inside of me.

Coach Johnny Carter

14

Going from the Gut

The hours, minutes, and then seconds leading up to the Regional IV Finals were winding down. As our team got their gear together, preparing for the short ride to Masters Gym, there seemed to be an air of confidence as my players joked back and forth, talking about our last game's high points, betting one another over their performances in the coming match; it gave me confidence. I realized that my team had never been here before. They had no fear, no tradition to live up to. They believed in the skills they had honed, all I could do was the same. If we could just continue our pattern of play for one more game! Hopefully, the foundation that we had laid all year would be rock solid for the intense pressure about to be applied that night.

As we started walking into the dressing room, Avinger's team arrived. One by one, they passed by our team, heading for their dressing room. Gary smacked the back of Herman's arm, his face twisted in disbelief.

"Man, that Herren is big! Coach, you said six-foot-five, he must be six-foot-seven or six-foot-eight."

"Well, they list him at six-foot-five, besides, he puts his pants on just like you do, son."

"Yeah, but Coach, when I put my pants on, I pull them up to here," his hands at his waist. "That Herren guy, he pulls his pants way up here!" Everyone was laughing as Gary held his hands around his neck.

Coach Johnny Carter

We were minutes away from the opening tip of the most important game of our season and a monster of a crowd had packed Kilgore Junior College Masters Gym, awaiting the Regional Championship. The sports writers had labeled it the "Upset Special." There was a current penetrating the air. The tension, pressure, and excitement were electric. After our usual pre-game prayer, we took the floor to a deafening roar. The feeling in the pit of my stomach was twisting my insides into knots. Nervously watching my team warm up, I ran over and over the checklist in my mind. Did I have everything covered? Had I left something off our game plan? I didn't have enough information or experience to be sure. All I could do was try to lead our team to yet another huge upset against the hardest competition in the tournament to complete this Cinderella season.

With our starting five on the floor, Avinger's Charles Herren proved more than equal to Haywood and forced the opening tip their way. Both teams changed baskets early on as Fred hit a jumper, followed by Tommy Qualls scoring for Avinger. For the first time in the playoffs, we were facing a team that took the early lead and were in total control of the first quarter. Just as I thought, they were working Herman, trying to keep the ball out of his hands. It showed good scouting on their coaches' part. We were in for a battle. Avinger dominated the first quarter as we picked the most important game of the year to have cold shooting, managing only 35 percent and trailing by four.

During the break, I was desperately trying to be positive. "Look, keep looking for the good shots and take them when they're there. Take your time, the shots will start to fall. We can't possibly shoot as bad the second quarter as we did the first!"

Little did I realize that our shooting woes would not only continue, they'd worsen. We couldn't throw one in the ocean shooting a meager 26 percent the second quarter. Fred barely managed to keep us in striking distance, scoring six of our ten points that quarter. We'd scored only twenty points the entire first half, considerably below our average. Avinger had played a smart game and coupled with our very poor shooting performance, it was no wonder they had the lead at halftime.

THE FIRST SEASON

Looking at the young faces of a team that had big doubts, I found myself re-living my senior year in high school. We'd come up against a very similar situation, in this very game, on this very date. We'd been playing the undefeated State Champions that night and our miraculous comeback had the biggest name team in Texas high school basketball, the Buna Cougars, on the ropes. When we tied the score with a little over a minute left, we could feel that trip to the State Tournament and the imminent championship deep in our souls. We had the ball, about to take the lead for the first time when the wheels came off and the dream died. Remembering the feeling that night, that memory rekindled a burning deep inside me to get past that game. My heart was racing and the pressure inside me was near eruption as I looked at the downcast faces in front of me. The big question facing me right then was just how I was going to convince them to reverse their present state of mind and realize that what we were facing was absolutely achievable. Unless they could see it, they would never realize it, regardless of the odds. It was the moment I'd talked to Curtis about, a game when a team plays poorly, when they're discouraged and when the true caliber of your players shines through.

Gazing at the looks of frustration and that dangerous air of negativity, I threw my hands over my head. "Get your heads up!" Haywood's eyes jerked open at the tone in my voice. "Look, we've played as badly as we've played all year and we're only five points down. Did you hear me? We're only *five points down."* I was almost laughing. "That's nothing! They should be at least ten or fifteen points up on us! You played poorly, but you played hard enough that you never let them take control. Let's make them regret that before this game is over. Look, one of the main reasons that I've loved coaching you guys is that whenever we have a down time, you always pick each other up. You always encouraged each other. Fellas, this is what has made the difference for us. We've still got a whole half to make up a measly five points! That's not exactly a mountain; that's not even a molehill." I looked at Fred. "Have we had one offensive run all night?"

"No, sir, we haven't."

I turned my attention to Roy, "Do you think we're gonna play a whole game without an offensive run?"

"Heck no, Coach, we'll have an offensive run before this game is over. We'll probably have more than one."

"Herman, I know those guys are overplaying you on defense, so you might as well expect it the second half. When you come off that pick on our offense, look for that quick shot because you're not gonna be open long. Fred, Roy, I know you two can get more buckets if they keep playing Herman the way they are. Haywood, you're doing a good job on Herren. You're physical enough to keep him in check. We've got to play good, sound, fundamental defense on him because he doesn't miss from the foul line. Nubbin, keep running the floor hard and you'll get some layups before it's over. Look, these Indians had us playing their game the first half and we had to circle the wagons. Let's get them on the run in the second half!"

With that, Haywood came up from his seat. "That's what I'm talking about, Coach." Suddenly, our dressing room was alive as players psyched each other up. That downcast look in the eyes of my young team coming off the floor was nowhere in sight, replaced by an air of confidence as we re-took it.

~~~

The second half started with a rush. We definitely had a little more fire in our step. However, Avinger had also stepped up their play. Fred hit a jumper off the high post, but Herren answered with a twelve-footer of his own. It seemed as if they had an answer any time we had anything resembling a run. Their consistent rebuttal increased their lead by another six points with about three minutes left in the quarter and I had to call a timeout.

That was that make-or-break moment of the championship game and we were hanging on by a thread. We had to make some kind of drastic change or it would be a very long, sad ride home. The only problem was that I had no backup plan. The Kennard huddle was very much down, reflecting once again that negative look. Every player looked to me for a shoulder to lean on. The Indians were as overpowering as the churning Red Sea. If I were Moses, I could cut right through them and head straight for the Promised Land! If only I had that particular expertise. If we were gonna make it to Austin, I had to come up with some plan to bring out the resiliency that I knew the team had deep within. Standing before a downtrodden group of kids with big doubts of my own, I could think of only one idea and it would be like reaching for rainbows. Still, I had to fake it. The road ahead was dark and narrow and it was up to me to shine the light. I squatted down with my clipboard, literally drawing up a makeshift, full-court press. I positioned each player where I wanted them.

"I know we haven't worked on this very much and this is something that we hardly use, but right now I think it's what we need." They looked on—already some of that negativity had been diverted into focus.

"Listen to me, fellas. We've got to play hard-nosed pressure defense. You've got to give these guys ninety feet of heat. I want to get in their heads, make them think that they're going to throw the ball away every time they try to move it down the floor. I want you to make them earn every inch. I don't want anyone in your area to receive the ball. Cheat toward the ball and be ready to run the floor when we don't get a steal. You can't afford to jog back. Hit the paint in a hurry. I don't just mean run. I mean *run.*" I was getting pumped despite my own doubts. I had a feeling and it was spreading.

"If you get tired, suck it up. You're in great shape, bust your butt. You can rest tomorrow. Fellas, right now is what it's all about." I pounded my chest with a clenched fist. "It's all about how bad you want it. This can be done, but not one of you can let up for a second. Look, this is going to put some razzle-dazzle in this game and give us a chance to score quicker." I pointed to Herman. "It should give you a chance to get some open shots.

"One more thing, Herren is in foul trouble. Whenever you get a chance, take it right to him. We've seen his offense, let's see if he can play smart *defense* under pressure. Look, all I want you to do is get two or three baskets before we start the fourth quarter. We've got to chip away at this lead right now. They have yet to see the real Kennard team. Let's give them a taste of what we're all about, starting now!"

I looked into the eyes of my players. It was a team that I had motivated many times in the past to get them through the pressure-packed situations, but this was for the Regional Championship—that one special game that very few teams and coaches even get a chance to participate in. I prayed that it would kindle the fire I knew was in them.

As play resumed, the full-court press paid some quick dividends as Nubbin got a quick steal and rifled a pass to his brother. Fred hit a jumper to cut the lead to nine. We immediately pressed again and caused a bad pass that became a turnover. Roy then got an athletic turnaround, off-balance jumper to fall in and in a flash, we'd cut the lead to seven. We traded baskets the last minute of the quarter as Herman retorted their basket with a jumper. When the buzzer sounded, the Indians were still in command, leading 42-35. Avinger's huddle was still high, even though cutting the lead at the end of the quarter was huge.

There were eight short minutes left for us to play the quarter of our lives. We were down but not out. Our chance to pull off a victory and move on to the State Tournament looked bleak, but the change in our game plan had shown a slow improvement. I knew that my guys were competitive, smart, and in great shape—the ingredients necessary to use the press, but I began to doubt that it would be enough. Hopefully, we would start the fourth quarter with a stepped-up intensity level, which is exactly what we had to do to have any kind of a chance at all.

As our guys took the floor for possibly the last quarter of the year, I only hoped that I had fanned the flame in each of their hearts. They were going to have to play great, both offensively *and* defensively, against a red-hot team hungry for State. We were seven down with eight minutes to play and it was time to turn on that faucet full blast because during the first three quarters it was barely a trickle.

The surge in intensity had been evident in our level of play the first minute of the concluding quarter. Hard-nosed, full-court pressure defense is only effective if every player has that killer instinct and is focused on the same piece of the puzzle. The incredible desire to win this game began to show early and it became obvious that we refused to roll over when we were down. We were going to make them earn their win.

The intense full-court pressure that we installed was starting to give the Indians a little trouble, but so far, not near as much as I had hoped. We managed to get a quick steal by Roy followed by a bullet pass to Nubbin and with a beautifully timed bounce pass to his brother, Fred, another easy two. I came off the bench with a fist pump yelling, "Defense! D it up! D it up! Press, press, press!" I did my best to *will* our team to a miracle finish. However, just like they had done all evening, the Indians returned the favor as Joe Ball scored on the other end of the floor and the gap remained unbridged at seven. We were desperate, looking for some kind of a break that might ignite our team to an explosive finish and it came with the shriek of sound as a referee blew the whistle at the four-minute and nineteen-second mark.

Charles Herren had four fouls and Fred had taken the ball right to him, drawing the fifth. It hadn't been the first time we'd tried for it and to Herren's credit he hadn't taken the bait until then. When Herren walked off the floor with his fifth personal, it was a psychological lift for our team, intensifying our already determined mind-set. Doubling the effect, it placed the fear of losing in Avinger's mind-set for the first time that night. They would have to play the last four minutes without the virtual backbone of their team. When they called a timeout at that juncture, our fans were exploding with a reaffirming, thunderous ovation. We had already seen a momentum change before Herren fouled out. I could only hope for what might be in store for us now.

During our timeout, there was an air of rebuilt confidence in the eyes of our players. They couldn't wait to get back on the floor and take care of business. I decided it was time to make a change in our press.

"Look, we've been double-teaming after the inbound pass every time. Right now, they're over there working on that. Now I want you to fake the double-team and go back to straight man. Look, Haywood, I want you to charge the ball, giving the impression of another double-team. Let the guy with the ball feel the pressure of a double-team coming and then I want you to quickly go back to the guy that inbounded the ball, look for that pass back to him. This should confuse them because they're being told to pass it up the floor. You play some aggressive passing lane defense with this change and you're gonna get some steals."

Our change paid some immediate dividends. The implementation resulted in a steal and yet another basket by Fred. With less than one minute to go we still trailed by three, but the Indians could feel their grip loosening. The intensity of our press forced another turnover at the fifty second mark and a layup by Haywood sliced the lead to one. I waved my arms, signaling for a timeout.

We changed our press once again, taking our point man off the ball, thus creating a five on four situation on the next inbound pass. "I want the most intense pressure humanly possible. I want you to make the guy you're guarding regret ever getting the ball. Roy, you cheat to where you think the ball is going to go and be a free safety. Watch the eyes of the inbounder. That will tell you which way to cheat."

On the front row of the Kennard side, my dad continued to ignite our fans. Hat in hand, swinging his arms in that clockwise, whirlybird motion, he once again had every fan on the purple side standing and cheering for our come-from-behind effort. Avinger's comfort zone was gone and everywhere they looked, there was a purple and white uniform. Almost every passing angle had been cut off. Wide-open dribbling space which had been plentiful early on was now nowhere to be seen. The question was, 'could we close the gap before the end?'

When play resumed, we cut off the lanes, blocking out any clear pass, forcing yet another turnover. It was coming down to a photo finish and the entire crowd was on its feet, straining to get a better view of the crucial final seconds of this remarkable Regional final game. There were forty seconds on the clock. The ball was quickly passed around the perimeter defense. Fred squared up for an open shot at the thirty-second mark.

Flipping his wrist, he put up the biggest shot of his life. The Kennard crowd was ready to explode as they anxiously awaited the result of this soft spinning one-hander. Bingo! It ripped the cords. With the flip of a wrist, we had miraculously taken the lead for the very first time that night: 58-57. Our crowd was roaring their approval and the colossal magnitude of the moment was absolutely magical. Our crowd was convinced that we had just accomplished the impossible, but the same couldn't be said for Avinger. Getting the ball through our press they quickly hit a shot to retake the lead, again ahead by one. We had enjoyed the lead for all of seven seconds, barely enough time to breathe it in. We inbounded the ball with twenty-one seconds left and rapidly ran it down the floor. I came off the bench, racing up the sideline, jumping about three feet straight up, calling a timeout.

This was the biggest timeout of the year. We had to call it so we could at least stop the clock and set up something for our best chance to score. The roar in Masters Gym at this point in the game had all four walls vibrating. It was deafening and literally felt like an earthquake. I set up a play to try to get the ball inside to Fred or Roy. However, I looked at Herman and made it clear what he was to do. "Look, when we run this play, if they're not open inside and you've got that quick jumper, go ahead and stick it because I know you can hit that shot."

Trying to emit more positive vibes, I said, "We're not trying to take the last shot. I want you to take the first good one you get whether it's Herman outside or Fred or Roy inside. Let's see some great off-side rebound positioning because if it comes off the rim, this would be the biggest rebound of the year. Haywood, that's your main job on the backside. Fellas, after we score, we're still going to press, but no reaching fouls. I want to see body position. Play with your feet, not your hands. It's our time fellas. One, two, three, let's go!"

With nervous tension filling the air on both sides of the court, our huddle broke and we headed back to the floor, attempting to execute the biggest offensive possession of the year. That was the one play that great teams always seem to make in that situation. If we could somehow pull off that miracle come-from-behind victory, well, that's what it truly would be—a miracle. Naturally, all of that was about to play out in the last twenty seconds of that spine-tingling game.

Herman Myers had been held to eight points by the superb Avinger defense. With perfect timing and position, Nubbin set up a screen, allowing Herman to get open. Receiving the ball, Herman quickly set his feet, preparing to take the biggest shot of his life. The roaring crowd was background music as my ace shooter, with ice water in his veins, leapt from the floor and flicked his wrist. In a smooth, spinning arc, the ball ever so gently rotated toward the rim.

Fifteen seconds remained on the clock—fifteen seconds to make or break a dream. Many fans sitting by the radio back in Houston County were anxiously listening to KIVY for a conclusion, hoping for a miracle finish. The incredible play-by- play that night sounded something like this:

"Herman Myers squares up, rocker steps, he pulls the trigger on a twelve-foot jumper. *Swish!* It's good! It's good! It's good! Herman Myers just put his young Tigers up by one, 60-59, with fifteen seconds left! Wow! What a shot! *What a shot!* Listen to this crowd; they're going nuts! Kennard is fifteen seconds away from going to Austin!"

A thunderous roar of exultation followed as our crowd, overflowing with passion, screamed and cheered. I was once told by an old coach that there would be no higher high or lower low than in the basketball business. I had just experienced both in a matter of seconds. If anyone had gotten up to use the restroom, they would have missed it all. My heart was pounding, my head was spinning, and the game wasn't over yet. Avinger called a timeout as soon as we'd scored and still had fifteen seconds to win the game.

Fifteen seconds is a lifetime when you only need one shot to secure a victory. We may have scored too early. All Avinger had to do was wait out the clock and take a clean shot. Yogi Berra once said, "It ain't over 'til it's over." In that moment, I realized the fear and excitement of his words. In that situation, defensively, you never know if you should continue to press and run the risk of letting them get through for an easy basket or back up and play conservative, which would concede more floor, but force a longer shot. Whichever route I took, it was going to be a choice that determined the game's outcome. It was a decision that if successful could send us nonstop to the State Tournament. *If it fails...* I shook the thought from my head. Now wasn't the time to think about that.

It was the press that got us there in the first place, so I crossed my heart, and told my guys to stick with it. Avinger was still having a lot of trouble with it and I didn't want to give them room to breathe and lose that negative mind-set. The press it would be. As Avinger attempted to inbound the ball, we continued with an aggressive, close-quarters defense, being very careful not to foul. They'd been lights out from the free throw line all night and a free throw would spell disaster. With determined entrenchment, our hawkish pressure defense was now covering the floor like a fresh coat of paint.

The sound of the crowd faded into the background. It felt like we were under water. Muffled cheers echoed around me as I watched the game as if in slow motion. The suspense filled the air; the enormous, overflow crowd awaited agony or elation equally. Avinger made its inbound pass. It shot through the air, a deep bullet pass. Nubbin, our reliable secretary of defense, stepped up to the top of the ladder, going from Mr. Ordinary in the eyes of many of our fans to the MVP of the moment. Using his cat-like reflexes, he stepped in the passing lane and got the biggest steal of his young life.

Nubbin's knack for coming up with the ball had come through for us again and his unselfish attitude blended seamlessly into our team chemistry as he shot the ball to Haywood. I could see the look of fear in our opponents' eyes as pride filled my own. We immediately shifted into our delay game, running out the clock, completing an amazing, miraculous, come-back win. Masters Gym exploded as the sheer outburst and volume of our fans over-whelmed us. Our players were jumping with joy and that one thought that I'd tried to suppress for so long shot through me like a rocket: *We're going to Austin! We're going to the State Tournament.*

The following morning, Stuart Wilson wrote in the *Longview Morning Journal,* "Avinger's championship hopes that glowed so brightly for three quarters lay crumbled at the Tigers' feet as the Kennard Tigers jumped on each other like so many frisky puppies. For the record, the Kennard team of Coach Johnny Carter posted an upset victory over Avinger, 60-59, before one of the largest crowds ever to see a Region IV Class B Championship in years."

Pandemonium reigned supreme that February night in that east Texas oil field city. The color purple shone in historic Kilgore, Texas, as the spotlight emitted a glow around my young team. The atmosphere surrounding that heart-filled finish defied description as our crowd swarmed us. With the main course now finished, our dessert was about to be served. The very unusual cork floor of Masters Gym was forgotten as fans, cheerleaders, moms and dads stormed it. People were cheering our players as much as they were each other. I watched as fans congratulated our players and staff, as our players were raised together by black and white hands, as our community came together to celebrate their team. There was a unity of togetherness that had been building all year around our young team and both races were now able to bask in its warmth and be proud of what unity could accomplish.

It seemed that moment was as important for my team as it was for my community. There was a togetherness there that night that I hoped would not be soon forgotten. Two of my former high school teammates descended on me laughing. Tommy Ferguson and Kenneth

Standley hoisted me up on their shoulders as the frenzied crowd cheered with approval. I was glad we could be there together because what we had come so close to accomplishing six years earlier was finally a part of us.

Tommy shouted up at me, "Congratulations, my friend!" His voice cracked with emotion. "We knew what we missed out on just a few years ago when we lost this game and now we know what it feels like to win it!"

As my feet hit the ground once more, people were coming up to me in droves, giving me hugs, slapping me on the back, shaking my hand. I had no idea who most of them were. Finally, faces I recognized peeked through. My dad came up to me and gave me a big bear hug and his congratulations. Mom was right by his side, following his hug with her own. "Oh, you did so great, Johnny! It must have been my weight vests!"

I hadn't noticed my brother James Otis as he rushed around my parents to me and gave me a huge hug. "What a game, what a comeback! Never a doubt, eh, Coach! Did you guys have a fourth quarter or what? That's one of the most amazing come-backs I've ever seen!"

In trying to make my way to the dressing room, I continued to be bombarded by well-wishers. Before reaching the entrance to the dressing room, I was mobbed by our cheerleaders for the second time that day.

Walking up to the dressing room, there was Curtis. "Couldn't you have made it a little bit closer?"

I burst out laughing. "We were doing everything we could!"

"I think you may be the only guy around that could have pulled it out for our team."

I looked for sarcasm in his eyes, but there wasn't any. "We got a lot of breaks tonight. We played good enough in the fourth quarter to win this game, but what do you think would have happened if Herren hadn't fouled out? That was a lucky break, Curtis."

"I was watching the game, Coach. I saw you take the ball to him over and over."

I shrugged, "Well, he's known to be foul-prone."

"When it's a strategy, I'm not sure how you can call it luck—that's just good coaching. You made all the right moves tonight. Time and time again I've seen these guys dig a little bit deeper when the situation called for it. Tonight, they had to play their best quarter of the year to pull this off and that's exactly what they did. I don't know how you brought this quality out of them, but it has become a habit. When there's a need to elevate their game, to get the job done, they do it. The chemistry between you and these guys—it's incredible!" He looked back towards the crowd, and breathed in deeply. "Thank you for coming to Kennard!"

Finally, I was able to walk into the dressing room after our Regional final win and it was a thing of beauty. The energy didn't know where to jump next and as the door closed, it was focused completely on me as my players cheered. They were high-fiving and jumping on one another. It was total joy coupled with complete jubilation. The first guy I came to was Fred. He had just played the game of his life and thanks to Avinger overplaying Herman, had scored twenty-seven points, just under half our total. I walked up to this highly competitive, extremely humble young man and reached for his hand. One look in his eyes said it all. Then, seemingly in unison, we took our hands back and just hugged each other.

Walking over to Nubbin, I took a high-five. "Who gets the biggest steal of his life to ice the game? *D* is the key!" With that, I saw that twinkle in his eye and the humility in his heart. It was quite evident that Nubbin appreciated what I said as we embraced with another hug.

I turned around and there was Roy with that priceless ear-to-ear smile. "We did it, Coach! How do you like integration?"

"How do I like integration? What I like is that there were some people out there tonight who've been struggling to decide if it's okay for black kids to play with white kids and what we showed them here tonight is how I see this team: I don't see black. I don't see white. I see basketball players—people I want in my corner when I go to battle. And who else would basketball players run with *but* other basketball players?"

Herman slapped me on the back. "How about that tea, fellas!" I turned on him, raising my pinkie in mock drink. "They were determined that you weren't going to be the guy to beat them and yet who hits *the* shot."

"It was about time they let me see some sky. They were on me like a leech. But Coach, you were right, it did open Fred. What a game he played!"

I pointed to Fred, clapping my hands, quickly followed by the team. "Did you guys know we hit ten of fourteen shots that last quarter? That's over 70 percent! That's incredible!"

A voice from behind me made me turn. "Coach, it looks like it's our year!" There was the well-sculptured body of Haywood. Before I could even get a word out he put a bear hug on me that popped every vertebrae in my spine, leaving me breathless as he lowered me to the floor. "How about that press, Coach?"

I took a moment to suck some breath into my aching lungs. "Haywood, son, please, after that—no more press!"

The team was laughing. "I'm talking about that Tiger full-court press, Coach! They didn't know what hit 'em!"

I winced as I straightened, nodding to him. "The press was the difference. We couldn't have done it tonight without it. And you were one of the main reasons that it worked so well. You gave one superhuman effort tonight. That's what I mean by intimidation!"

Haywood then looked up at me and asked a question that I thought I would never hear after winning the Regional Championship game. "Coach, what do we do now?"

The dressing room had gotten quiet. I looked around at their faces. They hadn't had nearly enough. A smile that practically stretched my face spread into place as I was finally able to release the words I held back for so long. "Well, now we go to the big house!" I pumped my fist in the air. "We're going to Austin to play in Gregory Gym. We're gonna play in the State Tournament!" The dressing room went crazy.

"Fellas, everyone over here and take a seat." They sauntered over, still too hyped to sit still, but I waited for them to settle. "When I was interviewed for this job, Mr. Bitner asked me what my goal in coaching was. I told him that someday I wanted to take a team to the State Tournament. You just handed me my long-range goal in my first season! Fellas, I started to fall in love with this team a few weeks ago, but tonight this goes far beyond what I ever imagined. You know my birthday is next week and you just gave me the best present that I could have ever received, by far. Thank you, thank you, thank you."

Haywood was the first to put his hand in the center, but the rest soon followed. Fred looked around the group. "Coach Carter on three." As I watched them cheer, I wondered if any of them realized how important that day would be to them as they grew older. If they knew that they would relate it to girlfriends and wives and children and grandchildren. The night I missed the game-winning shot when I was in high school, I hadn't realized the importance of that game. I hoped that these young men would.

~~~

I needed to get outside for a while, just to be alone, to take a deep breath of the crisp night air and thank God for that moment and that feeling. I was so lost in my thoughts that I didn't hear the soft crunch of grass behind me. I was surprised when suddenly my father's arm slipped around my shoulders.

"You okay, son?"

I nodded. "You know, Dad, I was just thinking...there are a lot of coaches who spend their whole lives trying to achieve what we've managed to accomplish in this first season. Don't get me wrong, I love what we just managed to do and I certainly would never even think of changing anything that happened here tonight, but you know something? It doesn't seem quite fair that a 23-year-old rookie coach should be about to take a team to Austin and play in the State Tournament."

He wheeled me around, gripping my shoulders and looked me in the eye. "Son, this is your time. Enjoy it, savor it because it may never happen again. Don't waste this moment second-guessing yourself. Live this moment because it's something that you'll remember for the rest of your life. Accomplishment is something to be relished. It's meant to be reassuring, not make us question how we got there."

I shook my head, thinking over the season. "I don't know. I know I've got an amazing group of kids, but I've made so many decisions strictly from the gut. I was guessing, Dad."

He let go of my arms, but wouldn't break eye contact. "Son, let me tell you something. The best, most experienced coaches in the country—including college and pros—many times a week make quick, gut instinct decisions and some of them have been coaching for thirty to forty years. If you coach that long—and I think you will—guess what? You'll *still* be making a lot of calls from the gut. You've made a lot of decisions this year that were right for your team. That's why you're 39-4 and are about to go to the State Tournament. Why do you think you won this game tonight? If you hadn't made some of those decisions, you and your guys would be feeling like Avinger right now. Whether it's because you have a feeling or because of stats or because you know your guys, what matters is that you are making the *right* calls. What I'm saying here is that you are making one heck of a good coach."

He smiled, and I gave him a big hug before we headed back in and out of the cold.

~~~

I couldn't help but sympathize with that very good Avinger team. They had played one great game, only to fall one point short. For the second straight year, they'd knocked on the door in the Regional final game only to be denied both times. I knew that they were heartbroken. I'd been there. Whether or not my family or friends would admit it, many times the best team in the state doesn't win that game. In some cases, the best team doesn't even manage to play in it. In playoff basketball, a bad game—a fluke—can determine if you realize your potential. I couldn't help but wonder if we were a fluke. If so, we would soon find ourselves overpowered in Austin.

As amazing as it seemed, the dream would continue and we would head to Austin in quest of a State Championship. With one miracle out of the way, would it be too much to ask for another? Could we possibly go up there and achieve the impossible? Could our inexperienced young team, not to mention its coach, take everything we had learned that incredible season, somehow structure it in the right direction and maybe, just maybe win the whole thing? It would require that special group of kids to continue to rise above their ability on the biggest stage of their lives at the highest level, and it would require me to make more decisions that I couldn't see past. Those thoughts haunted me for the remainder of the ride home as my father's voice mixed with Curtis's, attempting to reassure me.

It was one thirty in the morning when I got back to my apartment. A little over nineteen hours had passed since our remarkable pilgrimage had begun. I ached all over and I doubted it was entirely from Haywood's bear hug. It felt like I had aged ten years. It certainly didn't seem possible that it all could have happened in the span of a single day. It was almost too much for me to grasp. As I collapsed onto the mattress of my little garage apartment, I wanted sleep. I felt like I could use at least a day without waking, but as much as my body hungered for it, my mind was still playing the game, shouting and running the floor. I gave up and moved to the porch steps, staring into the chilly night. So much had happened in such a short period of time and with the emotion, splendor, and magnitude of the moment, my mind and heart were still trying to catch up and accept the reality of it. As I sat there on the porch embracing the stillness of the night, I stared in complete silence, trying to come back down to earth. I looked up, gazing into the darkness of the night. After thirty minutes of reflection, I was still too keyed up to sleep. Grabbing a Dr. Pepper, I got in the car and headed west toward Madison County and my parents' home.

~~~

I woke to eggs sunny-side up, sausage, biscuits, coffee, orange juice, and a lot of love from my mom. My dad and James Otis had already gone to church. We ate quickly and followed them to the service, sneaking in the back so as not to disturb anyone.

After the service ended, my mom and I waited for the others at the door. I couldn't believe the number of people that came up to me, offering their congratulations while wishing our team the best at the state tournament. My presence single-handedly stemmed the flow out of the church and we had to move farther out so that we wouldn't trap other members. Two such well-wishers were brothers Sam and P.M. Standley, two local businessmen and big-time basketball fans. They never missed a game when I played for the Mustangs.

Sam reached out, shaking my hand while offering his congratulations. "You know we're Madisonville fans, but with you coaching, Johnny, this is almost like the Mustangs playing in Austin!"

"Mr. Sam, this is as close as I'll ever come to playing at the State Tournament, but you know something? I think coaching will be a bigger thrill."

"I know it will," said P.M. Standley. "Every player out there has your brand on them and this team goes into every game playing *your* idea of basketball. Well, you'll be in our prayers."

Sam nodded. "And, of course, we'll be there to watch." He motioned to the church behind him. "We can put our hands together for more than one reason!"

Coach Johnny Carter

All my life, I had heard the expression, "What a difference a day makes." The game the day before had given me more than I could chew and I was still reeling, sure I couldn't take another bite, but there it was—State—looming before me—and I knew that I was about to make room for dessert. My dad's words were really sinking in as I looked around the church and at the smiling faces encouraging me. What a time to be young and alive. I would turn twenty-four on Wednesday, the day before the tournament. Could there be a better birthday present? *No way,* I thought. *No way.*

BOOK THREE

The Tigers' Trials

Coach Johnny Carter

15

A Close Call

Monday morning did indeed come early and I reveled in the early morning sunlight as I drove down the highway.

I stopped by Principal Jerry Phillips's office to check if Austin had called.

"Not yet," he said, "but they should be calling within the hour. Coach, I haven't had a chance to congratulate you. That was one heck of a game. We showed some kind of determination in pulling that thing out."

I laughed, leaning on the door frame. "Thanks, Mr. Phillips, I'll pass it on to the team. These guys just refuse to lose. If there was ever a game that we probably should have lost, that night was the one. I have to hand it to those guys, they do what it takes to win and now they believe they can beat anybody. We're going to Austin with the mind-set we need to win. The bad thing about that is that there are five other teams who are gonna have that same feeling and we'll have to beat three of them. That's what the State Tournament is all about."

Jerry nodded sagely and chose his words carefully. He tapped his steepled fingers against his lips and said, "Well, just go up there, coach the best you've ever coached in your life, and take every opponent apart." He shrugged, "Simple enough."

I rolled my eyes. "Oh yeah, right! Thanks a lot!"

Benford knocked on the doorframe beside me and entered, taking a seat. "Thought I heard some basketball talk. Coach, that was some game Saturday night. We played the fourth quarter like a machine. It was almost like we stepped up to a brand-new level to take that one."

Jerry was nodding in agreement. I agreed, but conceded that we had played three mediocre quarters before our incredible finish. Jerry looked like he was about to refute me when the phone rang. The three of us stared at it for the first two rings before Jerry cleared his throat, his eyes flicking towards me, and picked it up. "Principal Phillips speaking, who's calling? Ah, as a matter of fact, he's here in the office." He looked at me with a slight smile as he handed me the receiver.

I cleared my throat. "Coach Carter speaking."

"Coach, this is Dr. Bailey Marshall of the UIL. Congratulations on winning the Regional Tournament. You will open the Forty-Seventh Annual State Tournament at 8:45 a.m. on Thursday morning against the Avoca Mustangs. You'll be staying at the Stephen F. Austin Hotel. We have rooms already reserved for you. I would like to personally wish you the best of luck. One more thing, every team has a thirty-minute block of practice time at Gregory Gym on Wednesday. Your practice time is 9:00 a.m. Drive carefully. I hope you have a great time on your school's first ever trip to the State Tournament."

Almost immediately after hanging up, the phone rang again and I found myself tethered to the receiver for most of the day talking to newspapers, radio and television stations whose interviews took a lot more time than I thought they would. A television station in Lufkin wanted our team to be on the six-o'clock news in their leading sports segment. I spent what seemed like days on the phone answering question after question, giving answers I never knew I had. I'd never been on the phone that long in my life! Alexander Graham Bell would have been proud.

I had a bad case of super-cauliflower ears and took as many opportunities to rub some life back into them as I could. After I finished the interviews, I began making my own calls to coaches in west Texas, attempting to get some information on Avoca, our first round opponent in Austin. I also left a message with Caldwell High School to return my call, hoping to secure their gym for practice on Tuesday afternoon on our way to Austin. The day was passing quickly and it seemed there was much more to do than there was time to do it. I wasn't close to finishing my checklist when I realized it was almost lunch time and I hadn't been to one of my classes yet. I could only hope that this was the kind of pressure I was supposed to be under and that the other coaches were experiencing the same thing.

It was soon time for our last practice of the year in the Tigers' Den. I had done a lot of thinking about that day's practice in attempting to come up with a game plan for Avoca. We'd played our best ball of the season the last three games, attempting to establish a playoff tradition while once again our opponent already had plenty of tradition behind them. They had a previous State Championship under their belt and were ready for another. Our players came out of the dressing room and started shooting practice. After fifteen to twenty minutes, I blew my whistle, calling them over to the bleachers.

"By now, you all probably know that we're going to be playing the Avoca Mustangs. The first State Tournament that I ever saw was when I was in the fifth grade. Avoca won the State Championship that year. They were good. This year, they're good again. Right now they're 35-3. It will take a great effort to beat them. I'm sure they'll be the favorite."

"Frankston and Avinger were also the favorites and we sent them home!" said Herman.

Roy was rubbing his hands together. "I kind of like sending these so-called favorites to the house."

"That's what I'm talking about!" said Haywood. "Sending three favorites home in a row—that's okay with me!"

Nubbin was nodding. "It's hard to sneak up on a team when you're the favorite. I like being the underdog, giving them a little surprise."

I was overjoyed to see that a positive mind-set was already percolating among my players and I was beginning to develop one myself about the upcoming tournament game.

"Fellas, there's one very unusual thing about this practice today that I want you to be aware of. You've got to realize that there are only five other teams in Class B in the whole state of Texas that are practicing today. The rest are either in track or baseball already. You are one of a very select few and that makes this a very special practice, so enjoy this moment." I blew my whistle and we began to run the floor.

We were literally packing our bags, preparing to leave for Austin, when a student aide came by the gym, and waved me over. "Coach, Mr.

Bitner needs to see you-right now. He said it was urgent. He's in his office."

Why does the brain have to be pre-programmed to think the worst? I'm sure it's a coping mechanism, but couldn't my thoughts have drifted to Mr. Bitner just wanting to wish us good luck before we left? With black thoughts swirling in my head, I made my way down the hall and turned the corner. I looked up and there was Mr. Bitner, pacing the hallway. Our superintendent was nervous, looking over the top of his glasses, rapidly chewing the gum that he always seemed to have.

"Coach," he said in a very concerned voice, "there's a police officer in my office who needs to talk to you. Are you in trouble with the law?"

My eyes were popping. "No sir, at least not to my knowledge." Mr. Bitner was shaking his head, running a hand through his thin hair and letting out a deep sigh. "The officer didn't exactly tell me what he's here for, but he's not here to wish your team good luck in Austin." My thoughts went from bad to worse as I thought about my family—if something bad had happened. I'd talked to them only yesterday. There was a huge, hollow, very empty feeling in the pit of my stomach as we walked into Mr. Bitner's office. The officer was still standing and faced me as I entered. "Are you John Dean Carter, Jr.?"

I nodded, "Yes, sir, that's me."

He had a paper in his hands. "I have a warrant for your arrest."

Completely blown away, I was speechless.

Mr. Bitner put a hand on my shoulder. "Officer, do you mind telling us what the charge is?"

He looked over the warrant. "It says here 'non-payment of a traffic ticket.'"

Mr. Bitner was shaking his head. "Officer, you can't have him this week. We're about to leave for Austin to play in the State Basketball Tournament for the first time! Come back next week, you can have him then."

I'd managed to find my voice. "Officer, I paid that fine two or three months ago!"

The officer continued to look on, his face passive. "Can you prove that? Because if you can't, I've got to take you in."

One of my favorite television shows was *The Fugitive,* starring David Jansen as Dr. Richard Kimble, the innocent victim of blind justice. I never really knew how Richard Kimble must have felt until just then. My voice shook as I fumbled through my pocket. "Let me look in my billfold and see if I still have that receipt." I checked one small compartment right behind my driver's license. My prayers were answered. Lo and behold, there it was. Gingerly I pulled it out, unfolded it, and handed it over to the officer, breathing in deeply, trying to still my shaking hands.

He read it over and handed it back. "My deepest apology. Sorry to have inconvenienced you on such a big day for you and your school. I just take the papers and do my job. Between you and me, the judge is getting old and his record-keeping is starting to slip. This is the second time this month that this has happened to me. It's getting downright annoying." Apologizing again, he disappeared down the hall. It felt like a load of bricks had been lifted off my shoulders.

With an obvious sigh of relief, Mr. Bitner looked at me. "You know, Coach, all this weekend I kept telling myself all this was just too good to be true. For just a fleeting moment there I thought I was right. It's a good thing you know how to handle the pressure. My heart was beating out of my chest!"

With relief flooding my system, I couldn't help but laugh. "Mr. Bitner, coaching that Regional final game was chicken feed compared to what I just went through here!"

I was almost out the door when the whole conversation caught up with me. "Wait! What was that? 'You can't have him today, come back *next* week?' I'm about an inch from going to the jailhouse and all you can say is, 'You can have him next week'?"

Clearing the air, sitting behind his desk, he said, "Of course not, Coach. I was just setting the officer up with a proposition. If Kennard wins the State Championship, they drop the charges. But if we don't, he could take you away in cuffs as soon as we lose and you *double* whatever jail time there was!"

"Well at least I'd have the consolation of sharing a cell with you, what with you attempting to bribe a police officer."

We were both laughing, more from relief than anything, but finally Mr. Bitner asked, "Well, Coach, we're playing Avoca. Just how good are they?"

"They're real good. We'll probably be the underdog for the third consecutive playoff game."

Mr. Bitner pursed his lips. "Coach, do you remember when I interviewed you for the job back in August? I asked you what your goal in coaching was. You said taking a team to the State Tournament was your goal. Well I stand corrected, I told you not to expect that this year. Regardless of how you do in Austin, you have done one heck of a job. I have thoroughly enjoyed watching you take our...let's face it, mediocre team and mold it into something special and how you've motivated those boys. Coach, I honestly think this team has improved more than any team I've ever seen. You must be twenty points better today than you were at the start of the season. Congratulations." He reached out and shook my hand. "This could be a once-in-a-lifetime thing, so let's enjoy the moment and see if we can win the whole thing."

"Right now they really believe in themselves and I promise my head won't swell with all this flattery!"

"It better not! Just go down there and win three games and I'll let it swell as big as a house!"

Our last pep rally was coming to a close. Everybody was standing and cheering at the top of their lungs. The sound was deafening, echoing off the walls of the old Tigers' Den in a spontaneous eruption that was nothing less than inspiring. I leaned over to Gary and said, "All I need is a uniform and I'm ready to play right now!"

Gary looked at me and with a real big smile, "If you did, no one except our fans would know that you're not one of us. You could easily pass for a member of our team."

"Don't tempt me, Gary. There's no greater thrill than State."

~~~

The landscape of the east Texas countryside was a study in contrast. Tall native pine trees were underscored by graceful dogwoods and their sea of white blooms were punctuated as east Texas redbuds blossomed into an eruption of pink flowers. My birthday would arrive with the next day's rising sun and I was trying to squeeze every drop out of my last day of being twenty-three. It wasn't hard to do. I was traveling with the team that I loved, going to a place that I had always dreamed of, and had a tremendous passion for what I was doing for a living. Life was absolutely good.

As we approached Madisonville, one of the first things we saw was the sign in front of James Standley's famous Corral Cafe that read, *"Congratulations Coach Johnny Carter and the Kennard Tigers! Good Luck in Austin!"*

We took a small break at my parents' house for an opportunity to stretch our legs. Of course, we weren't prepared for the mountain of cookies pushed on us as we entered. With *my* mom, eating just one is an insult. The kids had no problem with being gracious and when it came time to leave, thirteen bags of cookies went with us, one for each of us. I think my players were just as much in love with my house as my own family was. Before we left, my mother warned me that Dad had planned something special for us but refused to say more.

Each of us was in our own cookie daze. Nubbin was the first to see the flashing lights of the police cars. Quickly we were surrounded with cars both in front and behind as they began to escort us toward the square of downtown Madisonville, complete with red flashing lights and sirens blaring. The kids got a kick out of it. I, on the other hand, felt that I'd seen enough police for the day.

As the escort guided us near the square, to my surprise, I saw my dad standing at the corner, along with all the employees of the store beside him, waving us on. We soon realized it was more than just *his* store, it was the entire street. Everyone was out of their shops, lining the roadside with cheer and smiles. "Coach, I feel like a celebrity!" Herman said with a big smile on his face. "I can't believe this. It's almost like a parade."

Fred looked at me. "Did you set all this up, Coach?"

I was grinning, waving at all the people I recognized. "I'd love to take credit because this is an awesome, absolutely great idea, but my mom told me my dad had something planned. The police must have been his idea too."

"I always thought that you were a pretty special coach and now I know why. You have two great parents."

I looked at Fred. "They've always been there for me. Back when I was playing, I don't think they ever missed one of my games. I'd always look around the gym to make sure they were there and when I saw them, it always made me feel safe and secure. It made me play harder because I knew I had good people to live up to, that I never wanted to disappoint. I don't know how children that grow up not experiencing this ever make it. You're right, Fred, they are really great parents."

Fred and I were both smiling as we made our way through downtown, but leaving the square, one more surprise was evident. Approaching the First Methodist Church, the sign in front read, *Go Kennard! Win State!* This was the church that I attended growing up and my dad had just a little influence with the members, so getting this sign done for one day was a given.

Herman slumped back in his seat. "This is crazy. We're not even at home and we're getting treated like we live here."

"Well, Herman, we're representing more than just our school. We're representing our community and our families, and my family happens to live here. But we're even more than that. Without our opponents, we would never have gotten stronger. We represent all the teams we've defeated because without them, we wouldn't be nearly as good as we've become."

My team rode in silence for a time, thinking about what I'd said. Finally, Herman nodded, relaxing in his seat, "I like it, Coach."

Our last practice in the Caldwell gym was a welcome back and a break from the monotony of the open highway, but soon we were back on the road and entering Austin. The young team had already experienced the spotlight thrust upon them last week at Kilgore and now their first look at the state capitol was colorfully magnified by the picturesque view of a majestic sunset.

"Is that a terrific view or what?" I said, looking at Fred.

"It's beautiful, Coach. Is that Austin over there?"

"Indeed it is. We're almost there."

"Isn't that the tower where that sniper was shooting at students?"

I nodded, a frown darkening my face, remembering the tragedy that occurred on the very day I interviewed for this coaching job.

Nubbin was pointing past us. "Coach, look at the sky. It's starting to turn purple!" He was right; the colors of the sunset were blending into Tiger purple. "Coach," he said with that now very familiar Nubbin smile, "That's gotta be a sign."

I laughed, shrugging. "Well, we had all the colors up there a few moments ago, but it looks like purple prevailed. Sounds like a winner to me, Nubbin. I'll take it." The sign post up ahead read *Austin City Limits* and we crossed over under purple skies.

Many times when high school kids are away from home, they tend to stay up much later than normal. Since we had the very first game Thursday morning and possibly for the next three games in a row, that was a major concern. We had no choice but to go to bed early because we would be getting up for breakfast *very* early. It would be the first time all year for us to play a game at 8:45 a.m. and that would severely alter our eating and sleeping schedule for the rest of the week. Since we had the 9:00 a.m. time slot for our shoot around at Gregory Gym, I decided to let Wednesday be our dress rehearsal for Thursday's game.

With that thought in mind, we were about to eat supper at approximately the same time we would be eating our evening meal hopefully for the next four days. But to even dream that, we had to win both Thursday and Friday morning. Even so, there was absolutely no choice but to plan for the possibility of a week-long stay, so that's exactly what we would do. We were one of six teams that had fought off all opposition in rising above the rest to reach this point. It was my job to do everything in my power to lead the team a few steps higher.

Soon we were off to the hotel's restaurant for our first meal in our new home. Our waitress couldn't have been friendlier—until we told her we were there for the tournament. Then she treated us like *family*.

We were thirty-nine hours away from our first State Tournament appearance as we dug in. I looked into the faces of each of the guys on my team. I didn't think they had a clue as to what they had already accomplished or about what lay ahead. Every high school player that ever played the game dreamed about being here. I knew I had always dreamed of sitting where those guys were. I remembered sending shot after shot at the rim at an imaginary free throw line, saying to myself, *This free throw is for the State Championship.* Of course, I would continue to shoot until I sunk it. So there we were, about to attempt the dream and I wanted to make sure that I had covered all the bases. I wanted my team to have a great time while they were there, but we couldn't let them forget that we had business to take care of.

~~~

Upon returning to the hotel, we had a short team meeting to talk about our plans for the next few days. "Look, fellas, there are going to be some changes in our daily routine for the rest of the week. The keyword that you should remember is 'early.' We'll be eating breakfast early, playing games early, eating our evening meals early, but first and foremost we will be going to bed early. This is not that big of a deal," I said, trying to downplay the change, but deep down, I was concerned. I gave them an early time for lights out and told them that they would receive a very early wake-up call because we'd be eating breakfast at 5:30 a.m.

Noticing a few continuing looks of negativity about the schedule, I stood firm. "Look, fellas, I don't set the time when we play. The UIL does that and I'm not about to let that affect our productivity level." By some of the looks, I was sensing that I had to do something to create a positive feeling about the whole situation. "Fellas, listen to me. We're not up here on a vacation. We're here to do everything in our power to win three straight games. We've got as good a chance as anybody up here to win this thing. Besides, we've played only two morning games all year long. Anybody remember who we played in those two games?"

Haywood's head perked up and his eyes narrowed. "Snook was the first one and now we've got a chance to play them again, right Coach?"

"That's a possibility, if we continue to win. Who was the other one we played?"

Herman nodded to himself. "Frankston."

"Snook is the two-time defending State Champion and Frankston was a former State Champion. You probably played your two best games of the year against these two very good teams—in the morning. It's true that Snook beat us, but it was also the best you had played then, by far. That game was the turning point of our year. We were a different team after that morning. And with Frankston, you took apart a really good team that morning—the first game at Kilgore. Fellas, there seems to be a pattern here. We just play our best in the morning.

Am I glad that we play all our games up here in the morning? You'd better believe it! Your first game is against another State Champ, our third straight morning game against one. Will we be ready to play? You'd better believe it! Thursday, when you play Avoca, I want you to deal them a personal case of morning misery. Is that clear, sports fans? This will be your schedule pretty much for this week. So we're going to get used to it a day early.

"Tomorrow after our early breakfast, we'll come back to our room, chill out for a little while, and then go to Gregory Gym for our morning shootaround. You'll get your first look at the gym where we'll play and guess what? You'll be doing that at exactly the same time as we'll play our first game on Thursday. The timing for our morning shootaround could not be more perfect. So let's get a good night's rest because tomorrow morning will come early. Any questions?"

I looked them over with a slight smile, "Don't make me come to your room and put some knuckles on top of your head! I just don't want anything *off* the floor to be the reason for a loss *on* the floor. Do any of you want that to be the reason that we go home early? Just get your butts to bed when I say to go." I had purposely planned this day full of things to do so hopefully they would be good and tired, ready to go to bed early. "Seriously, fellas, adjusting to this schedule is very important. We have no other choice. Our early game times dictate this, so get used to it! Good night, guys. I'll see you early tomorrow morning."

Coach Johnny Carter

16

Happy Birthday

Wednesday morning, March 1, 1967. My birthday had crept in before the sunlight. As I got up and put my clothes on, I got ready for breakfast and looked at my watch. We were twenty-seven hours from the opening tip of our game with Avoca. It was also the opening day of our adjusting to a different time schedule. To my complete surprise, most of my guys looked refreshed and wide awake for breakfast in the hotel's lobby. So far, so good.

Back in my room after breakfast, I flashed back to my first trip to the State Tournament. I'd been eleven and it was love at first sight. It became an ongoing dream of mine to play on that hardwood floor and lead the Mustangs to a State Championship, to have the hometown fans rush the floor and carry me off on their shoulders. I think every kid that ever played basketball probably envisioned hitting a twenty-footer at the buzzer for a one-point victory in the State Championship. That moment for the team had begun with a dream. Everyone needs dreams. They give you a starting point, an interest which leads to involvement, then to participation. They give you the determination to work hard and form teams that work together. You push yourself to attain them and, in turn, dreams give you pride in your accomplishment.

One thing athletics teaches is how to accept both victories and defeats, and in the long run that success is not measured just by winning games. Ben Sweetland, the author of *I Can* and *I Will* once wrote, "Success is a journey, not a destination." Whether my team won the State Championship or not, that year's journey had indeed been very fulfilling, very rewarding, and very special. The thought of losing a game at that juncture was with me constantly and something I had to battle to keep from my team, but I was already more proud of them than they knew.

Soon it was time for our team to head for Gregory Gym for our scheduled thirty-minute shootaround. We weren't that far away and we arrived at the UT Longhorn's home much more quickly than I anticipated. It made me wonder just what we would do with the extra time. *What the heck, we'll just go get dressed and check the place out until it's our time,* I thought.

When we got out of our automobiles, I told the guys to go up the ramp and wait in the lobby. "I'll be right behind you shortly." Before going up the ramp, I looked around. One of my players had left his travel bag. I picked up the bag and started jogging to catch up. Upon reaching the entrance, I approached a security guard at the front gate.

Looking at me with the travel bag in hand the guard nodded toward me, "Hey, boy, what position do you play?"

Having been mistaken for a player many times over, I didn't even bother to slow my stride. "Point guard, sir," I said and kept moving into the lobby.

Entering Gregory Gym, I couldn't help but notice the starry-eyed looks on the faces of my players as they gave this old, historic facility the once-over. Walter was pointing across the gym. "Look, Coach, there's a big map of Texas up there." A gigantic map rose from behind the bleachers covering a large part of the wall, little bulbs dotting the surface.

"Yeah, they don't have it turned on right now, but if you look real close, they have colored lights for all twenty-two teams that are geographically located on the map."

"Look, I see Kennard."

"How about that," I said. "This is the big time, fellas."

"Man, this is a big gym," said Haywood, who was strutting around the room with his hands on his hips.

"Wait 'til you see it full of people," I said. "It will be rocking and I'm going to tell you right now, you're going to play the best ball you've played all year, starting tomorrow *and* you're gonna have more fun than you've ever had in your entire life."

"I can't get over the size of this place," said Roy.

THE FIRST SEASON

"This is the State Tournament, not the Centerville Tournament. This place will be packed tomorrow. People from all over the state and beyond will be standing in line right out there," I said, pointing to the entrance. "They'll be waiting to watch you guys play." I could tell by their faces that my young players were in complete awe of what they were experiencing at the moment, but they still had no idea what they'd be experiencing the next three days.

Soon it was time for our thirty-minute shootaround, our first chance to test out the floor where within the next twenty-four hours we would be playing our first ever State Tournament game. I had instructed our players of the importance of this shooting session. We had to get as many shots as we possibly could in the allotted thirty minutes. As our guys aggressively hit the floor to do that, I happened to look up. Walking towards me was Leon Black, my old coach at Lon Morris Junior College. Presently, he was an assistant coach at UT and soon would become the head coach of the Longhorns. He walked up to me, reached out, and shook my hand.

"Congratulations, Johnny! Now this is the way all coaches wish they could make their debut! What a job you've done with this team. Any time you get up here by winning the Kilgore Region, you have done something very special."

I shook my head. "Coach, we got real lucky."

He nodded, still smiling, "Well, luck may be a small part of it, but the bottom line is that it takes a lot more than luck to get up here. Your team did a lot of things right last week or you wouldn't be here now."

"Thanks, Coach. What I learned from you has helped get us this far. By the way, Joe Turner told me to tell you hello." Coach Black just smiled. His eyes seemed far away, maybe reminiscing not only about Joe Turner at Kilgore, but about Floyd Wagstaff at Tyler, Leon Spencer at Henderson, and Vernon Horton at Jacksonville Baptist. There was a lot of Coach Black in the way I coached and approached the game. There was more than just Mustang in me, there was a collection of games, coaches, and teammates that had blended into what I'd tried to give to my team.

"Well, it's good to see you again, Johnny. Good luck tomorrow. From what I hear, you guys have a real shot to win this thing."

I scoffed. "Look, I don't know where you're getting your information, but if we somehow pull this off, it will be a major upset. It'll be a miracle, that's what!"

He looked at me and laughed. "You survived that Kilgore Region, which year in, year out is probably the toughest in the state. Anyway, I'll be here tomorrow rooting for you."

"Thank you, Coach. That means a lot." We shook hands one last time and I returned to our practice as he walked down the ramp and out of view.

Soon, our thirty minutes were just about up. I walked over to the official in charge and asked him how much time we had left. He glanced at his watch. "Two minutes and then you'll have to step aside for the next team."

Two minutes later, the second team had yet to arrive.

I walked back to the gym official." We're gonna keep shooting until the next team shows up and then we'll gladly relinquish the floor."

He nodded and took a seat on the bleachers. Twenty-five minutes passed and we just kept shooting. Every extra shot we took gave us an advantage for the game. It was a mental reprieve that I needed and the guys were definitely getting a feel for the space and the give of the floor. Eventually, we had to give way, but I was thankful for every extra minute.

~~~

After a great lunch and an enjoyable time, we were soon on our way to Johnson High School for a very light afternoon practice session. The session was crisp, quick, and to the point as we went over our basic game plan against a seasoned team that averaged seventy-nine points a game—a full twenty points above our average score. They obviously had a high octane offense, being able to score at will, so our number one goal would be to hold them below their average. Statistics can be very deceiving and sometimes not worth the paper they're written on, but the fact that those guys were averaging that many points a game definitely had me worried. We'd already beaten two teams in Regionals that statistically should have beaten us, so I hoped this would be one more. In a one-game elimination, your season stats boil away and it becomes about what you can do *today*.

Our second point of emphasis for the game would be rebounding. Our scouting report indicated that despite being outsized, we had a good chance to out-rebound them. It also indicated that we had a small edge in overall team speed. Their best player was Randy Thompson, an all-State candidate. The kid could score. Dennis Olsen and Larry Rister, their tallest players at six-foot-two, were two to keep an eye on. As it always had been, the key remained—defense. "I'm not emphasizing this to you, I'm telling you: either step up the defense or this will be your last game. If you guys play defense the way we've practiced, I guarantee you we'll keep them well below their average. Nubbin, what's your motto?"

He came out of the huddle, fist raised. "*D* is the key!"

I stabbed my finger towards him. "Nubbin's motto needs to be our motto tomorrow morning."

~~~

Later on that evening, we ate at the same restaurant where we'd eaten lunch and as luck would have it, we got the same waitress. I wanted them to feel secure and at home before our big game, so I was doing my best to create a familiar atmosphere. Everyone was just about finished with their meal when I asked if anyone wanted dessert. Hands went up like skyrockets. I ordered ice cream for the whole group.

My popularity had gone up a notch and Roy pointed at me with both hands. "Coach, you the man!"

Herman spoke between spoonfuls. "Coach, I always liked you a lot, I mean, from the very first day you started, but the way you're feeding us up here, I think the word now is 'love.' If you were a girl, I'd have to have a talk with your dad right about now." The team was laughing.

"Herman, if I was a girl, I'd have to have someone a whole lot taller than you, son!"

~~~

The game with Avoca was highly competitive to say the least. The great record they had compiled over the last two seasons was no fluke. They were giving us all we wanted and then some. It was late in the fourth quarter and we were down by one with seconds remaining. We'd called a timeout and set up an offensive play. We had one last chance to snatch the game from the jaws of defeat. Everything we'd worked on our whole year had come down to one last-second play. Avoca's defense tightened up, trying to keep us from scoring the winning basket. Executing our offensive strategy to perfection, we got the ball to Herman. He squared up, eyed the basket, and put up an arching one-hander. The game-ending horn sounded as the ball struck the front of the rim, bouncing up and coming back down. I held my breath, trying to will it to fall forward and through the net. It began to slowly circle the inner perimeter of the rim. It seemed to spin endlessly. I could feel my eyes watering. I blinked.

When I opened them again, I was in my bed in the hotel, the clock read two fifteen in the morning. It was a dream. I didn't even know what the outcome was. I laughed out loud. It was just under three hours before our wake-up call. There was no way I could get back to sleep. Even in my sleep, my mind wouldn't rest. I was like a kid trying to go to sleep on Christmas Eve. That day we'd be living the dream—in more ways than one, I guess. I could only pray that my players were having a better night of it than I was.

I answered the wake-up call fully dressed and a few minutes later was in the hotel's restaurant, ordering breakfast and that all-important pre-game drink for twelve young men. The waitress was the same lady that served my team yesterday. I'd learned her name was Susan and she was a godsend. "Coach, are you okay? You look a little edgy."

Looking at her, I held a finger over my lips. "Whatever you do, don't say that around my players. I'm trying to hide that little fact from them."

She took a seat across from me, gave me a reassuring smile and waited for me to continue. I shook my head. "You don't want to hear all this. You've got your own job to do."

She patted my hand. "Try me."

I gave a little laugh. "I'm trying to do something that I probably have no business attempting in the first place. I'm really way too young to be in this position anyway, but I'm trying to make the most of it."

"Coach, can I ask you a personal question? There's not a rule in basketball that you have to have X number of years of experience to win the State Championship, is there?"

I cupped my hands around my tea and shook my head.

"Well, there you go and if you *do* happen to lose, guess what? You have a legitimate excuse. You can always say, 'If I had a few more years of experience, we might have won it all!'"

We both were laughing as she walked back toward the kitchen. It did feel a little better to have someone other than my family and friends tell me their feelings.

The guys had made their way down with Haywood in the lead and Fred in the rear as they shuffled into the booth. Nubbin leaned in towards me, looking at the other players sipping their tea. "Coach, all these guys are talking about extra doses of honey in their tea so they'll shoot better. If I take a double dose, will that same thing apply to my defense?"

I went stone-faced. "Absolutely."

He lit up, "Coach, in that case, Avoca doesn't have a chance. If my defense gets any better we're going to hold 'em twenty to thirty points below their average. That'll probably *guarantee* a win!"

~~~~

Walking up the steps of Gregory Gym with its russet, reddish-brown exterior, I couldn't help but think back to all the times I had come there strictly as a fan. For the first time, I was there as a participant and it felt good. It felt real good! Heck, it felt great!

That giant structure had three main entrances at the front with skylights atop each gate entering the lobby. Each entrance had large Gothic arches trimmed in solid-colored brick, displaying a Spanish influence. It was the home of the Texas Longhorns, but on that very special weekend, it was the home of the Texas State High School Basketball Tournament. We would be lifting the curtain for the first game. It was all so impressive, almost overwhelming to these country kids from Kennard—or at least to their coach.

Soon we were dressed and on the floor, working on shooting. I watched with a gleam in my eye, giving an occasional word here and there, but mostly just warming the bench, sitting, wearing my lucky blue blazer, trying to look like a real ball coach. To my left, just entering the gym was the same security guard that just yesterday had asked me what position I played. He walked past the bench. When he got to me, he just nodded and kept walking. About six paces out, he stopped dead in his tracks. I could almost see the light bulb go on. Slowly turning around, we locked eyes and he began to retrace his steps. He was wearing a smile. "Point guard, huh?"

I laughed. "Well, that was four years ago, but now I'm the coach."

"You gotta be what, twenty-two? You don't even look that!"

"Turned twenty-four yesterday."

Still chuckling a little and scratching his head, he offered his hand, "Please accept my apology."

I took it, shaking my head. "It's really unnecessary, I never gave it a second thought. Believe me, you're not the first person to say that to me."

He looked out at my guys as they shot. "Well, who better to teach a team to play basketball than a player. It's still fresh in your mind. Best of luck, Coach. You know, if you guys win this thing you may be the youngest coach ever to win the State Championship."

"Hey, all we have to do is win three games in a row, right? Piece of cake!"

He wagged a finger at me, nodding as he walked away. "Something tells me that you guys may do just that."

The atmosphere, the aroma, the feeling at Gregory Gym was spellbinding. I had chills up and down my spine while the pit of my stomach was hosting a butterfly convention. I felt heavy, awkward, and so tense that I don't think a hurricane could have budged me. A few seconds later, my team was around me in the huddle. Looking up into the eyes of my players, my nerves began to unknot little by little. I looked into that special warmth in the eyes of my youthful team, saw the excitement there, and I remembered who we were and just what we were capable of accomplishing.

"Fellas, it doesn't get any better than this. Let's show this crowd, particularly Avoca, what Kennard Tiger Basketball is all about!"

In the background I heard the long-time PA announcer Phil Ransopher start warming up the crowd. "Welcome to the Forty-Seventh Annual State Basketball Tournament. From the high plains just north of Abilene, it's the Avoca Mustangs, winner of District 13B and Region II. Compiling a record of thirty-five wins and three losses, they're coached by Clayton Brooks. Their opponent and winner of District 45B and Region IV, from east Texas, smack dab in the middle of the Davy Crockett National Forest, it's the Kennard Tigers, coached by Johnny Carter in his very first season. Their record is thirty-nine wins and four losses."

After the player introductions, it was time to throw it up and play ball. With a ferocious beginning, we quickly took the early lead on the high-scoring Mustangs. Stealing their favorite role seemed to be the kiss of death for Avoca in the first quarter. Herman hit a jumper shortly after the tip and Fred followed with another two-pointer as we put a double deuce on the scoreboard with a couple of net swishers. At least at the beginning, it was not the galloping Mustangs but the streaking Tigers that m a d e a high-scoring start. Forcing numerous turnovers with some real intense half-court defense, we raced to a quick 11-0 lead and the quarter wasn't over yet. It marked the third time out of our four playoff games that we came out of the gate full speed ahead to take a good lead. Many times, the start of a game influences how the game will play out and this was certainly my hope when they called a quick timeout after a nightmarish start.

With intense and constant pressure, we totally dominated the remainder of the first quarter in all phases of the game. We out-rebounded them, caused several turnovers, and held a big edge in the all-important scoreboard columns. All that left us leading 19-5; however, Nubbin got his second foul and that was becoming a major concern. His presence in the team chemistry was an absolute necessity.

In the huddle again, I pointed to him. "Nubbin, don't give the ref a chance to call another foul on you. Play smart, sound, fundamental defense. If you get another foul, I want it to be one that makes the official have to think before he calls it. Don't you dare give him an easy automatic call, you understand?"

"Yes, sir!"

"Look, I fully expect them to play better this quarter. We've got a good lead. Keep up the pressure. This quarter may be the key to the game."

The second quarter opened just as I had predicted—the Mustangs started to make a run as Randy Thompson started showing why he was an all-State candidate. Slowly, they started to whittle away at our fourteen-point lead, but soon the tide turned back in our favor, another run re-establishing our place. Haywood and Roy continued their dominance on the boards as Fred and Herman continued to hit big shots. We refused to let them get a foot in the door, but it was only the second quarter and with the ref's whistle, Nubbin got his third foul.

I slapped my sixth man on the back. "Go in, Gary. Take Nubbin's place."

With Nubbin on the bench, Avoca started to slice into our lead. When they cut the lead to eight on a basket by Dennis Olsen, I looked over at my benched *D* man. He looked back at me, concern written across his face. Our team needed him. He wasn't a flashy player, but he was a hard-nosed, very aggressive defender and he always seemed to come up with loose balls. He was the reagent on the team—the thing that made the rest of the elements function to their full potential.

"Do you think you can play the rest of the quarter and not foul?"

He answered like any true player would. "Yes, sir!"

I looked him over, my stomach knotting. I knew it was a foolish question. Players always think they can play without a foul. It was on me to determine if I thought he could. In those seconds, I ran over and over his record through the year, about how he'd done in the big games when the adrenaline was at its highest. Even the smartest player can get a foul just by being on the floor. I decided to take the risk. I put Nubbin back in the game.

"You've got to play conservative. Back off a contested situation, don't force it. I know that's not your game, but I need to know you can play this way."

He nodded his head, staring out into the game. "I'll just have to, Coach." I nodded and he hit the floor. To his credit, Nubbin played exactly how I told him to and we shortly moved back to our fourteen-point lead, but I knew it could only be a matter of time. I had Gary at the scorer's table to replace him when he got his fourth foul.

I congratulated the guys at halftime for fighting off the attempted comeback. I also knew that we'd have to play the third quarter without Nubbin. "Listen up, I fully expect them to press you hard the third quarter. Look for the pass first on the press. If it's there, make it! If the ball is passed to you, never wait on the pass to get to you, go get it with authority! I mean, if one of their guys is going for the pass, you've got to go for it harder. If you collide, so be it. I've told

178

you before, the foul will usually be called on the defense anyway. You do this and we'll eliminate most steals."

We came out of the dressing room with a very positive feeling, but I knew deep in my heart that the third quarter without Nubbin was going to hurt. We'd be hard-pressed to hold our lead. Our fans had no idea just how important Nubbin was to this team.

Out of the dressing room came the real Avoca team and in the third quarter, they used a ferocious full-court press and began to reestablish their confidence. The momentum was gradually starting to swing toward the Mustangs and they started to make that sprint to the finish line. Those wild horses were thundering from behind, seizing every opportunity, cutting our lead to four.

Slowly, I turned to Nubbin. "Son, I want to put you back in the game, but I can't do it right now." I could see the disappointment on his face, but he accepted his role like a true player. We were in trouble—big trouble.

As we came to the sideline after the third quarter, I could see uneasiness in the eyes of my team as I tried to hide my own. The only positive about the third quarter that I could see was that we would have Nubbin fresh and ready to go in the fourth. But with four fouls, I wondered just how effective he could be.

I rested a hand on his shoulder. "We need you to play the rest of the game, so play smart. Remember, the key for D is body position. No reaching—and I mean no reaching, period! You got that?"

"Yes, sir."

"One more thing...Rister has four fouls and he's playing very well. When and if the opportunity arises, take the ball right to him. Let's see how *he* plays with those four fouls. Nubbin, if you can outlast Rister, this could be huge. Fellas, we've been in situations like this many times. They played their best ball in the third quarter and used a lot of energy in coming back. Now it's our time!"

The fourth quarter started just like the third quarter ended as Rister hit a six-footer to cut our lead to two. With the Avoca crowd roaring its approval and its high-flying offense now on cruise control, they were threatening to give us an early exit. Meanwhile, the Kennard faithful looked edgy, unsure, and tense, fearful of a loss. I only hoped that the Mustangs had spent too much energy trying to get back in the game. Roy Harrison was the third leading scorer on our team for the year, but he had made a habit of making that big basket when we had to have it.

When Roy received that nice entry pass from Herman, he squared up on the low post and prepared to take his patented, turnaround jumper. Having a true shooter's touch, his wrist flip nicked the front of the iron and then ever so gently rolled around the perimeter like a whirlpool, softly stroking the strings. It was our biggest basket of the game, but an even bigger thing happened on the same play—Larry Rister fouled out with six minutes and fifty-two seconds left on the clock. Our fans had just awakened and their cheers were the salve we needed. As they let out a blast of approval, Avoca's crowd, which had been riding the crest of the wave, was now sinking in the undercurrent.

With Nubbin back in charge as the secretary of defense, leading several consecutive stops, we started to resemble the team that dominated the first half. Herman hit a fifteen-footer to give us a 46-40 lead as we methodically regained momentum. Our crowd, which had sat in stunned silence as our lead eroded in the third quarter, was back into the game and on their feet, led by my dad who was standing and waving his arms wildly on the first row. Our level of play was now inspired to higher highs. With Nubbin playing exceptionally well with four fouls, our team chemistry was back on track as Fred took the ball near the free throw line. Squaring up with a rocker step, he left the floor, flipped the wrist and sent a spiraling jump shot straight toward the basket. The ball literally attacked the goal with the rim-riveting sound of a jackhammer. The hard reverse action of the basketball stretched the strings forward, then backward before dropping it to the floor for two. Nubbin had provided that much needed spark and the Mustangs were starting to see that they were attempting to stop what had become an out-of- control east Texas wildfire.

We were now up eight and in total command when we were dealt a severe blow. Nubbin fouled out with five minutes and thirty-five seconds left in the game. We were hoping that would not affect us the same way Rister's fouling out had hurt the Mustangs. Fred and Roy were both at four fouls, and we were walking a razor's edge. Even though Nubbin was now out of the game, the momentum had definitely swung back our way and when Gary went in for the second time, he didn't miss a beat. Outscoring the Mustangs seventeen to nine in the fourth quarter, we won the game convincingly by twelve. Walking over to shake Coach Clayton Brooks' hand, I could see the disappointment in his eyes as the great year for his Mustangs ended with the fourth and final loss of their season.

The first person to greet me with a big hug, followed by a handshake, was my dad, grinning and laughing. I really think he was having more fun with all this than I was. I walked with him over to my mom and gave her a big hug as she said, "I'm so proud of you, son! But then I was before you ever started coaching." She planted a kiss on my cheek and I started trying to force my way through to the dressing room. I couldn't believe how many new well-wishers clogged the path, offering congratulations, backslaps, and handshakes. Finally, I recognized a face among them.

"We're going to have to get a larger bandwagon if any more fans jump on board!" Mr. Bitner gripped my hand and walked with me. "Great job, Coach! I think we've got a real shot at this thing." We passed a trash bin and he spat the gum he'd been gnawing on into the can, along with the crumpled pack from which it came. "I went through a whole pack the third quarter. You almost gave me an ulcer!" He squeezed my shoulder and looked into my eyes. "Just one more win and we're looking at the final—the State final!"

After finally making it to the dressing room, I found it upbeat to say the least! As I walked in, I looked into the faces of the young players on my team. With a clenched fist high in the air, I came out with a yell that resounded across the room, soon finding echoes in each of their voices. *Yes!* That's what I'm talking about! I always wondered what this moment would feel like and now that I know, I *love* this, guys! Everyone get over here and have a seat. Guess what, Nubbin? We held the high-scoring Avoca Mustangs *thirty-two* points below their average!" Nubbin came out of his seat with both hands in the air.

"That's what it's all about Coach. O is for show, but *D?D* is the key!"

"We also out-rebounded them forty-five to thirty-three." With that Haywood, Roy, and Fred began exchanging high fives. Haywood pointed my way. "You wanted a war on that glass, Coach. Well, we brought it!"

"You bet we did. You soundly beat a very good team today and for the third straight game, we beat the favorite! Hey, fellas," I said in a very upbeat tone of voice, "can we make magic in the morning or what? I don't want to hear one more word about having to go to bed early! If ever a team was made for the morning, you are it! Now let's get ready to inflict some more morning madness on those tall guys from Plainview, same time tomorrow morning!"

Voices were chiming out. Gary came out with, "Same bat time, same bat channel!"

Herman went for *Casablanca.* "Play it again, Sam!"

17

One More Win

With the game history, my nerves—as well as those of our fans—were incredibly relieved. I walked down the corridor behind the bleachers, through the lobby, and made my way outside. I needed to get away, get out of the rush of the win for a moment and breathe some fresh air, attempt to somehow return to normalcy. It felt refreshing to get away from the furious celebration and just let my mind enjoy the beauty of the moment. I looked over the grounds and saw the mountain laurel was in full bloom, clusters of purple flowers hung all around me. I could only hope it was a sign. Taking a few deep breaths of the crisp, early spring air calmed my nerves considerably.

Upon my return, I met Curtis in the bleachers. My scouting partner looked at me with that familiar smile. "Well, Coach, you did it again. Congratulations! Were you ever worried?"

"Heck no, why should I be worried? Nubbin fouls out, Roy and Fred were sitting at four fouls each, Avoca makes a heck of a comeback after getting killed the first half, totally regaining the momentum, I look at the scoreboard and our lead dwindled to two. No, why would I be worried? And if you believe that, I'm gonna marry Ann-Margret!"

Curtis just continued to smile. "Well, I'll be at the wedding. Congratulations! She's a looker. I saw her a couple years ago with Elvis Presley. Then again, maybe you should call it off. It would make a lot of girls here in Houston County depressed if you went through with it." I tried to change the subject, but he wouldn't quit. "I'm not kidding. It seems like every day some young girl wants me to fix her up with you." He was wearing a big grin. "I tell them that I think you're old enough to pick and choose for yourself"

It took a while for me to get over that little shock, but we sat down to watch the Snook Bluejays play for their third straight State Championship. They were the odds on favorite to do just that. It had been three months since we'd lost to them in the semi-finals of the Madisonville Tournament and I knew my team, especially Haywood, was looking forward to possibly playing them again. If that matchup took place, it would be for all the marbles in the State Championship that would take place in about forty-eight hours. As Curtis and I watched, Snook eventually did take control of the morning's second game and knocked off stubborn Ackerly Sands, drinking deep of the same cup we had earlier that morning.

So the second-round matchups were set. We were down to the Class B Final Four. We would play Plainview Washington in the first game Friday morning, followed by Snook versus Krum. I turned to my partner, "Curtis, what do you think? The Bluejays are looking even better than when we played them."

Curtis just shrugged. "They're not unbeatable. I for one am looking forward to playing them again."

"Not more than Haywood, I'd expect, but let's not jump the gun. From what I found out, Plainview Washington is not only very good and extremely athletic, but they have size. They'll probably be the favorite on size alone."

"We're three for three against favorites so far. I wouldn't want to be Plainview right now."

I was thinking back to the team's roster. "If we don't block off the glass better than we've ever done in our lives, it could be a very long morning tomorrow. Plainview's got some guys that can hover around the rim like helicopters. They might as well bring some Windex with them for when they get bored; I mean they're already up there! They've also got one great athlete—Lawrence McCutcheon."

"Well, we've got an athlete, too. His name's Haywood, eh, Coach?"

I smiled, "True, true. I wouldn't trade Haywood for anyone. He's been a perfect fit for our team. And his value has been increasing with each playoff game. Hopefully, it will shine again tomorrow. There's something else about this game that really bothers me. This'll be the first all-black school to ever play in this tournament. You do know who won the NCAA Championship last year don't you?" The smile was gone from his face as he looked back at me. "That's right, Texas Western. All five of Coach Don Haskins' starters were black. Adolph Rupp, the Kentucky coach, had to eat his words. He said that no all-black team could beat them. And they didn't just win, they beat Kentucky *down.*"

Curtis was quiet for a time after that, but finally he turned, shaking his head. "But Coach, Kentucky was all-white. We're not. We didn't take *anybody* based on color. We did it on skill, and we got a blend of very special guys who you've focused in the same direction."

I nodded, "True, but I can guarantee you that the Plainview Washington's Coach has been preaching Texas Western to his team and if he's hasn't, he should be. That game changed basketball. It was an eye-opener for a lot of coaches, players, and fans. You know that Plainview Washington is thinking they could become the protegé of Texas Western and become the first all-black team to win a UIL State Championship."

"Well, that *would* be something, Coach, but I can do you one better. If *we* win our next two games, then we will become the first *integrated* team to ever win a State Championship in Texas."

"Curtis, I want to tell you, I really appreciate all your help this year, especially for consistently believing in our team. Every time I talk with you, I feel like we're gonna win the next game."

Curtis barked a laugh. "Then just keep talking to me."

~~~

Arriving at the Stephen F. Austin Hotel a few minutes later, I told my team that they had about forty-five minutes until we left for lunch. "How about a good old-fashioned hamburger?" Herman asked with a gleam in his eyes.

"How about one hickory smoked, charcoal broiled, about this thick?" I asked, indicating with my hands.

"Have we got to wait forty-five minutes?" Haywood asked. "I'm so hungry I could eat a horse!"

With that Roy chimed in. "Well, son, we just corralled a whole herd of wild Mustangs this morning, we could probably single one out for you!"

I was laughing. "Haywood, if you can hold off a few minutes, we'll make yours a double meat with cheese."

He sat down and began to twiddle his thumbs, becoming patience incarnate.

Roy wasn't about to let that slide. "Wait a minute, how come you're getting a double meat and I'm not?"

"Because I jump twice as high as you do, Roy. Isn't that right, Coach?"

I smiled and shrugged my shoulders. "I'm staying out of this one. You guys be down here in forty-five minutes."

As we walked through Friday's game plan, Lester looked at me with a very inquisitive look on his face. "Coach, just where is Plainview?"

"Just about as far north and west as you can go in this state," I said. "It's located in the panhandle, right between Lubbock and Amarillo. It's a long way from Kennard. In fact, it's a long way from Austin. Fellas, you are about to play perhaps the most athletic team you've played all year. They're quick, they're big, and they're very talented. All year long, we've done a pretty good job of blocking out and in the process, out-rebounded a lot of teams that should have been better rebounders than we were. Well, here's the deal. Tomorrow morning, you're going to block out the very best because the bottom line is, if you don't, our season will be over."

Herman thought deeply about that. "Does that mean no more charbroiled hamburgers?"

"That's exactly what I'm saying. If you want some more of those burgers, you'd better block out. Look, the object here is just what I've said all year. The key to rebounding is simple. When the shot goes up, you can't become a spectator. That's my job and the fan's job. The instant a shooter releases the ball, you have to get into position to rebound. There are two things you've got to use when you block out. Number one, your brain and number two, your butt! Your brain gets you in position and your butt keeps you there. The two easiest calls for a referee to make are reaching and going over the back. Guess what? If you don't block out, there's no over-the-back call and there's no reaching call. Washington has totally dominated the boards in their District games and fully expects to do the same thing to you.

Everyone I've talked to has said that if they could have gotten just a few more rebounds they just might have won. We've got to take away their strengths. Keep those jumping jacks behind you."

Herman put his hand in the group. "Okay guys, 'Block out for burgers!' on three." The whole group was laughing as I sent them to shoot layups. I knew that Haywood and Roy got the message loud and clear. As we left the gym and were coming back to the hotel, I heard the two of them making a bet about who would outdo the other rebounding-wise. Regardless of who would win the bet, the motivation would make the team the ultimate winner. With two of my fiercest competitors literally hungry for the win, I couldn't help but have a good feeling about the next day.

At dinner, I figured I would get a little more information just in case competition leaked over into being overzealous. I didn't want my players forgetting their proper function in the team.

I looked at Haywood. "Okay, what about this friendly wager between you and Roy. You want to give me the minute details or is this a secret?"

Haywood shrugged. "It's no secret, Coach. Look over there. Roy thinks he can out-rebound me tomorrow. He's a little crazy. He doesn't know that he doesn't have a chance. He doesn't have my size, my strength, my jumping ability, or my athletic skills." About that time, Roy realized what was being said and he came over to give his two cents.

"Coach, listen to me. Haywood is a little bit stronger and may jump an *inch* or two higher, but the thing I've got on him is that I *want* it more than he does." Haywood tried to challenge that, but Roy just kept talking. "There's one more very important issue—that's the fact that I just plain jump quicker than he does. When I go up, I explode off the floor like Superman. Now Haywood, he has to wind up like Bob Gibson."

Haywood settled back in his seat. "Well, what happens to all the hitters when they face Bob Gibson, Roy? Never mind, I'll tell you. They strike out."

Roy was laughing. "We'll see Haywood, but I'm gonna tell you right now, you'd better bust your butt tomorrow because I'm gonna out-rebound you and make you like it. Oh yeah, one more thing, you're Mr.

Super-Athlete, so technically you should out-rebound me anyway. So are you going to spot me a rebound or two? That's only fair."

Haywood leaned in, poking one big finger in the air. "Okay, I'll tell you what I'll do, I'll spot you *one* rebound and that's it. No more negotiations."

Soon, all of our guys were in their rooms and for the first time that day, I had a little time just to sit back, relax, and enjoy myself. Try as I might, I couldn't get my mind away from basketball. I soon found myself watching college ball in front of the TV. I kicked off my shoes, propped my feet up, poured a Dr. Pepper over ice, and let out the longest sigh of my life. I missed most of the game reliving my own memories and trying to think of what I needed to do to make sure my team was totally ready for Plainview and their Dragons.

That day, I'd felt the greatest high I could experience, and watched a much more seasoned coach walk away heartbroken. I was tiptoeing through the tulips with the big boys. The buzzer for halftime made me jerk out of a light sleep I hadn't realized I'd fallen into. I stretched my legs and walked over to the mirror, looking at my reflection. *So you're here. Your team just won its first game in the State Tournament and now you're in the final four. So what's next?* I almost stepped back when I found my reflection smiling back at me. I had to feel my own face to realize that it was really there. And why shouldn't I be smiling? We were playing the best we had played all year. Our confidence had also reached an all-time high. Could we pull off the unthinkable? Could this group of inexperienced unknowns somehow win this thing? My reflection was still smiling. *Why not?*

The Friday morning wake-up call rang with futility. Again, I had been wide awake long before the phone rang. In the restaurant, awaiting the arrival of my players, I enjoyed a cup of freshly brewed coffee. It wasn't Mrs. Baker's but it was good. One by one, the players came in for their breakfasts. Once again, they all looked fresh; so far I hadn't had to bust any skulls to get them into bed. Soon everyone was again enjoying their early bird breakfast and seemed to be in very good spirits. It was day three of being in this diner and it was beginning to feel like home.

I stood up. "It's time for dessert, sports fans."

Right on cue, Susan came in from the kitchen with hot tea and a smile. Whether my players were enjoying the hot tea and honey or just stomaching it, I didn't know. The important thing was that everyone was downing it. They *believed* that it would help improve their energy level-maybe that was enough to give us an edge.

Our team arrived at Gregory Gym about the same time we had the day before. A few minutes later, we were conducting our shootaround prior to tipping off against an athletic, very tall Plainview Washington squad from the wind-blown south plains of the Texas Panhandle.

I was trying really hard to duplicate our warm-up from the previous day. If it ain't broke, don't try to fix it. I walked up to Fred, "How's your shot falling today?"

He let one fly, sinking it cleanly. "I love playing in this gym. Every time I hit that big shot, I get to hear that PA announcer say my name." He placed a hand to his ear and deepened his voice. *"Basket by Fred Pilkington!* It makes me want to play harder. I think you'll be hearing it a lot this morning."

"You know, this has been some special year. I've loved every second of it."

"Me too, Coach." With a smile, he hit another jumper from the foul line.

I gave him a firm pat on the shoulder, "Now, let's see some of those after the opening tip!"

In our dressing room, it was time for our final chalk talk before going back out on the floor for our pre-game warm-up. I paced in front of the twelve players sitting before me. "You already know what our game plan is. What is it, Herman?"

His hands shot up. "Block out for burgers!" There were chuckles floating through the group and I was sure I heard someone say, "Mm-mmm."

"Look, one more very important thing," I said. "Even though you're playing a very talented team, they've got to be a little bit unsure of themselves." I paused, unsure of what to say, but it was my job to help my guys succeed any way I could. "They're the first all-black school to ever play in this tournament. They're under a lot of extra pressure from that fact alone. That's a double-edged sword. They're going to want to play hard, to prove themselves, but if we place some doubt in them, they just might crumble and get sloppy.

"Your job is to go out there and put pressure on them right from the start. You can make them even more unsure and compound all this pressure if you get after them extra hard the first few minutes of the game. You've beaten a lot of teams this year that were a lot bigger than you are. Just two weeks ago, we beat Grapeland, one of the tallest teams around, and we defeated them on their own floor. We did that at a time when we weren't even playing *near* as well as we are right now. Plainview isn't quite as big as Grapeland, but they're more athletic. They haven't played a team this year that can frustrate them more than you're about to do. You're going to go out there in a few minutes and make them have to work their butts off for every single rebound, got it? You're gonna take away their strength and make them play on equal terms. If you can do this, they won't be able to play with you. They're playing on your court guys, let's show them that."

Nubbin tentatively raised his hand. "How's this *our* court?"

"Well, think about it. We got our regular practice session like everybody else did on Wednesday morning and then we got a second session when the next team failed to show, then we got a third session by having a shootaround before our game yesterday and a fourth one this morning. So we've had four practice sessions plus one game under our belt. Plainview can't say that. Heck, they ought to change the name of this place from Gregory Gym to Tigers' Den!"

There were a few chuckles here and there, but it looked like they were ready to hit the floor. "Everyone grab a hand and take a knee; let's have a prayer."

As our team took the floor for our pre-game warm-up, we were greeted by a thunderous standing ovation from our faithful fans who seemed to be packed in even more tightly than the day before. The area behind our bench was completely stuffed, shoulder to shoulder— packed with purple. Looking down to the other end of Gregory Gym, I noticed that Plainview Washington was also going through their pre-game warm-up drills. As we went through our shooting drills, Haywood took a shot that struck the rim, ricocheting toward the sideline. It wound up bouncing right into the awaiting arms of Benford Frizzell. Tossing it back, he motioned across the court with his head. "Man, Haywood, those guys down there are huge! Do you think we can play with them?"

Haywood caught the ball and glanced down the court at the Plainview Washington team warming up. "Ain't no all-black team gonna beat us!" With his big smile, Haywood took the ball, got his game face on, and continued his pre-game shooting practice while Mr. Frizzell gave me a smile and a nod.

~~~

When the game started, we managed to capture yet another round of early momentum. True to his word, Fred got the show on the road as he hit two quick baskets early on, giving us a 4-2 lead. In fact, the next two trips down the floor, my silent senior leader continued his sizzling start with a personal onslaught of rapid-fire wrist action, shooting down the Dragons with a blazing beginning. Fred had scorched the cords for the first eight points, single-handedly giving us another first quarter lead. For the second straight day, we got off to a drag-race start, taking control from the outset. Fred pulled a foul, but his scoring was more than making up for it. We were also doing a great job on the boards, particularly blocking off the much taller Dragon board men. All those positives, along with some very good first quarter shooting, gave us the quick start we wanted and a 16-7 lead at the end of the quarter.

The second quarter started out just like the first as our offense continued to sparkle. Nubbin received an outlet pass from Haywood as he took the ball coast to coast for a fast break layup. A few seconds later, we caused a turnover, with Fred making a quick down court pass to Herman who bounce-passed to Roy for another easy basket. Fred got another foul on the next play but came back again with a pump fake shot for another two. I came off the bench with a clutched fist, sensing a major momentum moment for the Tigers. Haywood got a monster rebound and whipped a pass to Nubbin who, in turn, rifled it to Herman for a twelve-footer swish! We were dominating the quarter, forcing the Dragons to call a much needed timeout.

The Kennard fans behind us were exploding into a frenzy. The timeout did little to stem the flow of our scoring, but in the process, Fred received his third foul. I pulled him immediately, having Gary take his place.

Showing incredible scoring balance with baskets coming from every starter, we increased our lead to sixteen points, racing to a 37-21 lead at halftime. We jogged off the floor to another inspiring, thunderous standing ovation. Walking back to the dressing room, I couldn't believe that we had totally dominated a very athletic team for sixteen minutes and had completely negated their obvious superiority on the boards.

Entering the dressing room at the half, I saw a group of guys that could not have been more positive. "Super job, fellas! You totally took it to them in every fundamental aspect of the game. Don't let up. You blocked out well. We got those over-the-back calls that I thought we would. Why? Because we were in position to rebound almost every time. You made them earn every bucket they got. This third quarter coming up has now become the key quarter of the game. If you can increase the lead again in the third, they won't be able to recover." I pointed to the door, "Over in the Washington dressing room, they're talking about a comeback and I'm sure their focus is to get their train on track. Don't let that happen. Let's derail 'em before they leave the station. Leave no doubt that this is *our* game!"

It became obvious in the third quarter that Washington was indeed trying to get their rhythm back. They'd definitely put the beginning game jitters behind them and had kicked up the intensity. I tapped Fred back in the game and we met the Dragons' challenge. Roy and Haywood continued to grab their share of rebounds and Nubbin hit another fast break layup. Our effort continued to be team-wide as Fred hit a high post jumper and Herman got a fifteen-footer from the corner. Our lead was increasing with every minute. However, the very next play, Fred got his fourth foul and I replaced him with Gary. He'd barely set foot on the floor when he caught a bounce pass and hit a ten-footer and a free throw as we continued to increase our lead. The Dragons were continuing to score, but their big problem was that we were shooting the lights out in the quarter in high percentages. Resembling our last quarter comeback in the Regional finals against Avinger, we shot a sizzling ten for fourteen, increasing our lead to twenty.

~~~

THE FIRST SEASON

At the start of the fourth quarter, standing tall with sixty-one points, I thought I'd clear the bench. We had the game totally in our control and I wanted to give everyone a little playing time. I put five new guys on the floor. Play resumed with the referee's whistle and we were back in the game until Washington's coach began frantically waving his arms.

"Hold on! Hold on! Hold on! I'm having enough trouble with five of your kids, you know I can't beat *six!*" I looked around the court. I subbed five new guys in the game, but for some strange reason, six guys had checked in. The fourth quarter had started with six Tigers on the floor and I hadn't even noticed it. In fact, the referees hadn't noticed either. Immediately, the whistle blew and we got an embarrassing technical foul. This was the first mistake in the last quarter, and I prayed it would be our last.

Our error seemed to spark the Dragons and all of a sudden they had that look of fire in their eyes. With our starting five on the bench, Washington promptly scored three unanswered baskets and had a new lease on life, with plenty of time left in the game. Realizing I had made a major mistake, I had to go back to the starters. The lead had gone from twenty to fourteen in a flash, and that very athletic team had been given a taste of a comeback attempt.

With our starters back in the game, we slowed their momentum down, but they continued to whittle away at our lead. Harold Williams hit a jumper with four minutes and two seconds left in the game to cut our lead to eight. My heart dropped out of my chest with the next whistle as Fred drew his fifth foul. The Dragons seemed to truly be breathing fire now, sensing a major comeback in the works. I called a timeout. My guys huddled in around me.

"Look, fellas, they had their run. Now it's time to put the lock on the door and put this thing away. They've come as close as they're going to get. Gary, you're in for Fred. They're running that full-court press, so here's what I want you to do." Using my clipboard, I set up our press offense. "Look, work this the way I taught you in practice! Do not wait on the ball. Go get it with authority! Remember, pass first and dribble last. You know how to do this. We've worked on this press attack hundreds of times. Now go out there and execute! If we don't get a good, high percent shot off this press attack, take it outside and go into our delay game. Remember, you're not just trying to kill the clock, you're trying to get an easy basket. Get your hands in here and let's go!"

As the huddle broke, there was a hollow spot in the pit of my stomach, and although I didn't let my players know it, I knew that the outcome of this game was very much in jeopardy. For the second straight day, our team was going have to go through the crucial fourth quarter without one of our starters.

With our press attack working, we quickly got the ball down the floor to Herman. When he squared up to take a wide-open short jumper, my heart skipped a beat, even though it was a high percentage shot for him. Having cut our lead from twenty to eight, riding an avalanche of momentum, our talent-laden opponent was brimming with new-found confidence. If Herman missed that shot and they cut the lead to six—look out. There is a point in the latter stages of every close game when there's that one key basket that seems to turn the tide. As it arched through the air, I knew Herman's was that basket. Now if only Herman could stick it. Hoping for that momentum-ceasing jumper to connect, I watched his spinning one-hander gently rainbow toward the rim. With feather-like softness, there it was, a spinning swish, the ball barely tweaked the twine in its gentle fall to the wooden floor below. The psychological impact of a double-digit lead for some reason kills many a comeback effort and we held off their final push for a 77-67 win.

The crowd once again washed over us. I met my dad, who wrapped me in a hug. "You gave me a real scare starting the fourth quarter!"

"I gave *you* one?" I said with a sigh of relief. "I gave myself one. I learned my lesson though. I promise you that will never happen again! The next time I pull a move like that, the game will be decided."

My mom was wearing a big smile. "Just one more win!" she said. My other brother, Billy, had managed to make it down. He and James Otis found me next for congratulations.

Billy took a moment and looked into my eyes, "Yeah, it hasn't soaked in yet, has it?"

I shook my head, looking around the gymnasium, "No, it hasn't, but it better because I've got more work to do! Is this a fairytale or what?"

"I'll come by at halftime," I shouted back, only to find myself in a hand lock with Benford Frizzell.

"Well, Coach, we're in the finals. Congratulations! All you need now is just one more win. You're in the high cotton. You're rubbing elbows with the big boys now. Buy you a drink, Coach?"

I breathed in the moment. This was a time to celebrate. "I'd love a Dr Pepper."

"Ya know, Coach, if you'd taught these guys any faster, I think you could have beat Bob Hayes!" He shot me a thumbs up and walked away laughing, leaving me to push past cheerleaders and well-wishers before reaching our dressing room, politely excusing myself as much as I could.

When I finally reached our guys, the celebration was still in full force. I let the door slam shut behind me with a clang and saw twelve faces turn towards me. My hands were on my hips, "So, how about those Tigers?"

My team howled as I pumped my fist in the air shouting, "Yes!" over and over until I collapsed onto the bench. Forcing myself back to my feet, I made my way around to each player, congratulating them individually on the victory.

"Okay," I said, "everyone over here and have a seat. You used your brains and your bodies today. You followed our game plan to the letter and the results are on the board. Like they always say, the proof is in the pudding! It's amazing what can be accomplished when everyone is on the same page. This was a total team effort today. We had five guys scoring in double figures today, which lets everybody out there know that all our guys can score at any time. Whoever plays us tomorrow is going to know that they have to come after our whole team if they want to stop us. I am so proud of your execution. We took it to those giants and beat them on the glass. We got forty-five rebounds to their forty-three." I let them cheer before continuing.

"One last, but very important thing. We've dodged a bullet the last two days. In each game we've played, we've had a starter foul out. This is unacceptable. It better be the last time that happens. I'm telling you right now, tomorrow you're gonna play the most aggressive defense you have played this year, but you're also gonna play the smartest defense you've played all year." There were solemn nods and I felt that I might have taken the joy out of what really was an impressive win.

Herman cleared his throat and stood. "Coach, since we did what you said, does this mean that we get to eat those double-meat cheeseburgers?"

I smiled, clapping my hands together. "You bet!"

Smiles were once again showing all around and I breathed a sigh of relief. I pointed to Haywood and Roy. "So, who won the rebound war?"

Roy began shaking his head as a broad smile spread across Haywood's face. "Well, I had eleven rebounds; Roy only got ten." He jabbed Roy in the ribs. "I knew he couldn't beat me!"

Roy just rolled his eyes. "As big and strong as you are, you should have gotten five or six more rebounds than I did anyway."

"Were those scores *with* the rebound you spotted him?" I asked. Haywood's smile vanished while Roy's eyes lit up like a Christmas tree.

I couldn't stop laughing as Roy stood on the bench, both hands raised in fists above his head. "Stronger and faster, my butt!"

Haywood looked like he'd eaten a lemon, "Yeah, yeah, it's just a tie."

"A tie against you? I'll take it!"

Walking toward the dressing room door, I began motioning the guys out. "Okay, fellas, we're gonna watch the next game because we're gonna be playing the winner tomorrow morning in the State Championship!"

Haywood's smile had returned. "I can't wait to play Snook again. They're not gonna beat us twice!"

"*If* they win, you get your wish. If not, we play Krum. Meet me in front of the gym after the game and we'll go get those burgers."

Walking toward the bleachers to meet Curtis, I experienced a totally exhilarating feeling rushing through my chemical makeup. I felt like I was gliding, being pulled through each action effortlessly, like riding a breeze. It was like going to see a thriller—we'd reached the last act, but still didn't know the outcome. As I reached the bleachers, I looked up at Curtis, shaking my head to clear it. "Two down and one to go."

Smiling from ear to ear, Curtis said, "I told you to wear that blue blazer. I'm glad you listened."

"Well, since we're playing for the State Championship tomorrow, I thought I just might go shopping this afternoon and get me a new jacket, just for tomorrow."

Curtis's eyes bugged out. "Over my dead body!"

~~~

With our clipboards out and my team nearby, we watched the game progress intensely.. The early game clearly went Krum's way as they took a nine-point lead to the dressing room at the half. The Krum second half, however, turned out to be a cliffhanger as Snook made a strong run with a great comeback. Led by veterans Ervin See, Cedrick Nix, and Tommie Junek, the Jays slowly began to erase what had become a thirteen-point lead late in the third quarter. Cutting the lead to two points with forty-three seconds left in the game on a fifteen-footer by Junek, the Bluejays had the ball with a chance to tie the score. However, a key steal by Jack Hall and the ensuing court-length layup propelled the Bobcats to a surprising 45-41 upset. As Krum's crowd went wild, I looked at my team's next opponent.

Setting my clipboard down, I looked at Curtis, "Well, what do you think?"

He let out a long sigh. "They're big and they're good on the boards. They've got poise. It's probably gonna be a low-scoring game so we're gonna have to be selective with our shots. We've been pretty good all year at adjusting our play to our opponent; this will just have to be one of those games. We're going to need another great rebounding game like we had this morning. They beat Snook to death on the glass. They're not as athletic as Plainview, but they're just as big and more solid fundamentally. They're just a more polished team. I just hope that they reached their peak today. Beating Snook, maybe they're thinking that trophy is as good as theirs. We may be able to surprise 'em. You're going to need a plan to combat those big guys."

"Plainview was bigger and we somehow managed to out-rebound them. Our goal tomorrow is just to stay close with them on the boards. If we do, I think we have a real good chance."

Curtis nodded, "They remind me a bit of Grapeland—conservative, disciplined, and rugged rebounders."

He was spot on. They were more polished, but their style was very similar. They beat Snook playing that kind of a game, scoring forty-five points. In that warm-up game, we faced that same style of play against Grapeland, scoring forty-four points. I was sure that they'd try to force us to play a low-scoring game. They weren't as athletic. They wouldn't want to run with us so they'd try to slow it down as much as possible.

"If we try to totally rely on our running game, I'd say we we're in big trouble. We just have to show them that we have more than one tactic."

As we walked, Haywood made his way towards me, hanging his head. "I really wanted to play Snook. We owe them one. Now we'll never get the chance."

"They just didn't take care of business today, but we've already got two games scheduled with them next year. So now we've got to focus all our attention on Krum, got it?"

"Yes, sir!"

Soon, it was indeed burger time as the guys enjoyed their promised lunch. Sitting next to me, Fred looked a little down, poking at his food more than eating it. Finally, I forced him to say something.

"Coach, I'm sorry I fouled out today. It's looking like a Pilkington thing—Nubbin yesterday and me today. I promise you, it will not happen again tomorrow."

With that off his chest, he still wasn't eating and I sighed in exasperation. "Come on, son, that burger's not going to hop in your mouth if that's what you're waiting for. What's up?"

He shrugged, "I just realized that tomorrow will be my last game to play in high school. The rest of our starters have at least another year, but this is it for me." His brow furrowed as he skewered a French fry with a toothpick. "I've got to make it my best game ever."

"Fred, can you think of a better time or place or way to finish your career than playing for the State Championship?"

A small smile spread across his face as he shook his head. "Thank you, Coach, for making us believe that we could do this."

"The feeling's mutual."

18

Preparations

Soon we were back in Johnson High School's lobby for a quick practice that I'd managed to schedule. Our driver, Benford Frizzell, was beside me.

"Coach, an observation. We're the big cats—the Tigers—and Krum, they're the little cats—the Bobcats. So why is it that we've got all the little guys on our team and they have all the big guys?" I laughed, shrugging my shoulders.

He sighed, settling back into his chair. "Well, the good news is that we seem to be taking down bigger teams a lot lately. How many teams have we beaten in the playoffs that were bigger than us?"

With a smile, I faced him. "How many playoff games have we played?"

A few minutes later, we were in the gym for the last practice of the year. I had the guys take a knee before we began. I paced before them, trying to collect my thoughts. "The Boston Celtics." I looked over my team."They've won the NBA Championship six years in a row. Even if you're not a Celtics fan, you have to admire and respect that. Do you think they've won all those championships because they have the best players? Sure, they have some really good players, but so does every pro team. So what's the difference between the Celtics and the rest?"

My team was silent, but I had their attention. "The difference, I think, is that each player has a specific role and each one performs his accepted role better than anyone else could. Everyone has a strength, something they do better than any other, and when everyone does his job and plays to his strength, those individual efforts become a fine-tuned machine—a great team. "I don't know which team out there will have the best players and as far as I'm concerned, it doesn't matter. One of the main reasons that you have done so well this year is because every one of you has accepted the specific role that you've been given and performed it to the best of your ability, which for the last two weeks has been pretty close to perfection. I'm proud of what you've done this year and I'm expecting you to play your smartest game of the year tomorrow. Snook was the reigning State Champ and after taking them down, Krum probably thinks that we're just cleanup. They think that this championship already belongs to them. Well, I've got news for them. They're gonna have to play the best they're capable of playing to beat us. But the same is true of us. You all watched Krum today. They aren't here by accident. If you want that win tomorrow, you're going to have to play defense the way you did when you stopped Avoca. You're going to have to rebound the way you did when you beat Washington, and you're going to have to use some-thing we haven't relied on much in this tournament. You're gonna run our half-court offense with precision and discipline. Can we do this? Can we bring it to the guys who denied us our comeback game against Snook?" The cheer was led by Haywood, but it roared from all twelve of my Tigers.

The practice went smoothly and soon we were enjoying a meal at our hotel's dining room. We were welcomed, greeted, and congratulated by Susan, who was thrilled to be serving us for Day Four of our stay. "Another game, another victory! How about that, Coach? You guys play for the State Championship tomorrow morning, that's great! If I didn't have to work tomorrow morning, I'd love to see your game."

We had just started our meal when our cheerleaders walked in. I could tell my team was enjoying their evening meal a little more than usual. Nubbin poked his elbow in his brother's ribs, "The change of scenery is nice."

"Real nice," Fred grinned back.

THE FIRST SEASON

Gary seemed to be in a trance and I had to give him a little slap on the back on the head. "Gary, son, don't strain your eyes; we just might need those tomorrow."

He looked at me with a huge grin, "I'm just enjoying the view."

I just shook my head. "You have a lot to learn about subtlety. When I first looked over at you, I thought you were hypnotized. You didn't even blink for four minutes!" That possum grin was in place. "I'll bet you've got a crick in your neck right now because you were straining so hard to see." Everyone at the table was cracking up, which got a few looks from the cheerleaders. With any luck, they would want to be in on the joke and I might have just helped my kids' love lives a little.

Before paying for the bill, I had a short talk with the restaurant's manager. With a smile on my face, I left an extra ticket with Susan's tip. Her manager was speaking with her as we filed out the door, and I saw a smile brighten over her face as she threw her arms around his neck and turned our way. Our eyes met for a moment and she mouthed the words, "Thank you." I gave a short wave and walked out. We needed all the support we could get tomorrow, and having Susan there would probably be like having four or five regular fans.

We had one last meeting in the lobby and once again I stressed the importance of getting the proper amount of sleep for our last and most important game of the season. "Remember, we have an early pre-game breakfast and a shootaround, so get up there and lights out."

~~~

Back in my room, I finally had some time to call my own after another hectic day. We were only fourteen hours away from playing for the grand prize. I sat in the quiet of my room staring out the window at the Austin sky's emerging sunset. I was trying to get my mind off basketball, even for a short period of time. However, as I scanned the UT campus, it became impossible to imagine anything but the tide of spectators that would be soon walking its sidewalks, making their way to Gregory Gym. Unable to give my mind a rest, I decided to take the elevator downstairs to get something to read. I found a newspaper stand and scanned the articles. Nothing I read helped. Regardless of what it was, eventually my mind reverted back to our game. I wound up pacing the lobby and returning to my room to flick through the channels, hoping that my team wasn't experiencing the same case of nerves that I was wrestling with. I knew that I could coach the game whether I got one hour or eight hours of sleep. I had my game plan and I felt ready to adapt to whatever strategy changes were thrown our way. But if the guys didn't get the rest they needed, that was a different story.

I decided to make my rounds past their rooms to see if I needed to bust any heads, but everything was quiet, so I returned to my room and reluctantly picked up the paper I'd purchased. Suddenly, a door slammed down the hall, followed by the shuffling sound of feet and giggling. I tossed my paper aside and jumped to the door, easing it open, hoping to get a glimpse of someone. *Surely, it couldn't be one of my guys.* Walking down the hall all I could hear was the quiet of the evening, so I was forced to return to my room. About twenty minutes later, I heard the same slam and running feet. I was up like a shot, jerking open my door, only to see someone running through the exit to the stairs. The most important night of rest all year and I had a full-fledged track meet by some idiot in the hallway. I convinced myself that would be the last of it and pushed off the feeling that I should call security and complain.

I got a rude reply about fifteen minutes later when it happened again. Rushing to the door, I threw it open and saw two young girls running down the hall. "What are you doing?" They froze in their steps and slowly turned back towards me. "Do you realize that people are trying to sleep and you're acting like it's New Year's Eve? Look, my team has got a very important game tomorrow and they need to get some sleep. They can't do that with you two running around all night. I would appreciate it if you would go to your room and stay there; otherwise, I'm gonna call security."

The two girls quickly informed me that they weren't the only ones involved, but promised that they wouldn't make any more noise. I softened up a little with their promise, but got the room number of the other two kids involved in case the noise didn't stop.

Nonetheless, I did call the front desk, informing them of the problem. They assured me that they would investigate and take care of it. I finally managed to get to bed about an hour later.

Even without those two wreaking havoc, I had trouble falling asleep as my mind continued to dwell on tomorrow's game. I had just managed to doze off when I heard doors slamming once again. The covers flew off me as I dashed to my door just in time to see a door shut on the other end of the hall. Now I was incensed. As I stalked towards it, I realized it was the same room that the two girls had identified earlier. I rolled up my sleeves and rapped my knuckles on the door. It failed to open. I rapped again. "Hotel security...open up. If you don't, I've got a key."

It took a moment and I heard a whispered argument beyond the wood before the door eased open. With a terrible fake yawn, the kid rubbed his eyes with balled fists. I stuck my finger in his face, "Don't give me that bull!" His eyes grew wide. "I know what you guys have been up to. Obviously I'm not hotel security, but they will be called and you will be identified *right now*. If you so much as *open* this door one more time this evening, guess where you're gonna spend the rest of the night?" I bent over and looked the kid squarely in the eye. "That's right, the Austin City Jail." I heard the second kid gasp behind the door."So you've got two choices here: close the door, lock it, and don't come out the rest of the night or spend the night looking through bars! Do I make myself clear?"

The kid was rigid. "Yes, sir!"

I continued to glare at him. "You're a lot smarter than you look." I waited until I heard the lock turn before returning to my room, assured that we might finally have some peace for the night.

When I finally got back in bed, it was almost two in the morning. I continued to lay in bed, wide awake, a hectic pressure building behind my eyes as the day loomed before me. Reaching into the nightstand, I found the Bible and flipped it open. It fell to Matthew 6:34. "Therefore do not worry about tomorrow. For tomorrow will worry about itself. Each day has enough trouble of its own." I closed the Bible, closed my eyes, and closed that day as I fell asleep.

I rode the elevator as it slowly descended to the lobby. It was five o'clock on Saturday morning, March 4, 1967. I grabbed the paper from the same stall I'd found during my insomniac meanderings and got a table at the coffee shop. Opening the paper to the sports section, I could hardly believe what I saw. There was George Breazeale's column, "Sports by George." I'd been half asleep before I saw the article, but now I was wide-awake. There was a picture of me to go along with virtually every aspect of my life story in basketball.

As I started to read the column, Susan walked over, "Good morning, Coach, how about some coffee?"

Glancing down at my picture and then back up at me she leaned back, putting one hand on her hip. "Well, I didn't realize I was serving coffee to a celebrity!"

"A celebrity? I don't think so."

"Sorry, Coach, I've got news for you: If your team wins this game this morning, you're gonna be a celebrity whether you want to believe it or not." I looked up at her with a big smile as she poured the coffee.

"I've only served your team for four days and I feel like I've known them all my life; I don't think that the world getting to know them a little better is a bad thing at all. They are a great group of guys. I know you're very proud of them." I nodded, cradling the mug between my hands. She couldn't be more right. I felt blessed to be their coach.

"And you can bet the bank that I'm going to be there today, cheering you on. Thank you so much. You have no idea how much this means to me." With a smile, she disappeared back into the kitchen.

A few minutes later, our players started to come in for the most important pre-game meal that we would ever eat.

Roy walked by and rested a hand on my shoulder. "Coach, Curtis wanted me to ask you if that blue blazer is ready for one more game."

"It's ready, I'm ready. The question of the day is 'Are you guys ready?'"

Roy shot me a winning smile. "You know we are. I've been doing some heavy thinking about today's game. If there was a match with a little bobcat against a big ol' tiger, I'd put my money on a tiger, wouldn't you? We're going to send those Bobcats back home—assuming they can still crawl!"

A rush of confidence was swirling around the room as Susan returned bearing our breakfasts. "How did you sleep last night, Roy?" I asked.

"Great."

"All that noise in the hall didn't keep you awake last night?"

Haywood laughed. "Coach, a freight train could've come down the hall and it wouldn't have affected Roy."

"How about you, Haywood?"

"Oh, Coach, I heard it, but I just turned over and went back to sleep."

Fred leaned in from across the table. "The one you'd better worry about is Herman. He didn't sleep well at all." I finally noticed that our long-range man was missing from the table.

Fred must have seen my eyes searching the group. "He told me to tell you that he's really tired and needs some more rest. He wants you to call him."

Walking over to the house phone at the front desk, my stomach was knotting. *Great, my best outside shooter is going to be below par in the most important game of his life.* Herman answered groggily.

"Herman, you okay?"

"Coach, all that noise, I couldn't fall asleep all night. I'm so tired. I don't feel like I slept at all."

Wonderful, the game of all games is three hours away and this has to happen. "Herman, just slip on some clothes and get down here and eat. You've got to get something in your stomach and then you can go back to your room and rest until we leave."

A few minutes later, a weary-eyed Herman tottered into the restaurant and sat down for pancakes. "Looks like I'm the only one that couldn't fall asleep. I heard you out there corralling those idiots in the hall. Every time I was just about to fall asleep, they'd wake me up again. I heard you get on them the last time." A tired smile was spreading across his face. "You had those guys scared stiff. Fellas,

I'm not sure if you noticed, but we're eating breakfast with the new head of hotel security!"

Nubbin had been reading my paper from the across the table and forced his last bite down in a hurry. "Forget about hotel security, we're eating breakfast with a celebrity!"

Gary pushed back his chair from the table, brushing himself off, glancing up and down the guys. "Well, I didn't want to make a big deal about it, but if me eating breakfast with you guys means that much..."

Nubbin rolled his eyes. "Not you, Gary! I'm talking about Coach. Come look at this. It's got a picture and everything."

With that, all the guys crowded around, looking at the newspaper. Gary let out a low whistle. "Wow, Coach, can I shake your hand? I've never shook hands with a celebrity before. I promise I'll never wash it again."

I growled at the laughing crowd. "If you don't get your butts back in your chairs and finish your breakfast, I'm gonna shake more than your hands!"

~~~

Breakfast concluded and all my players back in their rooms, I sat in the silence and seclusion of my room contemplating just what was about to take place—the fact that in a little over two hours I would be walking on that floor, sitting on that bench, coaching my team in the game of their lives. My mind felt like it'd been through the wringer. I sat there in the early morning quiet, trying to clear my head, when the phone rang.

It was my dad calling to wish me a good morning and to ask if we were ready. I told him we were, talked about our game plan, and shared a prayer. At the end, he told me something that stuck with me. "I know you want to win this game. Heck, I want you to win this game. But regardless of the outcome, I want you to know how incredible this team is. I've been talking to a lot of people and we continue to be amazed at how close your team has become. I'm not sure if you know it, but they are together a lot more than just during practice. It means a whole lot to everybody to see your kids come together like that—and I mean more than just to your school. I guess I'm just trying to say, we're all proud of you, son." I was choked up, and though I tried to thank him, the words were stuck in my throat.

"By the way, that was a great article in the paper. I enjoyed reading every word of it. I'll let you go, son. You know that your mom and I will be praying for you today, just like we have been this whole season. Good luck."

My dad indeed was a very special man. You always knew where he stood regardless of what the issue was. Hardly a day went by that I didn't feel his influence help me down the road. Suddenly, my head was clear, my focus absolute, and I was glad he'd never stopped being my dad, even as I grew to be an adult.

~~~

The clock kept ticking and soon it was time to head for Gregory Gym. The early morning sun had already made its appearance as we slowly drove our way through the Austin city streets. A select few of the area's deciduous trees were showing beginning signs of spring as their buds were just starting to open. The short ride from the hotel seemed to take a little longer than the last two days. We arrived at the same time as our previous two mornings and slowly walked up the long flight of steps leading to the entrance.

Reaching the top of the stairs, there he was—the same security guard that thought I was a player. "Well, Coach, you've aged a lot the last three days. I don't think I'll confuse you with a player again.

"Thanks, I feel like I've put on ten years these last three days."

He laughed. "Like I told you the other day, I'll be pulling for you, old man!" He waved goodbye as we headed for the dressing room.

It was a little over an hour before the start of the game and that spacious old gym was virtually empty as the fans had yet to enter. "Fellas, get your uniforms on. We'll go out in a few minutes for some more pre-game shooting, just like before."

My players suited up for the last time of the season. Sitting there, slowly lacing up their purple shoestrings on their canvas Converse All-Stars, I looked at Fred and Nubbin. "Pilkingtons!" They looked up. "Don't either of you *dare* get in foul trouble again.

Your services are needed on the floor, not on the bench." Nubbin shot a smiling thumbs up while Fred just nodded solemnly. "There's no way I'm gonna spend any time on the bench in my last game. I want it to be one I'll never forget." The early bird fans had begun to trickle in as we took the floor for our warm-up shots.

As I walked back over toward our bench, I looked into the face of Phil Ransopher, the long-time public address announcer for the tournament. He shook my hand. "Coach, how do you feel?"

I shook my head. "I haven't been this nervous since...well, at least since yesterday's game."

He laughed. "Yeah, that Plainview Washington team made a little comeback on you guys."

"Little? They cut our lead from twenty to eight in a flash."

He pursed his lips together. "Coach, years ago I was a freshman right here at the University of Texas. At the last minute, Bill Whitmore, the scheduled PA announcer for the 1950 State Tournament was unable to do the tournament. Officials were at a loss as to who they could get for a substitute when one of them saw me folding towels in the gym. He knew that I had done some PA announcing when I was in high school. The next thing I knew I was behind the mic—a kid doing a man's job." He leaned in close. "Trust me, I know nerves. How old are you, son?"

"I turned twenty-four on Wednesday."

"Well, I was eighteen that year and this is the seventeenth straight year that I've done this tournament. Sometimes doors are opened for you when you feel you aren't ready for them. They won't wait for you. Open doors close again. You've just got to keep rushing forward as they appear. You've opened a bunch of doors in your coaching career already, don't stop pushing now."

"Thanks." We shook hands one last time and I started walking back toward our bench.

"Wait up, Coach." I turned back to face him. "I need to get your approval. How does this sound as the introduction for your team?" He went into a simulation of his announcing voice, "Introducing, from deep east Texas, it's the Kennard Tigers with a record of 41-4, coached by a very nervous first-year coach, *Jittery Johnny Carter!*"

"I've been trying to hide the fact that I'm nervous since the playoffs started and so far my game face has camouflaged it rather nicely, I think. Now you're about to tell eight thousand people that I'm jittery!" Still laughing, I wanted his assurance. "Come on now, you're not gonna do that to me are you?"

"Coach," his big smile fell away as he began backing away towards the officials' table. "You never know what's gonna come out of my mouth when it's game time."

I walked back to our bench with a smile. *Surely he wouldn't introduce me that way.* My smile faded. *Would he?*

I was soon joined on the bench by my two brothers, Billy and James Otis. Billy looked at me, ''Any new wrinkles in this game you wanna fill us in on?"

I shrugged. "Not really. We're just gonna have to be real patient. I've got the feeling that it could boil down to just how effective our half-court offense is."

James Otis was looking down court at Krum. "How about the rebounding battle? Those guys are huge compared to your team."

"I know. Fortunately, the game yesterday was good practice for today." I looked at my team still warming up. "One guy I'm worried about though is Herman. He got very little sleep and his shot doesn't appear to be falling like it normally does. We had a lot of noise in the hallway at the hotel and I think he's the only guy that didn't get his normal rest."

"Great!" Billy said. "It would have to be your best shooter."

As our players continued their pregame warm-up, a severe case of nervous energy was starting to work over me as I walked up and down the sideline. When I got to Herman, I called over my sharp-shooting guard. "Well, how's your shot falling, son?"

He shook his head. "Not as good as yesterday, but this is practice, Coach. I shoot better when they count."

To a large degree, the outcome of our game today was hinging on whether or not Herman had his regular game. Watching his shot carefully during our shooting practice did not give me much assurance as the ball clanged against the rim again and again. Herman was definitely well below par. I called my guys over as the shooting period came to an end.

Standing before my team that one last time, I could only pray for strength from above. I tried to open my mouth and deliver my pre-game pep talk, but nothing seemed to want to come out. I tried to feign calm as I walked to the water cooler to get a drink and took the opportunity for a deep, deep breath. Once again, I tried to give my pre-game speech. This time the words slowly began to fill the dressing room. "This has been one fantastic ride." There were nostalgic nods around the room. "A season that none of us will ever forget. We've covered a lot of territory and gone down many roads since that opening game in Zavalla back in October. It's hard for me to comprehend how much you have improved since the beginning of the season. Thank you for listening, thank you for your burning desire to improve, and thank you for allowing me to show you what it takes to get where we are right now. This is it." I squeezed the shoulders of Gary and Roy on either side of me and saw what it sent around the group, almost like we were all one animal.

"This is the last game of the year. This is the way every team wants to finish the season. You know, when this season started, there were probably five hundred teams in the state hoping to be in the position that you're in. Now there are two. The question is, 'Are we going to execute our game plan?" There was loud confirmation.

"I want to go over their personnel one more time. Ricky Knight, six-foot-four and averaging over twenty points a game. He's a solid player and an all-State candidate. You're going to show him some hard-nosed Kennard Tiger defense and today he's going to have a tough time scoring at all. You hold him to half his average and we take this game. Jackie Sandifer, six-foot-three, another good player. These two guys got twenty-five rebounds between them against Snook. You keep those two off the glass, cut their rebounds. Other starters are Jackie Hall, a junior guard, Allen Howard, and Donnie Merrifield. They're a very good team. They're 36-5. This is their fourth trip to the State Tournament and their second time to be in the State finals.

"Are these guys hungry for a title? You'd better believe they are. Are they solid fundamentally? There's no doubt about it. Are they confident after beating Snook? You bet—maybe a little too confident. You've got to put the fear of doubt in their minds in order for them to accept the fact that they can lose. This is exactly what you're going to do this morning. Let them know early that if they want to win this game they're gonna have to do a whole lot more than they ever imagined. They have an edge in height, so what else is new? We have an edge in quickness. I want you to look for the fast break and when the opportunity presents itself, go with it. But if it's not there, it's time to run some good, half-court offense and ours is good. Just go out there and execute and you'll be fine. Just remember, take your time, make your passes quick, and be selective on your shots. This is the key to half-court offense. Make every possession a quality one. You've done this many times through the season. There's no reason why you can't go out there one more time and do it again. Any questions? Everybody take a knee and grab a hand."

The sound of silence now engulfed our dressing room as those twelve young men knelt in prayer for our very last game of the year.

Coach Johnny Carter

19

State

As we jogged onto the playing court, the Kennard entourage behind our bench had massively grown in numbers and exploded with a totally electrifying standing ovation. I walked onto the floor and looked over at those absolutely delirious fans forming a sea of living purple. This fairytale season of one climax after another had led us to the very top of the mountain. The grand steeple chase was about to take place and now there was only one team left in our way. One team would be crowned as the State Champion and begin a celebration to be remembered for generations, while the other would be remembered as a worthy competitor, but only a champion that almost was.

Walking in front of our bench, all I could hear was cheering. One particular fan with a powerful foghorn voice could probably be heard in San Marcos. "Go get 'em, Coach! Just one more time! We're behind you all the way!"

I couldn't help but smile as I sat down on our bench. Watching my guys warming up, one thought entered my mind—that same thought that was there most of our games: I probably would be much more comfortable out there with a uniform on my back, shooting baskets with them, than sitting on this bench. But comfort wasn't what had gotten us this far and it was time to get focused.

There was less than a minute left as our players began to head to the bench. You could almost smell the energy as the crowd was engulfed with anticipation. The Kennard fans excitedly awaited the approaching moment of truth. It was almost game time. All the hype, the talk, and the preparation was history. It was time to put our plan into motion and let actions speak for themselves. It was time to lay all the cards on the table and let two momentum-driven teams play their hands.

Just prior to the start of this colossal clash, the Kennard huddle was emotion-filled as the mounting tension continued to build. We'd been here again and again, each new match replacing the last as the biggest game we'd ever played. Like dominoes, they'd fallen before us, now sweet memories, but I could see their impact in my team's eyes reflecting back at me. Each match was like a stroke across a whetstone, sharpening us into the team we had become that day. Looking across the Gregory Gym floor at the massive crowd in the background, I realized that would be our last pregame huddle.

"Fellas, everything we've worked on from day one led us to this point. Look out there at that crowd. Do you know how many players, former players, coaches, and former coaches are sitting out there wishing they could trade places with us right now? Thousands. I know because last year, in fact the last several years, I've been right up there sitting beside them. Let's go out there and enjoy this game because, one day, it's going to be you guys sitting up there. Live this game, this moment; have no regrets! Look, every one of you knows what your job is by now. So go out there, stay focused, and implement our game plan. Let's take care of business!"

About that time, Phil Ransopher began to welcome the crowd to the 1967 Class B State Championship game. I heard him begin the introductions. "From north Texas, with a record of 36-5, it's the Krum Bobcats of Coach Bob Derryberry." I pulled out of the huddle and looked over at Phil, waiting for the ovation for the Bobcats to die down. Just before he introduced our team, he looked right at me. He was really going to do it. I could see a smile spreading across his lips. With that familiar voice rippling through the packed house, he winked at me. "And from the pine tree country of east Texas, with a record of 41-4, it's the Kennard Tigers of Coach Johnny Carter in this his very first season!" I let out a sigh of relief as the crowd roared to its feet. We threw our hands in the middle and shouted for the Tigers. It was time to throw it up and get this thing started.

THE FIRST SEASON

Awaiting the opening tip, our highly partisan fans were now standing. Those very loyal followers just kept dramatically increasing in numbers with every playoff game. Today would be no exception because Pete and Deloris Hammons, two of our most devoted fans, had driven all night from St. Louis just to be here. I smiled as Pete walked in front of our bench. Looking at me through his travel-weary eyes, he stopped, shook my hand, and said, "You can start the game now; we finally made it. There's no way I was going to miss this. Good luck, Coach."

The clock on the side of the gym read 9:00 a.m. It was time for the two veteran officials, Mr. Scott and Mr. Kelsen, to take over. They would become both judge and jury for the time span of a little over an hour, ending in the inevitable execution. I hoped it wouldn't be *our* necks on the chopping block. Two teams left standing, everybody else having already been sent home with a heartbreaking end to an unrealized dream. With the crowd anxiously anticipating the start, there was a buzz in the air and hope in the minds of every fan that their team might take home the title. Eight players surrounded the center circle while the other two flexed their muscles in preparation for the opening tip.

Our hopes turned into reality as we started the game from the opening toss with a rush and for the third straight game of the tournament, had an amazing start. Galloping out of the gates, we sent the Bobcats the exact message I was hoping for. We let them know that they were going to have to work if they wanted to win. Herman, Fred, and Roy all connected baskets early in the game and once again we were in control at the outset. When Herman hit his second shot of the quarter, my worries about his lack of sleep were eased considerably. The importance of his productivity for the success of our team could not be overstated. But just like he said, he seemed to be doing just fine with the pressure on.

Krum opened the game with a pressing defense. On seeing that, I immediately stood up and signaled for our press break, shouting instructions. It worked like a charm. Their press failed to rattle us. Executing our equal and opposite theory with the box formation, we selectively made the proper passes to negate their defense. Precision was the key and we'd honed that skill nicely over the season. Nubbin took the ball on the dribble and looked down court. Seeing no one open, he quickly passed cross court to Haywood, who in turn hit Roy, cutting from the backside to the middle. Roy took the pass, pivoted, and found Fred open, coming to the ball. Knowing that Herman was open before he ever received the ball, Fred caught the pass and zipped it to him in one motion. His picture-perfect pass hit Herman wide-open, already squaring up from the right wing. His fifteen-foot wrist flip soon became two points on the board. It was Herman's seventh point of the first quarter.

We stormed through the Bobcat press like a tornado, racing to a 17-9 lead at the end of the first quarter. The over-confidence factor that we thought might enter into the picture definitely seemed to be in the mix for Krum. However, our surprise element would soon become a non-factor. We'd sent them an early morning wake-up call, a rude reminder that I was sure would have them more than ready to step up their game.

As the second quarter started, it became very obvious early on that not only had those sleeping giants awakened, but there was a new determination defining their new direction. They started the second quarter with fire in their eyes and immediately began to show a dominance that was totally absent early on. Krum's superiority in height began to come to the forefront as six-foot-four Ricky Knight and six-foot-three Jackie Sandifer started to dominate the boards. They began to display just why they were in the State finals as they not only tied the score, but went into halftime with a 29-26 lead. Having just put twenty points on the board, the Bobcats left the floor riding an emotional high to a thunderous ovation from their fans. They could sense that their fourth trip to the State Tournament might just be their first heretofore elusive State Championship. The favored north Texans had stolen the momentum, the lead, and the positive outlook that we'd enjoyed in the first quarter.

Carefully attempting to put my thoughts into words, I looked into the negative eyes of a group of downcast players. Their heads hung and shoulders were sagging. I knew that if I didn't do something to dispel the despair engulfing the dressing room, we wouldn't stand a chance in the next quarter. With a smokescreen of negativity staring me right in the face, I wondered just what I could say to get my team refocused. The sound of my foot stomping against the ground rang off the lockers of the dressing room.

"Get your heads up! I don't want to see anybody's head down again! They probably played the best they could play that quarter and we had one of our worst. How far ahead are they?" Roy raised three fingers above his head. "Remember last week in the Regional finals? We were eleven points behind late in the third quarter against Avinger and all that did was inspire us to change gears. The result of which was all this!" I extended my arms, looking around the room. "That's right! That's exactly why we're playing here today in the State Championship game!

"Okay, let's look at the second half. Number one, we have got to do a better job on the glass. They beat you by five rebounds and there lies a big difference in the half. Are these guys better jumpers than we are? I don't think so. They're just bigger. Plainview Washington was not only bigger than Krum but they were far better jumpers and who won that war on the glass?" The response was a faint murmur. I shook my head. "Who did?"

This time there were at least words in the mix. "We did."

"*Who* did?"

Now with Haywood leading the team, some smiles were starting to show through. "*We did!*"

Now was the time to clinch it. Their spirit was back up and now it needed a backbone to hold up the second-half battle on the boards. "Do you think these guys worked as hard on rebounding this year as we did? There's no way. I can promise you that. Why do you think I put you through all those weight vest workouts in the first place? I didn't do it so you would have your heads down right now, thinking you can't rebound with them! Look, every one of you is stronger, tougher, and a much better rebounder today than you have ever been in your lives. So go out there the second half and show me what we're capable of, what we've been training for. Look, you don't even have to out-rebound these guys to win this game, but you've got to close the gap and get your share!"

I looked at Roy, who was sharing a smile with Haywood. "Do you guys hear me? Just what do you plan on doing about it, Roy?"

Roy's chest puffed out. ''All I can say is that they had better work extra hard blocking me off the boards because I plan on making a rebounding run the second half!"

"That's what I'm talking about. Remember, you've got to aggressively position your body every time they shoot! I don't mean every other time, I mean *every time!* More rebounds equals more chances to score. If you don't, they very well could maintain the lead that they have right now. Are you going to let this happen?" I said that looking right at Haywood and Fred.

Haywood responded, saying, "We hear you, Coach. We'll take care of business this second half, right Fred?"

"You've got that right. Coach, you're about to see a difference in the second half We'll get our share of the rebounds."

"That's more like it. Another thing, they're running a 1-2-2 zone." I pointed at Roy and Fred. "When we run our overload on offense, if you don't feel open, step out one or two steps toward the ball. Make it a shorter and easier entry pass. Herman, if you're open on that corner offense, stick it! That's a high percentage shot for you. Remember, I want to see patience and when you're sure of an opening, I want quick passes. I want you to work for that good shot and you'll pick that defense apart. Defensively, we're gonna stay with our 2-1-2. You've done a heck of a job on Ricky Knight with that. As a matter of fact, I don't think he's even managed to score.

"I know they've slowed down the pace of this game, but look for the break on defensive rebounds. If it's there, kick it into high gear and go. We need to get some cheap transition baskets and utilize our advantage in overall team speed. Any questions? Look, we've overcome a lot of adversity this year and you've met virtually every challenge we've had to face. Well, guess what? We have a big second half facing us and I personally challenge you to go out there and take this game over. Reverse what they did to you in the second quarter. They've got their confidence back and it's up to you to take it away from them. Oh, one more thing: We have sixteen minutes left in this game, but we'll have a lifetime to talk about it, so give it everything you've got! Get your hands in here. One, two, three, let's go!"

You never know what effect a half-time motivational speech has on a team until you resume play. Many halftime speeches evolve into a sounds good, means nothing oration. I could only hope that what I'd said had registered with them. I really felt like our level of play would be significantly upgraded this last half, but feeling something is going to happen and actually seeing it take place are two entirely different ball games.

THE FIRST SEASON

Ralph Waldo Emerson once wrote, "What lies behind us and what lies before us are tiny matters compared to what lies within us." What we were attempting to achieve at that point was definitely within us and I knew that my team would do everything humanly possible to win this game. I just hoped and prayed that what they had left was enough to get the job done. Their effort was all I could ask for and I hoped my words had relayed the confidence I had in them and awakened some of the determination that had gotten us that far. I had witnessed the heart and soul that had grown within the team as it matured and I'd been growing up as a coach alongside them, step by step. Despite everyone's kind words, I knew that my coaching in the State finals was definitely putting the cart before the horse. If we were going to make it, our team's unity would have to overcome both player and coach inexperience. And why not? That unity had carried us to that point, allowing us to somehow overcome all the tension and side-step a myriad of favorites along the way.

~~~

As we headed back to the floor for the second half, once again I had more than used the allotted time, so once again there was no time left for warm-up shots. It was the third straight game in the tournament so it had become old hat for my team. I shrugged it off. Why change what's worked so far? With our issue of depth and lack of substitution, the extra rest they got at halftime was probably warranted. After all, the next sixteen tension-filled minutes would require all the energy that we possessed in our bodies. We would indeed find out just what was within us as the State Championship was riding on every decision and action that we made.

The true character of a team usually shows, sometimes dramatically, in the face of adversity and without a doubt, we had reached that point. We had handled pressure-packed situations like that many times before, but the stakes were higher than anything we'd ever come across. Momentum is a strange thing and it is indeed difficult to reverse the flow once it starts rushing downhill. Krum had the momentum in the second quarter, forcing us to fight an uphill battle, but we got a reprieve when the halftime buzzer sounded. It was like a breath of fresh air and at least temporarily had stopped the bleeding. It was an extended free timeout that we desperately needed and couldn't have come at a better time for our reeling team.

Unfortunately, the second half didn't start the way we'd planned. Jackie Sandifer slipped through our defense at the very beginning of the third quarter for an easy layup to put Krum up 31-26. I'd hoped the halftime break would cool off Bob Derryberry's fine-tuned team, but at least for now, it looked to be just the opposite. Like molten steel, their period of cooling had only made them stronger. With the Krum crowd continuing to fan the momentum the Bobcats had gained in the second quarter, it appeared that they were picking up right where they left off, their smoothly operating engine now on cruise control. All they could see up ahead was a sign post which read, *Full speed ahead to the State Championship.*

A basket by our team was now a necessity. We didn't want them to score two or three baskets unanswered because they already had the momentum of a freight train and it appeared to be accelerating! Our prayers were shortly answered as Fred hit a big layup to temporarily quiet their crowd. I came off the bench with a fist pump and an enthusiastic, "Yes!" I knew just how important that basket was. That basket by our only senior starter eased the pressure while giving my guys proof that the task before us was not as impossible as it seemed.

Defending the basket very well the next time down the floor, our 2-1-2 zone paid some immediate dividends as Fred rebounded, whipped a pass to Herman, who in turn found Roy on the run for another layup, bringing our score to thirty, just one point down with six minutes and eighteen seconds left in the third quarter. The Kennard crowd was back in the game and was making up for the cheering they'd missed out on during the second quarter. Seeing the team that they had ignited to a great comeback in the Regional finals, they shouted their approval, sensing their Tigers were making a move, getting ready to pounce.

The quarter proceeded with both teams answering basket for basket. With two minutes left in the third quarter, our half-court offense, with quick passes of precision, again opened Fred for another jumper. With a spinning swish, his shot ripped the cords, giving us the lead for the first time since the latter stages of the second quarter.

Krum was not about to be outdone and as the final seconds of the third quarter ticked away, we traded baskets yet again, both teams walking off the floor to their respective benches with the score tied. What had appeared a few minutes earlier to be the Bobcats' game was now a toss-up all over again.

In our huddle at the end of three quarters, I could sense a little more positivity than I saw starting the second half. We had successfully defended the basket, holding them to nine points. Since they had scored twenty in the second quarter, that was a major victory. Looking right at Nubbin, I said, *"D* is the key!"

"You've got that right, Coach!"

"Look, we held them to nine points in the first quarter and nine in the third quarter. You hold them to the single digits one more time and we're gonna take this thing. They are really sagging in on Roy and Fred, so Herman, it may be your time." Knowing the way the defense was playing, I just wanted to remind Herman that he had the green light with total freedom to shoot that open corner shot. I also wanted him to know that I had complete confidence in him taking those long-range ones too. For him, those were still high percentage. His eyes lit up when I said it and I could tell that if he could see some open air, he was going to take it.

Soon we were back on the floor to start the fourth and final quarter. That was it—the final quarter of the final game of the season. I took a deep breath and pushed the nostalgia aside. We had eight minutes to make or break us. Just as I had said in the huddle, their defense was all over Roy and Fred, so the ball went to Herman, who was open from the far right corner. He squared up, flicked the wrist, and the ball rotated straight toward the goal. It was beautiful, a shot you know was going in long before it reached the peak of its arc. Coming off the bench with a premature clinched, raised fist, I watched the ball spinning toward the rim. There it was, a magical mesh of orange through orange as his shot cut the cords with a swish of sweetness, giving us the lead at 40-38.

On the first row, my dad wouldn't let our following take a seat again. Waving them back up whenever they stopped cheering, his hat in hand, he swung his arm over his head, leading our choir. On the other end of the court, our defense kicked in and got a stop and a quick turnover. Running the same play on the opposite side, there was Herman, again squaring up. As soon as he shot, I was off the bench, about to give another early fist pump. His soft-spinning one-hander arched a semi-circular path toward the net and tickled the twine on its descent.

Just like that, we had a four-point lead with six minutes and thirty-six seconds on the clock. Krum called a quick timeout because they could sense the game getting away from them. The Kennard crowd was now exploding with eager approval in synchronized, unscripted solidarity!

After the timeout, to Coach Bob Derryberry's credit, Krum came back strong. Ricky Knight finally scored his first basket of the morning on a turnaround jumper for two and then made a free throw for one, slicing our lead to a single point. After we failed to score the next time down the floor, they brought it back and Jack Hall put them right back in front, 43-42. Krum's crowd was collectively cheering, hoping that this was the last momentum change of the game. It was our time to call a timeout as the Bobcats had stolen our thunder.

"Okay," I said, "we had our run and now they've had theirs. It's our time again. Look for Roy or Fred inside if they come out to cover Herman. If they don't, well, you know what to do."

With the crowd on the edge of their seats, we resumed play by working the ball patiently around the perimeter, eventually getting the ball to Roy. His patented turnaround fade-way jumper arched over the outstretched arms of the Krum defenders. The shot somehow went right through that maze of meshed hands before gently kissing the rim where it began a soft, smooth, merry-go-round ride around the rim's perimeter. Roy's shooter's touch marshmallowed round and round, touching all sides of the net as it spiraled down to the delight of the Kennard followers. We had just recaptured the lead. For the next few minutes, it was all defense as the ball changed hands again and again without scoring. However, the next time Krum got possession they got the ball to Knight for a short jumper and were back in the lead 45-44.

Just as I had feared, their talented top scorer had finally come out of his cave after three quarters of hibernation and Krum was reaping the reward of his rebirth, sensing a possible victory. The lead had zigzagged several times that last quarter and it appeared that whoever had the ball last might very well win the game. Working the ball with quick passes around the outside of Krum's 1-2-2 zone, we looked for an opening. Eventually we got the ball to reliable Roy inside. Using all the finesse and athleticism in his short body, the junior post man made an incredible move and put up a soft jumper that somehow found the bottom of the net. His soft swisher once again sent our fanatical fans right through the Gregory Gym roof.

Unfortunately, it didn't take Krum long to retaliate as they brought the ball down, got it to their all-State candidate Ricky Knight once again and he promptly put his team right back on top. Knight had just scored the biggest basket of the morning, his seventh of the quarter after being shut out for the first three. Krum was riding his wide shoulders right to a State Championship.

This pressure-packed seesaw game was now going into the last precious minute of action with Krum holding on to a precarious 47-46 lead. With the crowd reacting with every play, it looked like the game would go right down to the wire. Attempting to create a crease in their fired-up defense was indeed a tall order. The shot that we shortly took failed to connect, slowly rolling harmlessly off the side of the basket. Players shot into the air, arms outstretched, grasping for the ball. With the most crucial rebound of the game and the season, using his cat-quick feet, Roy aggressively positioned himself on the offensive glass. When the rebound came down, he skyrocketed with a superhuman leap between the much taller Bobcats. He said it would be his quarter to rebound and as his five-foot- nine frame shot past the towering Bobcat post men, he ripped a monster of an offensive rebound out of the air. Coming back down, he was only half done. Having just gotten the biggest rebound of our season, he was now about to attempt to score our biggest basket. With a determined look in his eyes and free-flowing confidence surging through his veins, Roy's feet barely touched the floor before he was squared up.

With six-foot-four Ricky Knight and six-foot-three Jackie Sandifer's extended arms casting giant shadows on my little post man, he dramatized a pump fake that would have made Robert Redford smile. Ricky went for it and as he came back down off balance, Roy followed up with a soft post shot that somehow got past all those arms and hands. The crowd was standing in anxious anticipation as all eyes watched the trajectory of Roy's possibly game-deciding shot. With the morning angels keenly guiding its flight, his prayer shot spiraled through the intense-filled air and landed right in that coveted halo ten feet above the floor, stretching the strings as it fell to the floor. We had gained the lead, hopefully for the last time. The gratifying eruption of our crowd certainly gave the impression that they thought that was the game-deciding basket. The thunderous roar that came from them far exceeded anything previous, rattling my bench on the floor. Raising the decibel level for the State Championship game to an all-time high, the noise of the crowd from the Kennard side was now so intense that I was sure the spectators on the top row would have ringing in their ears long after the game's conclusion. Sound waves of joy were literally bouncing off the walls as our crowd attempted to propel us right to a State Championship on energy alone.

That was the good news. The bad news was that it was Krum's ball with fifty seconds left. The way the last three minutes had gone, it was now their time to score. A Bobcat timeout was called. Our huddle was ecstatic, feeding off our delirious followers. With a forceful tone of voice and a fiery look in my eyes, I made a positive, but passionate plea. "Look, if you're ever gonna play the best defense that you can play, *now* is that time.

This is the key possession of the game. You hold them here and it could well be our game."

With his competitive juices flowing, Haywood looked around the circle, his head bobbing and voice full of emotion. "It's *our* game, let's do it right now. Let's put them away!"

Wiping sweat from his forehead, Nubbin was the last to put his hand in the middle. "Defense, fellas! *D* is the key!"

Inbounding the ball, Krum was now facing the most ferocious defense that we were capable of playing. Because of our hard-nosed, in-your-face pressure, they were forced to take a shot that they really didn't want and when it missed the mark, bouncing high off the rim, we got the rebound. I had already instructed my team to go into our delay game and we were soon in the process of running some clock. With thirty-six seconds left, Haywood was sent to the foul line. Our mass of muscle wing man had gone ten for eleven at the charity stripe

224

for the Tournament and with that kind of success rate, it seemed like they had just fouled the wrong guy. Haywood's shot was nothing but net, igniting our crowd again as they sent another blast of sound bouncing off the Gregory Gym rafters.

It would take yet one more super defensive stop on our part. We once again geared our defense up several notches as Krum had one more chance to make a shot and tie the score. "Intensity" was the keyword and once again we refused to give them a good shot. When they missed, Roy again climbed through the air for yet another huge rebound. He was soon fouled with eleven ticks left on the clock. There was an eerie tone of uncertainty looming in the air, particularly for the Krum fans as my little-big man slowly made his way to the line with a chance to ice the game.

With the Krum followers sending out a barrage of noise, attempting to break his concentration, Roy took a deep breath, bent his knees, and flipped the wrist. The ball clanged off the rim, bouncing to the backboard and off the right, our first miss from the foul line that day. Now the Krum crowd was really into it, hoping for another miss, full knowing that they were intensifying the pressure on Roy's second attempt. Roy looked over to me on the bench. He looked worried—an emotion I couldn't remember ever seeing on his face before. Knowing full well that Roy was a very good free throw shooter, I stood up, clapping my hands and nodding my head, trying to give him as much confidence as possible. He gave me a nod and turned back to the basket, closing his eyes and letting out a deep breath. Toeing the line for the biggest free throw of his life, Roy took the ball from the official. With his eyes focused on the rim, he dribbled the ball a couple of times before cocking it back. Staring at the rim with determination, he took a deep breath. With all the proper fundamentals and technique of a confident free throw shooter, he released the ball with the soft, spinning look of a perfect shot. This was our chance to put the icing on the cake, the ball spun forward, the picture of perfection until it struck the rim, rolling off to the side. Roy stood dumbfounded; I had to shout to bring him back into the game as players exploded into motion. Getting a huge rebound, Krum's earlier frustration now fishtailed into elation as they caught a reprieve and a third chance to tie the score.

With time slipping away, a quick outlet pass was made up the floor as Krum, out of necessity, uncharacteristically tried to hurry up the floor. Only eight seconds were left in the game as Jack Hall raced up the floor, dribbling toward mid court. Showing an uncanny sixth sense of being in the right spot well before the fact, Nubbin intuitively cut him off. Duplicating his late game heroics in the Regional finals just one week before, our secretary of defense was about to do it again. Demonstrating his shadowlike reaction time, Nubbin took that cat-quick big step, forcing what appeared to be a game-deciding double dribble. In a game of so many big plays, Nubbin had just stolen the show as the sound of the ref's whistle became the turning point. He had just made the defensive play of his life, giving us the ball with eight ticks left on the clock. For the second time in a week, Nubbin had turned the tide of the championship game. His superior defensive prowess had just taken away what appeared to be Krum's last chance.

We quickly called a timeout to set up our inbound play. Our team could feel it now. "Look," my voice shaking with excitement, "you execute what I'm about to tell you and this game is ours. When we inbound the ball, they are gonna try hard to foul immediately. I want quick passes. Don't keep the ball in your hands long enough for them to even have a *chance* to foul. The guy with the ball is almost always the guy fouled in this situation so don't give them time to do it. If you don't have the ball, set yourself up to be a receiver. Run that V-cut, then break to the ball. Whatever you do, don't stand there and wait for it to come to you. Go after it hard! Tell yourself that's *my* pass and *nobody...that's* right...nobody is gonna take that ball from me. Look, we want the clock to run and real quick passes will keep it moving. Let's go out there right now and finish the job. Is that clear, sports fans?" My guys could feel it and they were smiling as our huddle broke.

Nubbin stayed for a second longer, looking me in the eyes. "Coach, we take care of business right now and another favorite bites the dust!"

Our crowd was keyed up. They didn't need my father's help, they couldn't sit still if they tried. Their anxiety had reached an all-time high and they were barely holding back from rushing the floor. Inbounding the basketball while following my instructions, we effectively worked the ball like a hot potato. They tried desperately to foul, but failed again and again as the ball whizzed around the court. We ran seven precious seconds off the clock before they finally fouled Nubbin with only one second left. With a big smile, Nubbin calmly walked to the charity stripe.

The ref offered him the ball, but instead of taking it, he looked at me, then went stone-faced and pumped his fist in the air as he'd seen me do over and over through the year. I couldn't help but laugh. He took the ball and toed the line. The serious faces of our fans looked on as my left-handed defensive player bounced the ball a couple of times. He flipped his wrist. The ball came off his fingertips, arching a shot of spinning seams and leather, heading straight toward the basket. With an all-important follow-through, he looked down the barrel of his arm, pointing straight toward the rim as he watched the goal, awaiting the verdict. The entire season raced through my head, seeing those kids' faces for the first time at registration, watching them strive through each challenge, and coming to understand the hearts that pushed them to excellence. The ball reached the top of its arc and began its descent. I held my breath. The sound of the gym faded away. My hands clenched as I watched the ball pass right through the basket, quivering the cords with a soft, sweet swish as it dropped to the wooden floor below.

Sound exploded all around me as the crowd went crazy. The play-by-play announcer was shouting into his microphone, "It's good! It's good! James Pilkington just iced the game with a single second remaining on the clock. Listen to that crowd! They're going nuts!" Nubbin then hit his second free throw, which was just a formality.

At 10:11 a.m., Central Standard Time, on March 4, 1967, we won the Texas State Championship 51-47. Lester Hutcherson raced over and gave me a big hug. "Congratulations, Coach!" he said. "We did it! We did it!"

The Kennard Tigers were State Champions. I looked towards the rafters. *Thank you, God.*

Pride swelled in my chest, so intense I almost couldn't breathe. That team had gone far beyond what I thought humanly possible. There is no limit to what a team can accomplish when it has one heartbeat. John Keats once wrote, "A thing of beauty is a joy forever." I had to agree as I felt this moment etched into my memory forever. The horn finally sounded, concluding the breathtaking finish of that remarkable game. Even to the average fan with no interest in this game's outcome, it was truly a spectacle to behold. It was an on-the-edge-of-your-seat nail biter that the ordinary fan in the stands loves to watch, but to the coaches, it was mentally, physically, and emotionally exhausting down to the final seconds with the score zigzagging on every possession. It was almost as draining for the diehard fans of both teams as they experienced both the height of elation and the depths of despair with each basket down the stretch.

As that down-to-the-wire, fan-pleasing, see-saw finish between two relentless teams was history, there was a third team entering the picture that had already impacted the game's outcome many times over: our own delirious supporters. Even from the very top row of the balcony, a few of those late arrivals sitting that high up only because those were the only seats available, watched with utter astonishment as they saw a panorama of purple swamp the floor of Gregory Gym, stampeding down the bleachers toward our players. Every Kennard fan at the floor level was about to exemplify an ennobling flair as they headed to mid-court. An enormity of heartwarming effervescence filled the arena as our fans' bubbling laughter raised our spirits—and some players—on their shoulders.

Like honey on an ant hill, those delirious fans were charging the court just to get a taste of all of its sweetness. The madness of that March morning had reached a pinnacle of ecstasy as we were lost in a sea of affection. It took only seconds for that massive avalanche of harmonious humanity to saturate the playing court, obscuring it from view. Resembling someone hot-footing it at the base of a volcano, I was leapfrogging across the court just for the sheer pleasure of this miracle moment.

It felt like Thanksgiving, Christmas, New Year's, and the Fourth of July all merged into one. Our delirious fans were streaming down the aisles, flooding the Gregory Gym playing floor in huge numbers to join that once-in-a-lifetime celebration. All year long we had been climbing that emotional mountain and when we finally reached the very top, it was time to savor the excitement and enjoy the accomplishment. That truly had become the sunset of my dream.

It appeared that virtually every Kennard fan in Gregory Gym was on the floor. They were doing the one-step, quick jump, bunny hop as they leaped for joy, bobbing up and down like fishermen's cork bobbers. There were hugs, kisses, slaps on the back, handshakes, high-fives, smiles, and tears of joy. I saw my mom with tears streaking down her face, embracing my father before they turned to give me thumbs up. Curtis gave his mom a bear hug and was so overcome by all the emotion filling the gym that he too had tears in his eyes.

Roy was all smiles as he was hoisted into the air on the shoulders of one black guy and one white guy, both of whom at the beginning of the season, I happened to know were against integration. We had practiced, lived, and played as a team, and now were reaping the reward of our togetherness. In fact, it appeared that the whole community had come together in a very unique closeness with the sudden success of our basketball team. In the mass, they didn't see black or white, they only saw one c o l o r — purple. What a special moment, what a special time to be alive.

My dad rushed up to me and gave me a massive hug. We were both so overcome with what had just transpired that we were too choked up to speak. I'm sure the looks in our faces sent the message anyway because a picture is always worth a thousand words.

Herman was totally surrounded by his family and I could hear them fussing over how much weight he'd lost during the Tournament. Gary received a big hug and a kiss from his sister and head cheerleader, Gwen Parrish. Fred and Nubbin embraced each other like they hadn't seen each other for years, and Haywood got a big hug and a kiss from his girlfriend, Debra Denman, right at mid-court.

Suddenly, I was bowled over as my two brothers rushed in, giving me simultaneous bear hugs. "Great job, Johnny! Great job! Billy's voice was quivering.

James Otis followed suit. "What a game! What a finish!" I felt myself being hoisted up onto their shoulders as I reached for the sky with a clutched fist. I was totally lost in all the passion I felt in that moment. Having watched those celebrations after State Championship games year after year, I'd always wondered just how it might feel to be a part of it. I can truthfully say that whatever I was feeling, it went way beyond words. It was something I would never be able to re-create or imagine again. It truly was a once-in-a-lifetime moment.

When I finally came down from the clouds, I quickly walked over to Mom and gave her a big hug. "Congratulations, son! This is all so very special. I am so proud of you and your team!"

"Mom, we won by rebounding. We could never have done it without your help." The tears were free-flowing again as she held my face in her hands and hugged me one last time. My dad was beside us and I took both of their hands. "You can never know how much your support and encouragement means to me. Without you guys in my corner, I couldn't have done this. There were plenty of times I was sure it was impossible until I talked to you two. I love you, Mom...Dad...thanks for everything." We embraced as a family—James Otis and Billy grabbing hold before I pushed away to head to the dressing room.

~~~

Trying to make my way through that monster of a crowd, it seemed like every fan on the floor wanted to shake my hand and offer congratulations. In the end, I felt as if my arm might fall off. I had no idea that many people even knew where Kennard was, much less would be passionately cheering for our team. Upon reaching the edge of the playing court there was a tapping on my shoulder. Turning around, fully expecting to meet one more new fan, there he was—Curtis. With tears streaming down his face and joy in his heart, that young man embraced me with a compassionate hug that sent chills down both of our spines. "Is this special or what?" he said, attempting to wipe away even more tears.

Looking at Curtis through my emotionally-drained, weary eyes, I said, "Only because I can't think of any words stronger. Yeah, this is pretty special."

Susan found us just before we hit the dressing room, thanking me again for the tickets. There were tears in her eyes as she hugged me and made me promise to come by the restaurant before I left. I gave her my word.

Walking up the stairs toward the dressing room, we stopped in front of the door. I looked at Curtis and said, "You know something, if there is a basketball heaven on this earth, buddy, we're there!"

Curtis looked at me, smiling, "And you're about to enter the pearly gates. Maybe one day I'll be able to do that. I think I'd really like that. I can promise you one thing—I'll be applying to school. I want this, Coach. Now go in there and get your dessert!" With that, he pulled open the dressing room door and all smiles, I walked in.

~~~

Our dressing room was wall-to-wall sound. The amazing accomplishment of having just won the State Championship and the reality of the entire week was starting to sink in—and so was the exhaustion. We had all put our heart and soul into one gallant effort to reach the unreachable star and then we were there. The feeling within was absolutely magical.

Achieving the so-called unachievable by that amazing group of over-achieving youngsters had just stunned Gregory Gym, not to mention the shell-shocked fans of the Krum Bobcats. Our players were whooping and hollering, sharing the pure enjoyment of this moment of remembrance. Entering the dressing room, I let out a very loud, resounding *"Yes!"* It penetrated the air, giving off a feel of pure satisfaction. As I made my way through the enthusiastic group of youngsters, I walked up to Roy and gave him an emphatic bear hug.

"Hey, fellas, how about my man Roy, here? He made *back-to-back-to-back* baskets—each one more important than the last." Cheers rose around the room. "Here's the big thing. We were down each time he scored. He put us back in the lead three straight times—the last time for good. With a big smile I said, "Roy, you're the man!"

Amongst cheers of joy, Haywood came over and said, "Let me shake the hand of the Krum killer!"

I looked at Herman and said, "How about those corner jumpers? Did you do a number on Krum's zone or what? You made them pay for concentrating too much on our inside game."

"It was just like you said, Coach, when they backed off and gave me that open jumper, school was out!"

You lit them up like a Christmas tree!" With that I gave Herman a big hug. "You had a heck of a year. It's been an honor coaching you!"

I walked over to Fred and gave him a big hug. "Great game, big man! You showed them some kind of heart out there today."

"Not bad for a kid with a heart murmur, eh, Coach?"

"That's what I call going out in style."

"Just like you told me before, Coach, if you've got to go out, playing your last game in Gregory Gym before a packed house to win the State Championship is the way to go."

Looking at Haywood, I said, "How about all this, son? Is this incredible or what?"

"Coach," he said, "we just flat played together. I know that's why we won. Besides, Coach, you worked our butts off all year. You *made* us play together and, somehow, at the same time, you made us like it! Coach, you made us *believe* that if we played together we could beat anybody. And you know something? We could!" A grin spread across his face. " One more thing...we're gonna come back here and do this all over again next year."

I shook his hand and nodded. "Well, if we're gonna do that, we'd better start practicing."

Looking right back into my eyes, he had that fire still burning. "I'll be ready Monday, Coach!"

Continuing to walk around the room, I saw Nubbin headed toward me. Giving my unheralded defensive specialist a big hug, I said, "I want you all to know that my man Nubbin here made the big defensive play in both the Regional Championship game and today in the State Championship game."

In unison, our guys began chanting his name, tickling my short player silly. After the chant died down, Nubbin looked at me with a big smile. "I don't ever want to forget this feeling."

I nodded slowly. "Time passes on, but memories like this will last a lifetime. I'll tell you something else. Do you realize that twenty-five years from today, this team will go back to the State Tournament again?"

The entire team looked bewildered. "What do you mean, Coach? We'll all be old men then!"

"Well, you'll be in your forties and I'll be almost fifty. What I'm talking about is that every twenty-five years the team that wins the State Championship is brought back to be honored at halftime in the championship game. That will be in 1992. We'll have a reunion right here at Gregory Gym. Well, they'll probably have a brand-new gym by then, but regardless, we'll be honored at halftime and I hope to see you all here." Nubbin crashed into me for another hug as I fought back tears, thinking of meeting my players as men, but still brothers, who had done the impossible.

The dressing room door opened and there he was with a million-dollar smile—Mr. Bitner, our superintendent. After shaking hands with each player, he walked over to me. "Congratulations, Coach! You did one incredible job with this team!" A little softer, he pulled me aside. "But what is it with you and these championship games? You win Region by one point last weekend and today you win the State title by four in a game that was flip-flopping down to the last eight seconds! You got some kind of thing about close games?"

"Well, we just want to make the game as entertaining as possible." I wrapped a fatherly arm around his shoulders. "After all, this is a form of show business and we want to make sure that the fans get their money's worth!"

"Well, you about gave me a heart attack in the process! Oh, by the way, you owe me some gum. I went through *two* packs this game."

Looking around that joy-filled dressing room, I gathered everyone up, "Okay, everyone over here and have a seat. I want you guys to realize that this doesn't just happen very often. Only a very select few over the course of a lifetime have the privilege to sit where you are right now, listening to what I'm about to say. As we moved through the journey of forty-six games and many more practices, a very positive thing evolved. We started to believe—I in you and you in me. The togetherness that developed along the way is the main reason that I'm talking to you right now.

"I love this team. I love each and every one of you. Each of you has and always will have a special place in my heart and it's not because we won. I've loved every step that we've taken together. Thank you for taking my advice. Thank you for believing in me."

The room was silent as Herman rested a hand on my shoulder. "Coach, you just wouldn't let us stop believing in ourselves because it was easy to see that you always believed in us."

With a lump in my throat, my heart felt strangely warm when soft-spoken Fred said, "I'm sure that I speak for everybody in this room when I say that we believed in you from the start and thank you for being our coach."

Haywood stood and faced the group. "Let's hear it for our coach!" The outburst of cheers forced the tears that were threatening at the edge of my eyelids to finally fall. Wiping them away, I cleared my throat. "I've said a lot of things to you over the last six months and as time goes on, you'll probably forget most of it. But one thing I want you to never forget is how this moment has made you feel. This moment is what you should strive for your whole lives—it's the feeling of accomplishment."

Roy stood. "Coach, can I say something?" I nodded. "You're absolutely right. I think we've come a long way and we've met a lot of challenges and faced them as a team, so in my opinion..." He took a moment to play to the crowd. "This team is a *great* team."

There was a simultaneous eruption of cheering as everyone was standing with raised fists once again, bobbing up and down in another joyous show of emotion. When the cheering subsided, everyone was looking at me, collectively waiting for a response.

I cleared my throat. "You have played like a great team for a good while now, but are we a great team?" I looked in each of my player's eyes. "You'd better believe it! There's absolutely no doubt in my mind!" In the background, it started all over again as every player was now standing amid shouts of approval.

Holding my hands up, I quieted the group. "Hold up! I'm not finished! Sit down, fellas, I want you to truly understand what I'm about to say. Great teams are molded by how they play when the chips are down. They're made by how they perform in the now-or-never moments. They project greatness by how they react when everything goes wrong. Great teams are made by making their own breaks and understanding their opponents enough to know when to make them. They have the kind of players who, when facing astronomical adversity, rise to the occasion and play above their individual talents with a spirit of total team unity. Fellas, this describes our team. This is how you've played this year. The bigger the game, the better you've played. You have been playing like champions a good while now and it has been sheer pleasure just watching you mature from ordinary to the greatness you've reached.

"We all know that sometimes the best teams never even make it to the playoffs, so who's to say that we are the so-called 'best'? What matters is that we played like champions; we never became satisfied with our performance. Your hearts and your determination made you great."

Herman fought back tears. "Coach, I don't think that any of us thought that we were a great team until we heard you say it, but there's one thing that I do know. We have all thought you were a great coach for a long time."

My cup was running over. "I appreciate it, guys, but you have to understand that as a team you're judged by what you do in a season. Coaches are judged by how they do over a career. My career is just beginning. I'll tell you what though, there's no way that I could have gotten off to a better start than coaching you guys."

Roy stood up. "Well, right now I can say you've coached a very good game. I'll be here for another year, so I can tell you then if maybe, just maybe, you're on your way to being a *good* coach." He was immediately pulled back into his seat to rolling eyes and groans.

Herman took over. "I don't know about the future, but just like with some players, you can just *see* the talent. I think the same goes for coaches and you are a *great* coach and we can't wait to play for you again!"

I didn't want the day to end, but I knew that the sun would rise again tomorrow, just like it had that day. Robert Frost once said, "In three words I can sum up everything I've learned about this life: it goes on." And so it does. I knew that it wouldn't be long until that day would be just a memory, but what a memory it would make. You live a lifetime of memories, some good and some bad. That day, the precious moment was just placed on the very highest pedestal on the top shelf of my memories. When I first started practice, the very thought of what just transpired in this first season was, at most, a dream—a long-range goal.

Looking into the young faces of my crowned Texas State Champions, I had to say one last thing. I took a knee. "Most of you already know that I've had an ongoing dream since I was a little boy of playing and winning this State Championship. Very few people in this life get to live their dreams. I want to personally thank you for making it possible for me to live mine. Thank you. Thank you. Thank you."

Photos

1967-1970

Coach Johnny Carter

State semi-finals against Booker T. Washington High School, the first all-black team to play in the State Tournament. Lawrence McCutcheon rebounds; Herman Myers challenges while Roy Harrison watches. (Lawrence McCutcheon went on to be a great NFL running back for the Los Angeles Rams)

Coach Carter designs a play for the starters.
{left to right}
Fred Pilkington, James "Nubbin" Pilkington,
Herman Myers, Haywood Henderson, and Roy Harrison

Coach Carter with Region, District, and three tournament trophies.

Herman Myers attempts to score against Ricky Knight
in the State finals.

Fred Pilkington scores in Bi-District game against Anderson.

Coach Carter holds the State Championship trophy.

Herman Myers

Haywood Henderson

James "Nubbin" Pilkington

Fred Pilkington

Roy Harrison

Coach Johnny Carter

Coach Carter inspires his team against Avinger
in the regional final game at Kilgore, Texas.

John Dean and Mary Frank Carter
Coach Carter's parents hold the State Championship trophy.

Fred Pilkington hits high post jumper over Krum's 1-2-2- zone.

Coach Carter speaks to student body
at pep rally for State Tournament.

Roy Harrison scores against District rival Lovelady

Pre-game warm-up for District Championship game against Apple Springs.

Fred Pilkington hits a big basket in the State final
as Herman Myers (20) and Roy Harrison (10) look on.
Pictured for Krum are Howard, Knight, Merrifield, and Standifer.

The 1967 State Champion basketball team
{left to right}
Danny Smith, Jerry Parrish, Herman Myers, Gary Parrish, Fred Pilkington,
Leeland Strban, Eddie Pilkington, Haywood Henderson, James Pilkington,
Roy Harrison, Walter Denman, Lester Hutcherson.
Coach Johnny Carter

Roy Harrison scores against Krum in the State final as
Herman Myers (20) and Haywood Henderson look on.
Pictured for Krum are Knight, Hall, Standifer, and Merrifield.

Coach Carter, Kennard's only coach, is pictured with trophies
earned by his boys, girls, high school, and junior high teams for the year.

EPILOGUE

June 4, 2011

Our first book signing took place on June 4, 2011, forty-four years after I last stepped foot onto the Kennard Tigers gym floor. The players and I were stunned by the magnitude of the crowd that was waiting for us there.

Many of the people were children and grandchildren of the original players and fans. I was sad to see that some of the fans and people that I mentioned in the book had passed on—Mr. Bitner, Nona Baker, and her son, Curtis. It almost moved me to tears as I remembered back to the packed gym of excited fans that greeted us after winning the state championship in 1967.

Larry Bruce, a member of our 1970 undefeated team, introduced me and I received a very warm reception from the nostalgic onlookers. I tried my best to express the depth of my feelings and love for the school, for the community, and especially for the players that I had coached in my four years there.

The book signing was an overwhelming success with supply not being able to meet demand as all books were sold and a waiting list taken. All the players thoroughly enjoyed signing every book while re-living the wonderful time when a determined minded team, through the grace of God, somehow achieved the impossible. The outpouring of support that special Saturday morning brought back beautiful memories, seemingly making time stand still. It really touched my heart as well as the players involved. I just wished my Mom and Dad were still alive so they could have been there. After all, without their help and support this miracle would have never happened. Thank you, Kennard, for letting me be a part of "The First Season"!

Coach Johnny Carter

Reunion Photos

June 4, 2011

Coach Johnny Carter

The 1967 State Champions, forty-four years later.
{left to right}
Gary Parrish, James "Nubbin" Pilkington, Haywood Henderson,
Coach Johnny Carter,
Leeland Strban, Roy Harrison, Herman Myers, Fred Pilkington

Former players listen to Coach Carter address the crowd.
{left to right}
Jeff Myers, Roy Harrison, Herman Myers,
Fred Pilkington, James Pilkington

Former players and Coach Carter await a long line of admirers.

The crowd purchasing books was enormous.

Former players
{left to right}
Roy Harrison, [Coach Carter], Fred Pilkington,
Gary Parrish, James Pilkington,
Jeff Myers, Leeland Strban, Herman Myers.

Three members of the 1967 State Championship team.
{left to right}
Roy Harrison, Herman Myers, Fred Pilkington

Larry Bruce introduces Coach Carter

Coach Carter speaks to the crowd.

Benford Frizzell, Herman Myers, Roy Harrison

Roy Harrison, Nancy and Herman Myers,
John Reid Carter, Sallie and Coach Carter

James ("Nubbin") Pilkington is the only one still working!

Coach Johnny Carter

About the Author

Coach Johnny Carter was born and raised in Madisonville, Texas, and graduated from Madisonville High School in 1961. After an excellent basketball career at Madisonville, he went to Lon Morris Junior College on a scholarship. He graduated with a Bachelor of Science degree from the University of Houston and finished his master's degree at Sam Houston State University.

Coach Carter's first coaching job was at Kennard High School in 1967. In four years there, his teams compiled a record of 160-13, winning three State Championships in 1967, 1968, and 1970. The 1968 Kennard Tigers set three Texas State Tournament scoring records, the last of which—most points scored in a three-game series—still stands.

Carter served as an assistant coach at Howard Payne University in Brownwood, Texas for three years. They were the Lone Star Conference Tri-Champions in 1971 and played in the National AAU Tournament.

Carter was head coach at McLennan Community College in Waco, Texas, for seven years, finishing second in the conference in his first season in 1974. Thereafter, his teams won six consecutive conference championships. They qualified for the Regional Tournament every year, reaching the National Junior College Tournament in 1976. He was voted Junior College Coach of the Year by the Texas Association of Basketball Coaches that season. In 1980, his team was the winner of the highest scoring game in the history of basketball:

169-165 against Kilgore. The game ball is in the trophy case at the National Basketball Hall of Fame in Springfield, Massachusetts. He coached two players at MCC who went on to the NBA: Vinnie ("The Microwave") Johnson and Sam Worthen. Vinnie, the seventh player taken in the draft, played on two NBA championship teams for the Detroit Pistons in 1989 and 1990. Sam is on the coaching staff with the Harlem Globetrotters.

Coach Carter was an assistant coach at the University of Oklahoma for two years, reaching the NIT Final Four in 1982.

Carter was head coach for twenty-two years at Madisonville High School and had sixteen playoff teams. In 1995, they reached the State finals.

Throughout his career, Carter's teams were known for their aggressive full-court pressure defense, which he used every year after that memorable first season. His teams compiled an overall record of 903 wins and 241 losses.

Several of Coach Carter's players went on to have outstanding coaching careers. Among those are Danny Kaspar, Tony Mauldin, Eddie Nelson, and Randy Weisinger.

Carter is married to Sallie, his wife of fifteen years. They have three children: Candice, Ben, and John Reid.

* * *

Visit my website: www.coachjohnnycarter.com
Watch Interview with Coach Carter
http://www.youtube.com/watch?v=hsDlx4whLxc

In May 2014, Coach Carter will be honored at the Texas Association of Basketball Coaches convention in San Antonio, Texas when he will be inducted into the Texas High School Basketball Hall of Fame.